The Peopling of Hawai'i

The Peopling of Hawai'i

SECOND EDITION

Eleanor C. Nordyke
Foreword by Robert C. Schmitt

 University of Hawaii Press • Honolulu

Library of Congress Cataloging-in-Publication Data

Nordyke, Eleanor C.
  The peopling of Hawaii / Eleanor C. Nordyke ; foreword by Robert
C. Schmitt. — 2nd ed.
    p. cm.
  Bibliography: p.
  Includes index.
  ISBN 0-8248-1191-7
  1. Hawaii—Population—History. I. Title.
HB3525.H3N67   1989   88-38927
304.6'09969—dc19   CIP

Camera-ready figures and tables were prepared by the
Population Institute of the East-West Center, Honolulu,
Hawaii.

To our grandchildren
   Aimee, Nalani, Cameron, Trevor, and Larissa

and

To the children and
   grandchildren of Hawai'i

and

To the people of Hawai'i
   on whom its future depends

CONTENTS

FIGURES

TABLES

FOREWORD

In the first edition of *The Peopling of Hawaii,* published in 1977, Eleanor C. Nordyke stressed two major themes in Hawai'i's demography. One was how the Islands' original Polynesian settlers were followed, and partly supplanted, by successive waves of new arrivals from America, China, Portugal, Japan, Korea, the Philippines, Samoa, and other areas. These in-migrants, largely maintaining their separate ethnic and cultural identities, had over a two-century period contributed to a rich population brew offering significant insights to sociologists, public health analysts, and researchers in a variety of other disciplines. The second theme, equally important, was the need for a coherent and effective population policy to address the imminent threats of soaring densities, congestion, environmental degradation, and the loss of cherished Island values and lifestyles.

Much has occurred during the past twelve years, a good deal of it anticipated in the original edition and some clearly unforeseeable even by the most prescient analyst, but these topics remain central to the author's concerns. Migration streams have ebbed, shifted course, and sometimes reappeared in new manifestations. Fertility, after more than a decade of decline, has stablilized at a new low level. Death rates, although low by current standards, reflect emerging ethnic patterns and at least one cause of death, AIDS, not even recognized in 1977. Rapid increases in the resident population have been surpassed by an even greater growth in the number of visitors present, and both have contributed to densities, congestion, and assaults on the environment that seem to portend an ecological crisis.

Any study of this nature must inevitably depend on a wide range of statistical sources, and here the author has been relatively fortunate. Full-scale population censuses were instituted by American missionaries, beginning in 1831–1832, and then, from the late 1840s through 1896, by the Hawaiian government. Birth and death registration became legal requirements as early as the middle of the nineteenth century, and migration statistics date from the same period. Since 1900 Hawai'i has been included in the decennial counts and annual estimates of the U.S. Bureau of the Census. Detailed visitor statistics have been compiled since 1950 by the Hawaii Visitors Bureau (HVB), providing data unequalled in any other jurisdiction on the size and characteristics of our large nonresident population. Beginning in 1964 and continuing to the present, the Hawaii Health Surveillance Program (HHSP) has offered annual sample survey data on the demographic, social, economic, and health characteristics of Island ethnic groups.

At the same time, Hawai'i's statisticians and data users have become increasingly aware of erosion in the availability, quality, and meaningfulness of some of our most important series. Budget cuts have forced drastic reductions in sample sizes used in the decennial censuses, the HHSP, and HVB Basic Data Survey. The 1950 census was the only such effort in the twentieth century to collect comprehensive data on race mixture, and in 1970 the Bureau of the Census deleted the category of "Part Hawaiian," which had appeared in all seventeen official enumerations from 1849 through 1960. As a result, the 1970 census was comparable neither to its predecessors nor to the birth, death, marriage, divorce, and related statistics regularly compiled by various state agencies. Further definitional changes occurred in 1980, with still others in prospect for 1990.

These cutbacks in statistical programs occurred at the very time that Hawai'i's population dynamics were becoming ever more complex, further complicating a situation that was already badly tangled twenty years earlier. Interracial marriage and a growing population of mixed bloods had been characteristic of Hawai'i since at least the 1820s, but prior to World War II most of these unions and their issue could be conveniently classified as "Part Hawaiian." For the past half century, however, all groups have participated in such heterogeneous mating. As a consequence, according to the State Department of Health, 46.5 percent of the resident marriages occurring in Hawai'i in 1986 were interracial, and 60.6 percent of the babies born to civilian couples of known race that year were of mixed race. Based on tabulations from the HHSP, fully 31.2 percent of all persons living in households were of mixed parentage—19.9 percent Part Hawaiian and 11.3 percent of other origins. Yet neither the 1970 nor 1980 censuses provided any indication of such developments.

These statistical gaps, in combination with the growing complexity of demographic events, have seriously handicapped Hawai'i's demographers. Even such a fundamental (and ostensibly simple) question as "Which groups are growing, which are declining, and by how much?" can no longer be answered, even in the most approximate terms: shifting and often arbitrary racial definitions have rendered decennial census tabulations almost useless, and annual data from the HHSP, now our sole source of population estimates by detailed race, have been marred by high sampling variation and unexplainable (and sometimes unreasonable) fluctuations in group totals. Calculation of accurate birth, death, and other rates has consequently become exceedingly problematic. These difficulties are especially daunting in a work like the present one, which relies to an uncommon degree on accurate, consistent, and meaningful ethnic statistics. It is a tribute to Eleanor Nordyke's skill and perseverance that, in the face of such intractable underlying data, she has been able to fashion any kind of reasonable and defensible conclusions.

The importance of this analysis is underscored by the irresistible impact of the changes now sweeping Hawai'i. Not only are the state's once-distinctive ethnic groups—under the influence of pervasive intermarriage—turning into a racial chop suey, but even those maintaining a fair degree of endogamy are becoming indistinguishable from their neighbors, as their third, fourth, and fifth generations succumb to cultural "haolefication." These trends, plus the growing irrelevance of ethnic statistics, suggest that this may be our last chance to capture the significant differences among Hawai'i's peoples. When these differences can no longer be charted, either because the population has become biologically and culturally homogenized or because government no longer collects meaningful data, Hawai'i's value as a social laboratory will vanish.

When I drafted the foreword to the first edition of this book, I went to some pains to justify "still another work on the population of Hawai'i," but this concern is no longer valid. My own book on *Demographic Statistics of Hawaii: 1778–1965* appeared twenty years ago. Andrew W. Lind's seminal volume on *Hawaii's People* was last revised in 1980, before results of the census conducted that year were released. A new edition of *The Demographic Situation in Hawaii* is in the works but will appeal to a readership different in significant ways from that anticipated for the present publication. *The Peopling of Hawai'i,* second edition, faces no real competition.

The problems and issues discussed in this book are ultimately among the most important now confronting the people of Hawai'i, even though public recognition of their significance may lie dormant or appear in other guises. Eleanor Nordyke deserves our gratitude for her efforts to attack them and, through this volume and its predecessor, to bring them to the attention of a wider readership.

ROBERT C. SCHMITT
State Statistician
Hawaii Department
of Business and
Economic Development

PREFACE

Mark Twain, who toured Hawai'i as a journalist in 1866, wrote with eloquence and humor of his enchantment with the Islands:

> . . . . the Sandwich Islands—to this day the peacefullest, restfullest, sunniest, balmiest, dreamiest haven of refuge for a worn and weary spirit the surface of the earth can offer. Away out there in the mid-solitudes of the vast Pacific, and far down in the edge of the tropics, they lie asleep on the waves, perpetually green and beautiful, remote from the work-day world and its frets and worries, a bloomy, fragrant paradise, where the troubled may go and find peace, and the sick and tired find strength and rest. There they lie, the divine islands, forever shining in the sun, forever smiling out on the sparkling sea, with its soft mottlings of drifting cloud-shadows and vagrant cat's paws of wind, forever inviting you. . . . What I have always longed for, was the privilege of living forever away up on one of those mountains in the Sandwich Islands overlooking the sea.[1]

For over half a century our family has experienced the rare delight of living Mark Twain's dream, sitting high on a hilltop overlooking Honolulu on the island of O'ahu, enraptured by the beauty of this unique paradise of the world. The panorama is ever-changing: by the late 1980s only a small glimpse of Waikīkī's white sands and curling waves were visible between a wall of high-rise hotels, condominiums, and business structures; the plains of Mō'ili'ili and Kaimukī were blanketed with private homes, apartment dwellings, and traffic-laden highways; the sharp peak of the promontory Diamond Head, protected from visual obstruction by legislative regulation, stood in stately grace over urbanized Honolulu, Hawai'i's state capital; and Mānoa Valley, with its lush green foliage, soft breezes, delicate and misty rainfall, and double vivid-hued rainbows, retained the charm of my childhood haven.

From our hillside vista we have observed firsthand the unrolling scene and felt some of the consequences of population and economic growth on a small island. The numbers of people, increasing fivefold from 200,000 persons in 1930 to about a million residents and visitors on Oʻahu in 1988, have intruded insidiously for the past half century with complex repercussions on a limited environment.

Hawaiʻi's growth mirrors a world problem. On an international scale, the rapid increase of world population is considered to be one of the most serious concerns facing mankind. Thomas Robert Malthus, English demographer and economist, in 1798 published his thesis, *An Essay on the Principle of Population as it Affects the Future Improvement of Society,* in which he argued that the human species has power to grow geometrically, while subsistence can increase only arithmetically. Hawaiʻi can be viewed as a microcosm of world demographic change: the populations of both the world and Hawaiʻi have been growing at a historically unprecedented rate.

The demographic study of Hawaiʻi extends beyond a statistical review of population numbers. Interwoven in the figures is the fascinating history of different peoples who have abandoned their homelands to cross a broad expanse of water and inhabit a small chain of islands in the north Pacific Ocean. The transition from an ancient Polynesian feudal society dependent upon a subsistence economy to an urban industrialized community of multiethnic derivation has occurred in just two hundred years. Since the arrival of Captain James Cook in 1778, recent history records the depopulation of the native Hawaiians, the rebuilding of a society by the infusion of new blood through subsidized importation of labor from nations across the globe, and the present threat of overload from population and economic pressures on a finite land.

Since the preparation of the first edition of this book in the early 1970s, Hawaiʻi's population has continued to increase rapidly, and the neighbor islands have experienced an unprecedented rate of expansion. The close correlation of growth of population in response to economic policy has become more clearly apparent with the publication of the state model of population–economic projections, which holds steady the variables of births and deaths while migration patterns vary in relation to economic assumptions of labor needs. Unlike most of world population growth that is related to more births than deaths, Hawaiʻi has reduced its fertility below replacement level while experiencing rapid expansion in numbers of people in response to economic growth and job development, especially in the service-based visitor industry. As a resource-dependent society, Island inhabitants have become dependent on the fragile balance of imported food, energy, and finances in accommodation to expanding numbers of people.

This book is the result of personal concern and professional interest. Although the natural beauty of Hawai'i still offers pleasure to the resident and tourist, there is reason for concern about the impact of continued population growth on environmental quality. By presenting the demography of these Islands from a historical and environmental perspective, I hope to show that current population trends cannot continue indefinitely and to give the reader a broader understanding of factors and implications of rapid growth on an Island community.

The researcher of population in Hawai'i is fortunate to have a rich assortment of resources from which to draw information. Perhaps the most difficult problem in the analysis of this broad subject is to present the facts objectively and with simplicity for the non-technically trained reader. To facilitate this purpose, mathematical and quantitative material with discussion of methodologies and techniques have been minimized.

This book offers information to complement the studies in the multidisciplines of Hawaiian scholarship. It does not attempt to duplicate the writings of history, ethnic studies, Hawaiian studies, sociology, anthropology, population geography, or other areas of population interest; nor does it propose to suggest solutions to problems of urban planning or environmental overload.

In response to guidelines of the 'Ahahui 'Olelo Hawai'i, a committee of teachers who seek standardization of the Hawaiian language, diacritical marks have been included to provide orthographic modifications to Hawaiian words.[2] The glottal stop *('okina)* represents a missing consonant, and the macron *(kahakō)* indicates a long vowel sound. Unfortunately the presentation is not entirely consistent, since quotations from older writings did not use this spelling method.

The problem of ethnic definition presents a serious challenge to analysis of Hawai'i's people. With the continued miscegenation of races in the Islands it becomes increasingly difficult to assign precise ethnicity, and accurate interpretation of demographic measures is blurred. This study presents findings from counts using U.S. census and state health survey definitions, but the reader should be aware of the limitations of the underlying data. For example, while the U.S. census may have undercounted Hawaiians in 1980, the Hawaii Health

Surveillance Program (HHSP) suggested a much higher number with a sex ratio of Hawaiians that was wildly erratic, a tabulation of Filipinos and Koreans that was lower than would be expected when migration figures are considered, and an undercount of Samoans. Future counts of ethnic groups in Hawai'i will become even more complex and unreliable.

The preparation of this book was dependent upon the assistance, advice, constructive criticism, and moral support of many people to whom I wish to express my sincere thanks and appreciation. Robert C. Schmitt, State Statistician and "walking encyclopedia" of Hawaiian facts and figures, has been the pillar of my knowledge of the demography of Hawai'i. His voluminous writings on historical Hawaiian statistics, his compilation of facts in the annual *State Data Book* and in the *Statistical Report,* and his spontaneous and cheerful personal communications in response to frequent inquiries provided the essential information, cooperation, and support that enabled completion of this publication.

Special acknowledgment is given to my colleagues at the Population Institute of the East-West Center. Robert W. Gardner, coauthor of *The Demographic Situation in Hawaii* and its revised edition (forthcoming, with Robert C. Schmitt and Michael J. Levin), kindly gave permission to use some of the material from that publication and offered assistance in the preparation of this work. Richard K. C. Lee, coauthor with Robert Gardner of *A Profile of Hawaii's Elderly Population,* permitted use of graphs from that paper and offered enthusiasm for this project. Sandra E. Ward, senior editor, provided technical and editorial assistance and steady friendship to steer the course through the myriad of details.

I am also grateful to administrative, computer, library, cartographic, and stenographic staff at the East-West Center. Appreciation is expressed to Lee-Jay Cho, Director of the Population Institute, and to Victor H. Li, President of the East-West Center, for their support of this project. Special acknowledgment is given to Victoria C. H. Ho and Judith A. Tom for computer programming; to Alice D. Harris and other members of the Population Institute library staff; to Joan M. Choi, Rubye Benavente, Wendy A. Nohara, Jennifer Higgins-Ross, Linda Y. L. Loui, Joan M. Komatsu, and Jill Kajikawa-Kent for staff support; to Morley H. Gren and Keith E. Adamson for administrative backing; and to Jackie D'Orazio, April W. L. Kam, and Lois M. Bender for graphics and production services.

My gratitude is extended to those who endorsed and assisted in the editorial and publication process at the University of Hawaii Press, with special appreciation to Iris M. Wiley, Jean A. Brady, and Janet Heavenridge. I also wish to express my thanks to Milan I. Heger for assistance on cover design.

It would have been impossible to complete this book without the helpful guidance of many persons in the community. Dedicated librarians and their staffs graciously retrieved information and pictorial material, including Agnes C. Conrad and Carol Silva of the Hawaii State Archives; Lela Goodell of the Hawaiian Mission Children's Society Library; Barbara Dunn of the Hawaiian Historical Society Library; Cynthia Timberlake and Marguerite Ashford with the book collection and Lynn Davis, Betty Kam, Stuart Ching, and Clarise Mauricio with the visual collection of the Bernice P. Bishop Museum; and Bea Kaya of the library at *The Honolulu Advertiser.* Invaluable information was obtained from Abraham Pi'ianaia, Rubellite K. Johnson, Richard Kekuni Blaisdell, Lilikalā K. Kame'eleihiwa, Larry L. Kimura, and Haunani Bernardino of the University of Hawaii Center for Hawaiian Studies, and from others at the University of Hawaii Ethnic Studies Program, the Hawaiian and Pacific Collection of the University of Hawaii, the Multicultural Center of the Hawaiian Foundation for History and the Humanities, and the Hawaiian and Pacific Room of the State Library of Hawaii. Appreciation is expressed to Thomas K. Hitch, economist, for constructive suggestions. Members of the staffs of the Research and Statistics Office of the State Department of Health and of the State Department of Business and Economic Development (formerly the State Department of Planning and Economic Development), and of the former Governor's Commission on Population and the Hawaiian Future have contributed in significant ways to this publication.

Special appreciation is expressed to the photographers and artists whose pictorial materials have added a visual dimension to this study. The work of each contributor has been credited beneath the appropriate illustration. I am grateful to *The Honolulu Advertiser,* the *Honolulu Star-Bulletin,* and the Hawaii Visitors Bureau for making their pictures available to this project, as well as to Senator Daniel K. Inouye and his cooperative staff in Honolulu and in Washington, D.C.; to Governor John Waihee and his public relations officer, Carolyn Tanaka; to Lieutenant Governor Benjamin Cayetano and his secretary, Janeen Nozaki; to Marilyn E. Kali, public information officer for the State Department of Transportation; to Major Tim Pfister of the Public Affairs Office, U.S. Pacific Command; to Virginia Staley of Corporate Communications, Hawaiian Electric Company; to Norman Kanada of The Bus System Division, and to members of the Rapid Transit Development Project, Department of Transportation Services of the City and County of Honolulu; to Larry Lee of the Elderly Affairs Division, Office of Human Resources of the City and County of Honolulu; and to Edna Bechert, Helen G. Chapin, George Chaplin, Irmgard Hormann, Lee and Will Kyselka, Deacon Ritterbush, Blase Camacho Souza, and many others who facilitated the process of acquisition of graphics.

In conclusion, a word of special aloha is expressed to my patient family. My kind husband supplied a personal computer for word processing, giving encouragement and thoughtful criticism, and our helpful adult children and curious grandchildren tolerated a cluttered dining room table for an extended period.

The Peopling of Hawai'i

Introduction

Hawai'i is a unique place. As the fiftieth state of the United States, it is the only region where all racial groups are minorities and where the majority of the population has roots in the Pacific Islands or Asia instead of Europe or Africa. Since the opening of Hawai'i to the Western world by Captain James Cook in 1778, waves of immigrants of different ethnic groups have come to the Islands. Recent rapid immigration from foreign lands and the U.S. mainland along with intermarriage and culture-mixing continues to dilute racial identities and distinct cultural patterns.

Since 1900, when only 154,000 persons resided in the Hawaiian Islands, the population has increased at a comparatively high average annual growth rate of 2.3 percent and is now approaching 1.5 million inhabitants. The rapid rise in population caused by continued in-migration, natural increase, and economic policies that favor growth have led to profound changes in the physical environment of the Islands as well as in the economy, social structure, and lifestyle. The effects of unrestrained population expansion on the finite island community are readily visible.

This brief review of the history of Hawai'i's people offers a demographic perspective on the native inhabitants, the immigrants of the nineteenth and twentieth centuries, and the present resident, military, tourist, and de facto populations in the Islands. The illustrations accompanying the text give evidence of the striking impact of increased population on a limited environment.

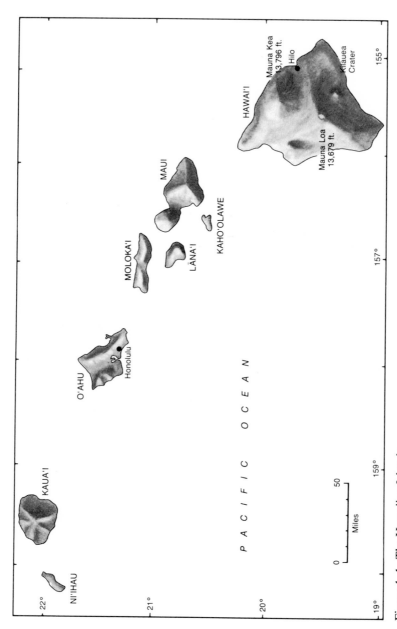

Figure 1–1. The Hawaiian Islands

CHAPTER I

Early Polynesian Immigrants

The Hawaiian Islands were probably the last large, habitable land-mass in the Pacific to be occupied by man. The volcanic chain of islands emerged, weathered, and eroded for millions of years without incursion by humans.[1] The presence of people in Hawai'i is a phe-nomenon of the past fifteen hundred years, and the major influx of new residents has occurred since statehood in 1959.

A mountain range stretching nearly 2,000 miles erupted through a rift in the north Pacific about 25 million years ago, gradually rising as much as 18,000 feet from the ocean floor to sea level and protruding above it.[2] The Hawaiian Archipelago of shoals, reefs, and 132 islands extends 1,523 miles (2,451 kilometers) from Kure Atoll and Midway Islands in the northwest to the island of Hawai'i in the southeast, reaching in longitude from 178° 25' W to 154° 40' W and in latitude from 28° 15' N to 18° 54' N.[3] The eight major islands—Kaua'i, Ni'ihau, O'ahu, Maui, Moloka'i, Lāna'i, Kaho'olawe, and Hawai'i —surfaced perhaps 5 million years ago in the southeast region from 159° 46' W to 154° 53' W longitude and from 22° 14' N to 19° 04' N latitude. Volcanic action continues even now on the youngest, largest, and easternmost island of the group—Hawai'i, and geologists report the early formation of a new submerged landmass to the southeast of Hawai'i that is not expected to surface for thousands of years (Fig-ure 1–1.).[4]

Over a period of 5 to 10 million years of above-water history for the entire Hawaiian chain, plant and animal life was carried to the deso-late volcanic surface of islands by trade winds and storms, migrating birds, and currents of the sea.[5,6,7] Living seeds and spores dispersed and evolved to form native plants.[8] Close examination of native Hawaiian flora and fauna reveals features that are adaptable to long-distance transport. The presence of flowering plants may be attributed to seeds carried by birds, either internally and excreted upon arrival or externally dropped after random attachment to feathers. Most coastal flora in Hawai'i has seeds or fruits that could have drifted to the Islands on ocean currents and then taken root along beaches, such as the *hala* (pandanus) tree and the *pōhuehue* (a pink-flowered morning glory). Later some plants evolved inland and became established in upland forests.

In 1948 naturalist E. C. Zimmerman postulated the probable quantity of immigrant ancestral species of insects, land snails, land birds, ferns, and flowering plants as numbering about seven hundred, with evolving descendants and others discovered approaching ten thousand plants and animals.[9] In recent years the unique biota of Hawai'i has been destroyed at an increasing rate by commercial, agricultural, and human activities. Introduced insects, animals, and crops, and the development of vast residential and business areas, have altered the landscape and irretrievably replaced much of the native growth.

Ancient Hawaiian mythology gives varied accounts of the coming of people to the Islands. The legend of Hawai'i Loa tells of the creation of man: "The gods, seeing the man without a wife, descended on earth, put him into a sleep, took out one of his ribs and made it into a woman." This tale was probably influenced by biblical teachings of the missionaries without authentic basis in Hawaiian tradition.[10,11]

David Malo, a nineteenth-century Hawaiian scholar, reported contradictory genealogies that attempted to explain the origin of the first inhabitants.[12] According to the genealogy called *Kumulipo,* a creation and genealogical chant, the first human being was La'ila'i, whose union with Ke-ali'i-wahi-lani (the king who opens heaven) created the ancestors of this race. The genealogy called *Lolo* describes the first native Hawaiian as Kahiko, whose son Wākea and his wife Haumea (also known as Papa) were progenitors of the race. A study of the *Kumulipo* by Hawaiian literary scholar Rubellite Kawena Johnson explains that this extensive chant "was not a specific genealogy so much as a concept of some point in time from which genealogies might start as they may from Pali-kū or Lolo, whichever was the discretion of genealogists who were responsible for composing chants in honor of new-born or dying chiefs."[13]

In his study of the origin and migration of the Polynesian race, Abraham Fornander traces fifty-six generations from the time of Wākea, dated at about A.D. 190, to 1870.[14] Another historian, nineteenth-century Hawaiian Samuel M. Kamakau, wrote that a man named Hulihonua and a woman named Keakahulilani are said to have been the first inhabitants of Hawai'i, preceding Wākea by twenty-eight generations.[15]

Oral tradition describes the migration of the Polynesian ancestors of the Hawaiians. Through the disciplined ritual and recitation of the learned priests, the *kahuna,* knowledge of navigation and heroic achievements of long-distance voyagers were reported to succeeding generations.[16] Although no written history exists to document these movements, data from archeological, botanical, and linguistic studies trace their probable origin to South Asia. Similarities of Babylonian, Arabian, Indian, and Chinese lunar nomenclature to Hawaiian thirty-six ten-day week calculations leads to presumptions of ancient historical ties to Euphratean-Egyptian Decan stars and calendar.

A Caucasian offshoot is believed to have moved eastward from south of the Himalayas, mixed with Mongoloid people of South Asia and the Malay Archipelago, and then pushed into the Pacific.[17] The languages of Polynesia have a common origin with those in Melanesia, Micronesia, and Indonesia, and similar food plants and animals can be traced to southwestern islands.

When Austronesians began their open ocean voyages eastward into the Pacific as long as three thousand years ago, they did not penetrate the inhabited area of Melanesia but moved on to a home group of islands—perhaps Tonga and Samoa. There they developed common traits of culture, physique, and language.[18] Whether motivated to move by warfare; catastrophic mishaps such as tsunamis, earthquakes, or volcanic eruptions; a search for land with more plentiful food; or the lure of adventure, the ancestors of Hawaiians migrated across vast stretches of the Pacific. Research on voyaging and navigation has pinpointed more precisely the movement of people into the Pacific, and archeologists have provided supportive evidence for information on Polynesian migration.[19]

About a thousand years after the settlement of Tonga and Samoa, Polynesian migrants traveled across vast stretches of the Pacific to the Marquesas Islands, to Tahiti and the Society Islands, north to the Tokelaus, and northwest to the Ellice Islands. They inhabited Easter Island off the South American coast in the southeast Pacific and Hawai'i in the northern hemisphere in about A.D. 500, and they established settlements in New Zealand in the southwest between A.D. 500 and 750.[20]

The seafaring pioneers of Polynesia (a Greek word meaning "many islands") possessed unsurpassed instrument-free knowledge of navigation.[21] Covering long distances, they relied on the locations of the rising and setting sun and stars, the positions of the stars in the southern and northern hemispheres, the limits of the ecliptic, the weather at the equator, the winds, and the swells and currents of the tides.[22] Trained judgment and keen observation enabled them to identify land by the color and dispersal of clouds, the flight of birds, and the *te lapa* or underwater lightning streaks that dart out from island positions.[23] The position of sunrise and sunset, wave direction and swell interaction patterns, reef locations, and other natural phenomena assisted in their passage across uncharted waters.[24] These courageous seafarers showed unusual courage, endurance, and confidence. Their society accorded them high prestige for their competence.

With the emergence of increased Hawaiian cultural pride in the late-twentieth century, and with the popular rise of groups such as the Polynesian Voyaging Society, there is a sharpened awareness of the remarkable skills of the early ocean travelers.[25] By reconstructing the double-hulled canoe in the prototype *Hōkūle'a,* and demonstrating

Skill in boat-building and navigation made it possible for the ancient Polynesians to carry families, animals, and provisions across thousands of miles of the Pacific Ocean. *(Herb Kane painting, Hawaii State Foundation of Culture and the Arts)*

successful Pacific voyages, increased interest has peaked in the unique feats of Polynesian ancestors of the Hawaiians. The boat builders designed sturdy seagoing vessels that could carry men, women, children, and some animals. Provisions such as dried fish, breadfruit paste wrapped in pandanus leaves, coconuts, edible roots, fruits, and water-filled gourds enabled the voyagers to survive for several months at sea while traveling thousands of miles over the ocean. It is possible that the large physique of the Polynesians was the result of selective pressures that required natural insulation to withstand the rigors of the long voyages.[26,27]

Hawaiian genealogies do not say how or when people arrived on the Islands, but Malo suggests, "It is thought that this people came from lands near Tahiti and from Tahiti itself, because the ancient Hawaiians at an early date mention the name of Tahiti in their *mele* [songs or chants], prayers, and legends."[28] The Hawaiian language bears a close resemblance to Tahitian, Samoan, Tongan, and New Zealand Maori words, indicating a common homeland for eastern and western Polynesian groups.[29] The Hawaiians' physical features, their traditions, and the names of their deities and places are similar to those of the Tahitians, and artifacts such as fishhooks, adzes, and ornaments closely resemble those of central Polynesia.

In the ancient Hawaiian legend of Kumuhonua and his descendents, the Polynesians are called *ka po'e Menehune,* or "the Menehune people."[30] A Marquesan legend also refers to a group of people with a similar name, and in Tahiti the term *Manahune* referred to the laboring class, or commoners. It is possible that the Manahune of Tahiti were in the employ of early chiefs who settled the Hawaiian Islands. Later legends described the Menehune as mythical, elflike creatures who built a *heiau* (temple) or a fish pond in a single night and performed other superhuman feats.[31]

New techniques in linguistics, physical anthropology, ethnobotany, and archeology are being used to unravel the mysteries of the origin and migration of Polynesians to Hawai'i.[32] Genetic connections can be classified in linguistic terms using glottochronology, which presumes a measured rate of change between languages separated from a parent language. The use of blood groups in physical anthropology to determine ancient ties has been applied to the Hawaiian race, and complex analysis of blood types has shown common gene pools. Inquiries into the origin of the *'uala* (sweet potato) have resulted in varying explanations of the manner and course of its distribution throughout the Pacific. Many of the plants considered "native" in

Figure 1-2. Routes of Early Polynesian Migrants
Source: Kyselka 1971, pp. 38–39.

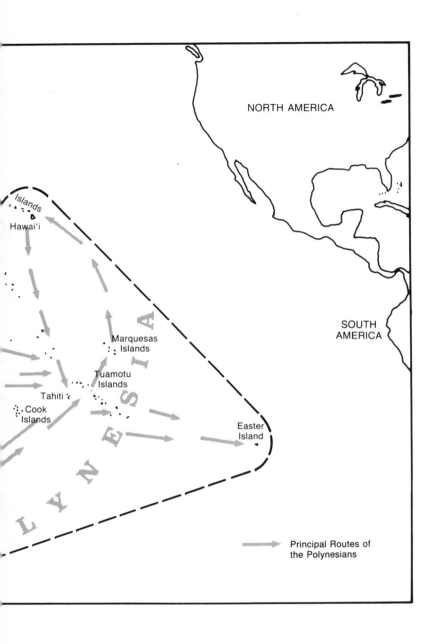

NORTH AMERICA

SOUTH
AMERICA

Islands

Hawai'i

Marquesas
Islands

Tuamotu
Islands

Tahiti

Cook
Islands

Easter
Island

LYNESIA

Principal Routes of
the Polynesians

Hawai'i, such as *'uala, kalo* (taro), *niu* (coconut), *ulu* (breadfruit), *uhi* (yam), *mai'a* (banana), *wauke* (paper mulberry), and *kukui* (candlenut) were brought to the Islands in successive migrations of early settlers.[33]

Archeologists have determined that the first traces of human habitation in the Marquesas, Easter, Society, and Hawaiian islands occurred between 200 B.C. and A.D. 700.[34,35] Using charcoal, shells, wood, bones, sea urchin spines, and other organic material found in ancient campsites, scientists have assessed the radiocarbon age of many localities and provided a solid framework for chronological history.[36] It is believed that the first settlers may have come from the Marquesas, and that Tahitians may have arrived between A.D. 900 and 1300.[37] Archeological theories suggest that the original migrants increased in population and then initiated voyages of exploration and conquest.[38] The 2500-mile sea route between Hawai'i and Tahiti was

Early inhabitants of Hawai'i, such as this Hawaiian who is pounding poi from a taro root, used natural resources with care and maintained life in harmony with the environment. *(Hawaii State Archives)*

repeatedly negotiated until perhaps the fourteenth century when the voyages gradually ceased (Figure 1-2).

Legendary Hawaiian history offers no reliable population figures. Various assumptions have given figures of slow, gradual habitation to rapid population growth.[39] State Statistician Robert C. Schmitt and Lynn Zane hypothesized the calculation of a pre-contact population growth based on other Oceanic societies, using an annual crude birth rate of 45 births per 1,000 population and a death rate of 38.7 deaths per 1,000 people per year, or a growth rate of 0.63 percent per year. Considering migration in the population growth equation, Schmitt assumed a figure of 100 persons as initial entrants to the Hawaiian Islands in the year A.D. 500, with an average of 25 in-migrants annually for 1,000 years, resulting in a population that doubled approximately every 110 years (Table 1-1).[40] This steady increase paralleled world population growth, with small numbers of people in the early period of settlement, followed by rapid expansion accompanied by intensified food production and the establishment of social and cultural systems to accommodate increasing population.

A preindustrial or agrarian society is expected to have high fertility, fluctuating and high mortality, and static to low population growth.[41] An excess of births over deaths and an absence of contagious diseases accounted for a growth in numbers by natural increase, while warfare, sacrificial killing, and limited health measures restrained the rate of growth in pre-contact Hawai'i. A slight lowering of fertility and an increase of mortality could produce vast differences in the net annual growth assumption. The maternal and infant mortality rates were comparatively high. Some out-migration occurred during the era of long voyaging in the eleventh to fourteenth centuries. Death was related to diseases such as pneumonia and gastrointestinal disorders, lack of sanitation, unstable nutrition associated with drought and famine, homicide, accidents, and wars. Life expectancy of about thirty years was low.[42]

The first census is said to have been conducted on the island of Hawai'i in the fifteenth century by King 'Umi to determine the sizes of the population of his various districts.[43] He directed all of the people to come to his temple and each to bring a stone representing the bearer's strength. The rocks for each district were deposited in a pile at the *heiau* of 'Umi, located on the slopes of Hualālai mountain. According to tradition, the district of Kona was represented by the largest pile of stones.

Over a period of more than one thousand years, the early Polyne-

A Hawaiian fisherman spears fish at Kāneʻohe Bay, Oʻahu, in the 1890s. *(Charles Crane collection, Hawaii State archives)*

sian inhabitants of Hawaiʻi developed a self-sustaining, distinctive culture.[44] Despite the absence of a written language and the lack of natural resources for production of metal products, they created a subsistence economy in a cooperative society. With the end of the era of Pacific migration by large voyaging canoes in the fifteenth century, the Hawaiians became isolated from ancestral ties and established a community of complex social, religious, and cultural practices.

CHAPTER 2

The Coming of Westerners and the Depopulation of the Native Hawaiians

For over one thousand years the Polynesian immigrants to Hawai'i remained relatively isolated on their northern Pacific islands beyond the lanes of early exploring expeditions. Myths and legends describe the coming of the Hawaiian settlers and the infrequent visits of long-distance voyagers. The unwritten literature of pre-contact Hawai'i was transferred from one generation to the next by carefully trained storytellers who received knowledge through their ears as societies that use the written word receive information through their eyes.[1] These esteemed bards were members of the court of the *ali'i* chiefs and kings, and through the spoken word they preserved the history and traditions of ancient Hawai'i.

King Kalākaua, who compiled authentic stories to record the unwritten events of Hawai'i, described the arrival of the first Polynesians as follows:

Nanaula, a distinguished chief, was the first to arrive from the southern islands. It is not known whether he discovered the group by being blown northward by adverse winds, or in deliberately adventuring far out upon the ocean in search of new lands. In either event, he brought with him his gods, priests, prophets and astrologers, and a considerable body of followers and retainers. He was also provided with dogs, swine and fowls, and the seed and germs of useful plants for propagation. It is probable that he found the group without human inhabitants.

During that period—probably during the life of Nanaula—other chiefs of less importance arrived with their families either from Tahiti or Samoa. They came in barges and large double canoes capable of accommodating from fifty to one hundred persons each. They brought with them not only their priests and gods, but the earliest of Polynesian traditions. It is thought that none of the pioneers of the time of Nanaula ever returned to the southern islands, nor did others immediately follow the first migratory wave that peopled the Hawaiian group.

For thirteen or fourteen generations the first occupants of the Hawaiian Islands lived sequestered from the rest of the world, multiplying and spreading throughout the group. They erected temples to their gods, maintained their ancient religion, and yielded obedience to their chiefs. The traditions of the period are so meagre as to leave the impression that it was one of uninterrupted peace, little having been preserved beyond the genealogies of the governing chiefs.[2]

Kalākaua also describes the arrival of the second migratory tide in the tenth or eleventh century, which continued for about one hundred and fifty years: "Near the close of the twelfth century all communication between the Hawaiian and southern groups suddenly ceased. Tradition offers no explanation of the cause, and conjecture can find no better reason for it than the possible disappearance at that time of a number of island landmarks which had theretofore served as guide to the mariner."[3]

Abraham Fornander, another transcriber of ancient Hawaiian history from chants, prayers, and legends, tells of the wanderings of Hawaiian voyagers to foreign lands, and one tale relates their return to O'ahu with two white priests. These priests were described as: *"Ka haole nui, maka alohilohi, ke a aholehole, maka aa, ka puaa keokeo nui, maka ulaula"* ("Foreigners of large stature, bright sparkling eyes, white cheeks, roguish, staring eyes, large white hogs[4] with reddish faces").[5]

Shipwrecked Japanese sailors are said to have landed on O'ahu and Maui in the thirteenth century.[6] According to records transmitted to their homeland during the Kamakura era, Japanese drifted in battered boats to Makapu'u Point on the island of O'ahu in the year A.D. 1258. Twelve years later, in A.D. 1270, a separate Japanese group of two men and three women, aboard a disabled ship carrying a cargo of sugar cane, were reported to have gone ashore at Kahului, Maui, with the first supply of sugar cane for Hawai'i.[7]

During the sixteenth century, another legend tells of new residents arriving in the Islands:

In the time of *Keali'iokaloa,* king of Hawai'i and son of *'Umi,* arrived a vessel at Hawai'i. *Konaliloha* was the name of the vessel, and *Kukanaloa* was the name of the foreigner (white man) who commanded, or to whom belonged the vessel. His sister was also with him on the vessel.

As they were sailing along, approaching the land, the vessel struck at the

Pali of Ke'ei, and was broken to pieces by the surf, and the foreigner *Kukanaloa* and his sister swam ashore and were saved, but the greater part of the crew perished perhaps; that is not well ascertained. . . . The strangers cohabited with the Hawaiians and had children, and they became ancestors of some of the Hawaiian people, and also of some chiefs.[8]

Some researchers believe Spanish vessels reached Hawai'i as early as the sixteenth century. In 1555 a Spaniard named Juan Gaetano, the captain of a Spanish galleon, may have found a group of islands that were located at the same latitude as the Hawaiian Islands.[9] Their longitude was placed several hundred miles farther eastward, but because Spanish charts of that period were not considered precisely accurate, the error in mapping may have been a problem of design, calculation, engraving, or misidentity.

Other researchers have disputed the presence of Spaniards in Hawai'i, suggesting that such an important discovery by Spanish explorers would have been internationally reported.[10] However, early Hawaiian historian James Jackson Jarves explains: "Their position was directly in the course of their rich Manila galleons, and would have afforded an inaccessible retreat for the buccaneers and their numerous naval enemies; consequently it would have been a matter of policy to have confined the knowledge of their situation to their own commanders who navigated those seas."[11] Indications of early contact include the Hawaiian helmets and feathered cloaks that bear a striking resemblance to those worn in medieval Europe. However, according to Swedish researcher E. W. Dahlgren in 1916: "No historical fact proves, nor is there any sort of probability, that the Hawaiian

The crews of the ships of Captain Cook's third voyage of discovery in the Pacific first saw Hawai'i upon their approach to Waimea, Kaua'i, on January 18, 1778. This watercolor, *A view of Atowa [Kaua'i], one of the Sandwich Islands,* is by William Ellis, the surgeon aboard the HMS *Discovery. (Bishop Museum)*

Islands were ever visited, or even seen, by the Spaniards before their discovery by Captain Cook in 1778." Dahlgren concludes that the traces of European influence on appearance, language, dress, and customs of the natives "are due to loose hypotheses without any scientific value."[12]

Two hundred years ago Westerners opened the isolated sphere of the Hawaiian community and permanently altered the course of civilization in the Islands. On January 18, 1778, Captain James Cook, aboard HMS *Resolution* and accompanied by HMS *Discovery*, observed land while on an expedition in search of a northern sea passage from the Pacific to the Atlantic. Cook wrote: ". . . an island made its appearance, bearing North East by East; and, soon after, we saw more land bearing North, and entirely detached from the former. Both had the appearance of being high land. . . . Our latitude, at this time, was 21° 12′, North; and longitude 200° 41′, East."[13] The accuracy of Cook's determination of longitude is related to his use of an octant to measure angular distances between moon and prominent stars in relation to Greenwich lunar time tables and to his use of the chronometer, which provided accurate time at a prime meridian.[14]

The next day, in his description of the natives, Cook reported: "In the course of my several voyages, I never before met with the natives of any place so much astonished, as these people were, upon entering a ship. Their eyes were continually flying from object to object; the wildness of their looks and gestures fully expressing their entire ignorance about every thing they saw, and strongly marking to us, that, till now, they had never been visited by Europeans, nor been acquainted with any of our commodities, except iron; which, however, it was plain, they had only heard of, or had known it in some small quantity, brought to them at some distant period."[15] He named the group of islands the Sandwich Islands, in honor of his patron, John Montagu, fourth earl of Sandwich, who was then first lord of the British Admiralty.

The Hawaiians treated the visitors with awe and respect, identifying Cook with Lono, their god of agriculture. They referred to the ships as floating islands, and the chiefs called upon their people to contribute provisions and to supply the other needs of the foreigners. Cook described the islanders as frank, cheerful, and friendly people who used the language of Tahiti. He was impressed by the affection the women and men showed toward their children: "It was a pleasure to observe with how much affection the women managed their infants, and how readily the men lent their assistance to such a tender

Captain Cook's ships, HMS *Resolution* and HMS *Discovery,* brought Western ideas and culture, industrial implements, tools of war, and unfamiliar diseases to the Islands. *(Hawaii State Archives)*

office."[16] On a return voyage in 1779, a tragic altercation with the Hawaiians at Kealakekua Bay resulted in Cook's untimely death, but the detailed accounts of the discovery of the Islands and their inhabitants by Cook and his men awakened world interest and opened the door to international migration to the Islands.[17]

An estimate of the population of Hawai'i in 1778 was made by Captain Cook's officers, based upon the average number of persons in each house multiplied by an average number of dwellings per village. Cook wrote: "From the numbers which we saw collected at every village, as we sailed past, it may be supposed, that the inhabitants of this island [Kaua'i] are pretty numerous. Any computation, that we make, can only be conjectural. But, that some notion may be formed, which shall not greatly err on either side, I would suppose, that, including the straggling houses, there might be, upon the whole island, sixty such villages, as that before which we anchored; and that, allowing five persons to each house, there would be, in every village, five hundred; or thirty thousand upon the island."[18]

Cook's population totals varied from William Bligh's figure of 242,000 to James King's estimate of 400,000.[19] Other early voyagers, as well as Pacific Island researchers, have presented estimates ranging from Norma McArthur's 100,000; Peter Buck's 100,000–150,000; George Dixon's 200,000; Captain V. M. Golovnin's 200,000 (for 1818); and David Stannard's 635,000–875,000.[20,21,22] Population scholars Romanzo Adams, Andrew Lind, Bernhard Hormann, and Robert Schmitt offer traditional thinking, giving a total of 250,000–

300,000 persons residing in Hawai'i during the period of first Western contact. If this number is relatively accurate, the population by island in 1779 may be estimated:

Population by Island, 1779

Island	Population
Hawai'i	120,000
Maui	60,000
O'ahu	50,000
Kaua'i	30,000
Ni'ihau	1,000
Moloka'i	10,000
Lāna'i	5,000
Total Inhabitants	276,000

In 1823 an English missionary, William Ellis, toured the Sandwich Islands and reported a population of about 85,000 on Hawai'i; 20,000 on Maui; 2,000 on Lāna'i; 3,000 on Moloka'i; 20,000 on O'ahu (with 6,000 or 7,000 inhabitants in Honolulu); and 10,000 on Kaua'i (including Ni'ihau)—or a total of approximately 140,000.[23] Censuses conducted by American missionaries in 1831–1832 and 1835–1836 showed a decline from 130,313 to 108,579 persons, and according to the official government census of 1850 the population had decreased to 84,165.[24] An all-time low of 56,897 residents was recorded by the census in 1872, but the actual nadir was probably the 53,900 total population in January 1876, almost a hundred years after the arrival of foreigners (Table 2–1; Figure 2–1).[25]

The coming of Westerners had a fatal impact on the Hawaiians. Although foreigners made many contributions to the society, such as introducing metal, cloth, and manufactured goods, offering a Western education, and developing a written language, they also brought alcoholic beverages, militaristic equipment of firearms and gunpowder, and destructive diseases for which the native Hawaiians had no natural immunity. The seventy-five years between 1778 and 1853 saw political consolidation and the establishment of the Hawaiian monarchy, but it also produced complex changes in religion, land use, the economy, and health practices that permanently altered Hawaiian culture.

The rapid depopulation of the Hawaiian race is traced to many causes. Missionary Ellis described deserted villages and abandoned

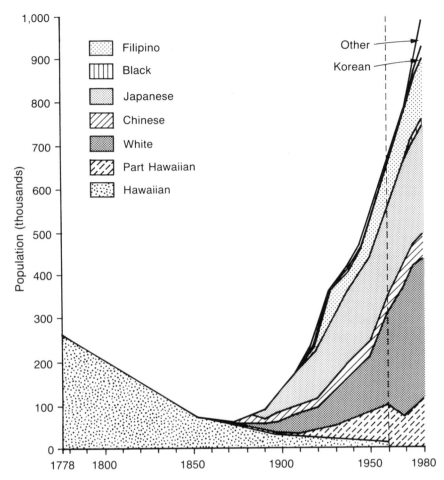

Figure 2-1. Resident Population by Ethnicity, Hawai'i, 1778–1980
Note: The dotted line represents changes in definition of race by the U.S. census in 1970 and 1980 that resulted in figures that are not directly comparable with earlier years.
Source: See Table 3-1.

enclosures, which he attributed to "the frequent and desolating wars which marked the early part of Kamehameha's reign, the ravages of a pestilence brought in the first instance by foreign vessels, which has twice, during the above period [1778–1823] swept through the islands; the awful prevalence of infanticide; and the melancholy increase and destructive consequences of depravity and vice."[26] Hawaii State Statistician Robert C. Schmitt has explained the severe depopulation as a result of declining fertility, high infant mortality, and emigration.

Such factors as wars, famine, and natural disasters—including the devastating 1790 volcanic explosion of Kilauea Crater—have been exaggerated as reasons for population decline, causing altogether only about a thousand deaths during the first fifty years following the Hawaiians' early contact with Westerners.[27] Catastrophes, including earthquakes, tsunamis, volcanoes, wars, marine disasters, fires, transportation accidents, storms, and violence, have taken fewer than six thousand lives in the Islands in two hundred years.[28]

The natural increase of the Hawaiian population was severely retarded by a decline in births and by a high incidence of stillbirths and fetal deaths. The ancient Hawaiians prayed that their race might "increase and flourish, and sprout from the parent stock. 'Thriving seedlings *ka po'e kahiko* [the people of old] bore; great gourds filled with seeds they were. But today they are poison gourds, bitter to the taste.' "[29]

Diseases introduced by early visitors took a heavy toll on the unprotected natives. Venereal diseases, such as syphilis and gonorrhea, were brought first by men on Cook's ships and later by crews and wayfarers on vessels from many parts of the world.[30] Captain Cook declared in his journal: "The order not to permit the crews of the boats to go on shore was issued, that I might do every thing in my power to prevent the importation of a fatal disease into this island, which I knew some of our men now laboured under, and which, unfortunately, had been already communicated by us to other islands in these seas. With the same view, I ordered all female visitors to be excluded from the ships. Many of them had come off in the canoes. . . . They would as readily have favoured us with their company on board as the men; but I wished to prevent all connection, which might, too probably, convey an irreparable injury to themselves, and, through their means, to the whole nation."[31]

In 1779, upon Cook's return to Hawai'i, he and his officers observed "melancholy evidence" that efforts to prevent the spread of the disease had failed. According to historian J. C. Beaglehole, the gloom of Kealakekua Bay sailed with them, and they knew that they were leaving behind in the Sandwich Islands "visibly and horribly alive, a disease compared to the ravages of which musket-balls were gifts of love." He added: "the Hawaiians were not such fools that they could not put cause and effect together."[32] Charles Clerke, who assumed command upon the death of Cook, wrote: "Captain Cook did take such preventive methods as I hop'd and flatter'd myself would prove effectual, but our Seamen are in these matters so infernal and dissolute a Crew that for the gratification of the present passion that affects them they would entail universal destruction upon the whole of the Human Species."[33]

Reverend Artemus Bishop lamented the decrease of the Hawaiian population that resulted from the introduction of venereal disease and alcohol. "It is not civilization, but civilized vices that wither the savage," he said in 1838. "He drinks into them like water, without knowing that their attendant diseases are cutting the tendrils of his heart, and drawing away his life's blood."[34] Bishop claimed that alcohol had murdered thousands, but licentiousness had slain hundreds of thousands. Hawaiian women who had sexual relations with members of Cook's crew contracted syphilis, which caused prenatal infection, congenital defects, and impaired health; and gonorrhea, which caused inflammation and scarring of the reproductive tract, resulting in sterility.

The depopulation effect of lowered fertility is stressed by Schmitt.[35] According to the earliest reliable statistics of births and deaths in 1834–1841, the crude birth rate was only 19 and the crude death rate per 1,000 population was near 77. This low birth rate is about 60 percent lower than rates characteristic of societies that have no effective contraceptive methods; hence this low rate of fertility was a significant factor in the steep decline of the number of Hawaiians.

The incidence of venereal diseases among the natives reached a peak between 1820 and 1840.[36] In 1824 E. Loomis, a missionary, wrote that an order was published to prohibit women from going on board ships, but sailors from the ships in port "insisted that they must have their girls and would seize and carry them off by force."[37] Bishop in 1838 appealed to foreign visitors to help the Hawaiian nation remain a distinct nation by aiding in the destruction of licentiousness through refraining in its indulgence, disapproving its practice, and upholding laws for its suppression.[38]

Another cause of depopulation was high infant mortality. The disruption of the ancient social system and the discarding of old *kapu* (taboos) that controlled kinship and dietary patterns reduced protective measures and increased the susceptibility of Hawaiian infants to disease. In 1838 Bishop reported that "the great majority of children born in the islands die before they are two years old."[39] Historian Samuel M. Kamakau wrote that some Hawaiian women had as many as ten or twenty children, but few of them grew to maturity.[40] Even in the early twentieth century, the infant mortality rates of 226.5 deaths per 1,000 live births in 1910 and 108.8 deaths per 1,000 live births in

1920 were excessively high (Table 4–7). Although infanticide was described by the missionary Ellis and Hawaiian historian Kamakau, its effect on depopulation was considered minimal.[41,42]

Emigration was also a cause of population decline. Young men, drawn by prospects of adventure on the high seas, joined the crews of transport, fur-trading, and whaling ships. Kamakau tells of the departure of some of his people who felt oppressed by new land laws. "The foreigners were benefited and they have stayed here because they like new lands, but the people of Hawaii waited for the benefits of the government under the law from strange lands. For fear of the law they went, and were not seen again in this Hawaii."[43] Historian Kuykendall reports that about two thousand Hawaiian young men enlisted as seamen on foreign vessels in 1845–1847, and many of these voyagers never returned to the Islands.[44]

Statistics on out-migration of Hawaiians are speculative. The number of Hawaiians who left the Islands was not systematically recorded, although Hawaiian names were included in crew tabulations. An 1829 expedition of the Hawaiian chief Boki is known to have been lost at sea with 479 aboard. Romanzo Adams reported absent Hawaiians as 200 in 1823, 300 in 1825, 400 in 1832, 600 in 1836, 3,500 in 1848, and 4,000 in 1850.[45] Schmitt points out the significance of these 4,000 missing men as representing almost 5 percent of the total Hawaiian population and 12 percent of all Hawaiian males of working age eighteen and over.[46] With the deliberate importation of laborers during the middle of the nineteenth century, the Hawaiian government initiated the compilation of statistics on migration and naturalization.[47]

The high mortality level among Hawaiians was a basic factor in depopulation. Because the islanders possessed no natural immunity to the diseases of foreigners, they became victims of contagious illnesses, such as measles, whooping cough, and mumps, which were rarely fatal to Europeans and Asians. The crude death rate ranged between 32 and 60 deaths per 1,000 total population, with higher rates during epidemics.[48] The steep decline in population during the first fifty years after Cook's opening of Hawai'i to the Western world has been attributed to wars during the period of Kamehameha's conquest and control of the Islands, famine that occurred as farmers changed jobs from agricultural development to the gathering of sandalwood for export, and natural disasters. In reality, the total loss of life from these events was minimal, and the major cause of the high mortality was a series of epidemics introduced by persons on visiting ships.

In 1804 the *ma'i 'ōku'u* (to sit in pain, or squatting sickness), a dysenteric disease that probably was cholera, reduced the population by 5,000 to 15,000 lives.[49] An epidemic of "cough, congested lungs, and sore throat," probably influenza, killed thousands in 1826; and mumps and whooping cough struck the Island population in the 1830s.[50,51] Measles, which had fatally struck Kamehameha II and his wife, Kamamalu, while they paid an official visit to England in 1824, was one of the factors responsible for the high death rate of 98 per 1,000 persons in Hawai'i in 1848, or a loss of more than 10,000 residents.[52,53]

Smallpox was brought to the Islands in 1853, where it cut a swath of death, especially on O'ahu where about 15,000 people died before vaccination was carried out.[54,55] A Board of Health with three commissioners was hastily organized, a system for ship inspection and quarantine was developed, and an extensive program for vaccination was established. Government and voluntary organizations joined efforts to strengthen public health and reverse the high rate of mortal-

Public health physicians provided inoculations for the populace at Camp Wood in Kahului, Maui, in 1887. *(Magoon collection, Hawaii State Archives)*

ity. In the 1880s whooping cough returned and another smallpox epidemic of smaller proportion was brought to the Islands by Chinese immigrants.[56]

Many other contagious diseases had devastating consequences for the unprotected Hawaiians. Influenza, bubonic plague, rheumatic fever, scarlet fever, and Asiatic cholera attacked the natives. Reverend Charles S. Stewart in 1823 described inhabitants of Honolulu who were disfigured by eruptions, sores, and disorders of the skin. Dr. A. Mouritz, leprosy specialist, identified the presence of the disease in Hawai'i: "The description of them clearly indicates that the Nodular form was the disease in evidence (swollen, lumpy face, large and pendulous ears, no eyebrows, large, swollen hands and feet, and peculiar musty, offensive odour from their persons). To my mind, this is clear proof that leprosy prevailed to a moderate extent in Hawaii as early as the year 1830; also that some of the 'remediless and disgusting cases' observed by the Rev. Charles Stewart in the year 1823 were quite possibly a double combination of disease, to wit, leprosy and syphilis."[57] Called ma'i pākē (Chinese sickness) by the Hawaiians, it is believed that the disease was carried by Chinese crewmembers who came to Hawai'i in the late eighteenth century and by subsequent immigrants from Asia. As a public health measure to combat the spread of the disease, leprosy patients were involuntarily confined at Kalaupapa, Moloka'i, from 1866 to 1969. The disease became known as ma'i ho'oka'awale [separation disease].[58] With improved methods of treatment, the mortality impact of leprosy has been reduced, and patients are no longer held in isolation.

Tuberculosis attacked lungs and organs, causing chronic illness and death. In the second decade of the twentieth century it was still uncontrolled and listed as the leading cause of mortality in Hawai'i with 400 to 500 annual deaths.[59] The Hawaiian medical practitioner, the kahuna lapa'au, was not familiar with infectious diseases and their treatment.[60] Although Western physicians settled in the Islands, Hawaiians were confused and wary of their medical practices and resisted their care. A government physician wrote in 1892: "There are many cases of serious illnesses among the natives that never come under our observation, because of their indifference to receiving medical aid." In 1914 the superintendent of the Anti-Tuberculosis Bureau described problems relating to the health of Hawaiians as follows:

[Tuberculosis] seems to be directing its deadly aim at one section of the community above all others—at the very class that this community is in duty bound to protect against all others—the Hawaiian race. The death rate amongst the Hawaiian race from tuberculosis is 66 per 10,000 (in contrast to 17.3 per 10,000 for the whole Territory). Two factors operate to produce this high death rate—first, an absence of race immunity; tuberculosis finding in them a virgin soil—they have inherited no resistance from their ancestors as other races have done. This is strongly borne out when the death rate of Part-Hawaiians is noted—the admixture of the suscepti-

A *kahuna lapaʻau* teaches an apprentice the anatomy of the human form. Drawing by Joseph Feher, from *Ka Poʻe Kahiko/ The People of Old* by Samuel Kamakau. *(Bishop Museum)*

ble Hawaiian with the more resistant races brings the death rate per 10,000 down from 66 to 11.2. The second factor is undoubtedly the adverseness of the Hawaiian race to submit to treatment or seek aid when ill, and often there is a seeming active evasion in order to seek treatment, and a reluctance to accept advice.[61]

The treatment by the *kahuna lapa'au* was empirical medicine combining ancient healing methods with spiritual power. Hawaiian scholar Mary Kawena Pukui explained that *kahuna* with *ha'aha'a* (a sense of humility) often referred their patients with *ma'i malihini* (foreign sicknesses) to a *malihini* doctor. She added: "The danger that lurks today when some Hawaiians pray and conduct *ho'oponopono* in sickness is that they turn spiritual enablement into 'faith healing'. While prayer can certainly facilitate recovery in many illnesses, prayer should go hand-in-hand with medical diagnosis and treatment. Too many Hawaiians today call in only the minister and forget the doctor."[62]

Medical services are provided to workers and their families at a plantation dispensary on O'ahu in 1915. *(Edgeworth photo, Bishop Museum)*

In the two hundred years since the entrance of foreigners to the land settled by ancient Polynesians, the race known as Hawaiian has been almost completely depleted by high mortality, low fertility, out-migration, and intermarriage. The coming of Western man had a fatal impact on the culture and numbers of the Island inhabitants. The native population was reduced from about 276,000 in 1979 to 11,294 pure Hawaiians in 1960, the last year in which they were counted as a separate ethnic group by the U.S. census (Table 3-3.d). At that time the pure Hawaiians represented only 1.7 percent of the total population in Hawai'i. University of Hawaii sociologist Bernhard L. Hormann explained: "Groups which are statistically recognized are the ones which are sociologically rather than anthropologically recognizable. The fluidity of race relations is indicated by the fact that in the past decades certain races have 'disappeared,' because in the first place they have become merged into wider groupings, e.g., Germans, Spanish, Portuguese, and all Caucasians as Caucasians, and Asiatic and Caucasian Hawaiians as part Hawaiians, these, in turn being in process of becoming once more simply Hawaiians . . ."[63] By the end of the twentieth century persons of pure Hawaiian blood had almost completely disappeared, and the ethnic group tabulated as Hawaiian by the U.S. census was a composite of many races of the world.

In 1887 King Kalākaua lamented the loss of his people and anticipated the merging of racial, economic, and political ties:

In the midst of evidences of prosperity and advancement it is but too apparent that the natives are steadily decreasing in numbers and gradually losing their hold upon the fair land of their fathers. Within a century they have dwindled from four hundred thousand healthy and happy children of nature, without care and without want, to a little more than a tenth of that number of landless, hopeless victims to the greed and vices of civilization. They are slowly sinking under the restraints and burdens of their surroundings, and will in time succumb to social and political conditions foreign to their natures and poisonous to their blood. Year by year their footprints will grow more dim along the sands of their reef-sheltered shores, and fainter and fainter will come their simple songs from the shadows of the palms, until finally their voices will be heard no more for ever. And then, if not before—and no human effort can shape it otherwise—the Hawaiian Islands, with the echoes of their songs and the sweets of their green fields, will pass into the political, as they are now firmly within the commercial, system of the great American Republic.[64]

Nineteenth- and Twentieth-Century Immigrants and Admixtures

The growth of a sugar-based economy in the kingdom of Hawai'i during the mid-nineteenth century was contingent upon the availability of a large labor force. Economic and political attention was focused on the need for more cane workers and the problem of declining population in the Hawaiian Islands.

"The decrease of our population is a subject in comparison with which all others sink into insignificance," declared King Kamehameha IV to his legislature in 1855. He encouraged bringing in Polynesian immigrants to replenish the native Hawaiian blood.[1]

The decision by island businessmen to grow sugar as the primary source of economic revenue set the course for population, politics, and commerce for almost a century. The California gold rush of 1849 offered a market for the early cane sugar planters in Hawai'i, and the 1861 Civil War blockade of the Confederacy that cut off sugar supplies from southern states provided a demand for Hawaiian sugar in the northern United States.[2] From the production of only two tons of cane sugar in 1837, the industry in Hawai'i expanded rapidly and became the third-largest producer of cane sugar in the world by the early twentieth century.[3]

The successful development of the new sugar industry was threatened by an insufficient number of capable workers. A large, dependable, and cheap labor force was needed to achieve a viable business. Early plantations employed from fifty to two hundred men; later, the larger plantations used over three thousand persons.[4] Hawaiians were recognized as industrious and competent workers, but their declining numbers were inadequate to meet the increasing demand for field employment. Isabella Bird, a visitor to a plantation on the Island of Hawai'i in 1874, said: "The natives are much liked as laborers, being

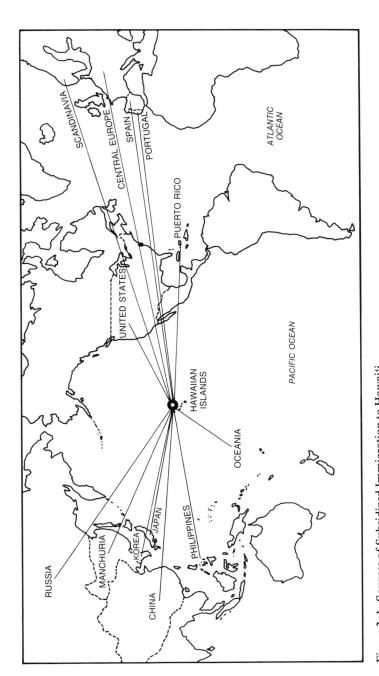

Figure 3–1. Sources of Subsidized Immigration to Hawai'i

Sources: Ivers 1909, Table 1; McLaren 1951, p. 91; Kuykendall 1967, pp. 117–185; Clifford 1974, Table 1; Schmitt 1977, Table 3.1.

docile and on the whole willing; but native labor is hard to get . . ."[5]
One report showed that more than 50 percent of the able-bodied
Hawaiian male population of the Kingdom in 1873 were employed on
plantations, yet this represented fewer than three thousand men.[6] In
the absence of an adequate supply of native workers, recruitment of
new workers from various locations around the world was considered
necessary in order to expand the economy of Hawai'i (Figure 3-1).
Merchants, missionaries, and officials of the royal government joined
in a cooperative effort to bring new life and blood into Hawai'i.

This chapter focuses on the major racial groups that settled in
Hawai'i during the nineteenth and twentieth centuries. A demographic profile of each ethnic classification is discussed in the order of
historical arrival and adaptation to life in the Islands. While census
information on voluntary and refugee immigrants is limited, some
statistics on Asian and Pacific movement is included in the section
titled "Other Ethnic Groups."

Hawaiians and Part Hawaiians

For over a thousand years the ancient Polynesians settled and mingled
on the isolated islands they had found in the North Pacific, uniting
their tall, brown-skinned, strong physique and their alert tempera-
ment to become the Hawaiian race. In the last two hundred years
since the arrival of persons from other parts of the world, Hawaiian
blood has blended with many nationalities.[7] The miscegenation of
Hawaiians during ten or more generations has confused the anthro-
pological identification of this race and altered the biological factors
of their genetic continuity. Presently most Hawaiians are Part Hawaiians who can trace mixed background with Whites, Chinese, Japanese, Filipinos, Portuguese, and other ethnic peoples who came as
foreigners to the land of the Hawaiians.

A new pride in Hawaiian heritage emerged in the last quarter of the
twentieth century in Hawai'i. The recent renaissance of Hawaiian culture sharpened appreciation for the values of a remarkable Polynesian civilization. George H. S. Kanahele, Hawaiian scholar, civic
leader, businessman, and writer, discusses the effect of cultural transition and reaffirms the dignity and self-esteem of his people:

> One of the greater tragedies in our history lies in the fact that many post-
> contact Hawaiians believed in their racial and personal inferiority and

therefore were ashamed of their ancestors' practices and ideas. We can understand now the psychological reasons for that shame, although we cannot accept their judgments about the quality of Hawaiian civilization in the days of old. Today we can demonstrate through a broad sweep of activities in the traditional Hawaiian culture—from religion and mythology, cosmology, time and space, philosophy, natural science, technology (from mechanics to mathematics), economics, management, to politics and leadership—that *ka po'e kahiko* [the people of ancient times], considering their historical period, location, population, and available natural resources, managed to achieve levels of development equal to and in many cases greater than those reached by comparable societies.[8]

The resurgence of Hawaiians has occurred in politics, education, cultural interests, and business. In 1986 John Waihee was elected as the first person of Hawaiian ancestry to serve as governor of the state

King Kamehameha I united the Hawaiian Islands in 1795. Drawing by Choris, during the Russian Expedition of Kotzebue in 1816. *(Hawaii State Archives)*

of Hawaii. This achievement provided strength to counterbalance some of the loss of power felt by post-contact Hawaiians. "The greatest impact of foreign colonization was perhaps the loss of the indigenous authority structure," said anthropologist Jocelyn Linnekin in a 1975 comprehensive study of a rural Hawaiian community that continued Hawaiian agricultural and social practices.[9] In 1987 Governor Waihee helped Hawaiians celebrate their growth and accomplishments: "This race was near extinction a century ago and has made a remarkable recovery since then. . . . As the first elected Hawaiian governor, I clearly understand that I am a symbol of Hawaiian pride in what we are in the present and what we can become in the future.[10]

Who are the Hawaiians and how many live in the Islands? A tragic loss of pure Hawaiians since 1778 was attributed to high mortality, low fertility, out-migration, and intermarriage (see Chapter 2). Hawaiians, known as kindhearted, affectionate, and hospitable people, were unsuspecting victims of diseases brought to the Islands by visitors.

John D. Waihee, the first person of Hawaiian ancestry to be elected to serve as governor of the state of Hawaii, took office in 1986. *(Courtesy of the Executive Chambers, State Capitol, Honolulu, Hawaii)*

Missionary Artemas Bishop wrote in 1838 of the tragic depopulation of Hawaiians by venereal diseases: "Without a means of cure, the greatest influence [of these diseases] has been to destroy the power of procreation, thus writing childless a vast majority of Hawaiian families."[11] He spoke of large numbers of barren marriages and said that infertility and high mortality had left not more than one in four families with any living children. During this period of social disorganization, he reported: "Many, if not a majority, of the elder and middle aged women have no children of their own." Bishop blamed the seafarers for the ravage of the Hawaiian race: "The unbridled rage of lust [of the seafarers] fastened upon them [the Hawaiians] this curse of foreign depravity. . . . The crisis is now approaching, and the question will soon be decided, whether the Hawaiian nation is to remain a distinct people, or be annihilated."[12]

Hawaiians intermingled with peoples from many nations. The descendants of the early White seafarers were relatively few, in consequence of high infant mortality and high death rates; however, about twenty men from Great Britain and the United States were given positions of rank in the Hawaiian Kingdom and received wives whose procreativity had been carefully protected to preserve the genealogy of the *ali'i* (chiefs).[13] These women were fertile and produced large families. Chinese crewmen also settled in the Islands, took Hawaiian women as wives, and had many children.

Early missionary censuses did not indicate the number of persons of mixed blood. The 1832 count gave Honolulu a foreign population of 180 and other localities showed 15 non-Hawaiians, but there was no identification of ethnicity.[14] It is probable that many half-Hawaiian children were adopted and accepted as pure Hawaiians. "Doubtless the descendants of these pretty fully Hawaiianized half-white children were in the first and second generation almost wholly of the dark mixture, and, having no ground for pride of ancestry, many permitted the memory of their white ancestry to perish," wrote Romanzo Adams.[15]

In 1853, when the number of pure-blooded Hawaiians dropped to 70,036 from the almost 300,000 natives who are believed to have populated the Islands at the time of Cook's arrival, the first census tabulation of Part Hawaiians was 983 (Table 3-1). During the next half-century, the count of Part Hawaiians increased at only a moderate rate. Social standards set by the White community of that period were averse to out-marriage, some immigrants brought wives with them, and fewer Hawaiian women were available for the increasing number of male foreign residents. By 1900 pure Hawaiians were counted at 29,799 and Part Hawaiians numbered only 7,857 persons (Table 3–3.d and Table 3–3.e).

The classification of "Part Hawaiian" has been modified many times by successive censuses. The 1853 census applied the terms "natives" and "half-natives" to the people later called Hawaiian and Part Hawaiian. Between 1860 and 1890 the term "half-castes" was used. The U.S. censuses between 1910 and 1930 adopted a special classification system for Hawai'i, attempting to differentiate between "Caucasian-Hawaiians" and "Asiatic-Hawaiians." In 1940, 1950, and 1960 the United States census and the Hawaii Department of Health reported any Hawaiian admixture as Part Hawaiian, regardless of percentage.[16]

The 1970 U.S. census eliminated the traditional distinction of (full) Hawaiian and Part Hawaiian, since pure-blooded Hawaiians were very few in number and of questionable identity. The Part Hawaiians

Children of Hawaiian ancestry are photographed in Honolulu in the 1920s. *(On Char photo, Bishop Museum)*

were merged into the single category of "Hawaiian" or classified with other races. The census also changed the method for gathering data, from conducting household interviews to mailing questionnaires, which permitted individuals to self-identify their race.[17] The present trend in data-gathering has been to resolve biological and sociological heterogeneity by assuming that persons with mixed genes are in many cases part of only one subculture, which can be identified with reasonable accuracy by each respondent.[18]

The Hawaii Health Surveillance Program, an on-going survey by the Hawaii Department of Health, uses different standards from the census for racial definitions, interview procedure, sample design, and coverage. This sample survey excludes persons in institutions or military barracks, on Niʻihau, and in Kalawao on Molokaʻi. Persons of mixed race are classified by self-identification or by race of mother. These differences in methods of recording race have resulted in confusion and lack of precise comparability of statistics for Hawaiians. Since the state health survey figures are so disparate from the U.S. census tabulations, it is important for program and policy planners in such activities as housing, health, education, and welfare, as well as private businesses, to identify their source of information when using statistics about the Hawaiian population.

Because the ethnic classification systems used over the decades in Hawaiʻi have been altered repeatedly, trends from data in successive U.S. censuses since 1950 cannot be charted with any degree of accuracy. The 1960 census figure of 11,294 Hawaiians and 91,109 Part Hawaiians dropped (artificially, by definitional change) in 1970 to 71,274 Hawaiians, or a loss from 16.1 percent to 9.3 percent of the total state population (Table 3–1). By 1980 the U.S. census counted 115,500 Hawaiians, or 12.0 percent of the state population.[19] This rapid 4.8 percent average annual growth rate for Hawaiians in the 1970–1980 decade reflected natural increase and definitional shifts by self-identification of race or editorial procedures that favored Hawaiian classification.

In contrast, the Hawaii Health Surveillance Program (HHSP), conducting a sample survey of about 15,000 persons representing about 2.5 percent of the households, tabulated 9,366 unmixed Hawaiians and 166,087 Part Hawaiians in 1980 (Table 3–2). A 1986 HHSP sample survey showed a loss of unmixed Hawaiians to 8,093 persons and a gain of Part Hawaiians to 203,355 residents, or almost 20 percent of the total population.[20] State planners prefer use of this higher tabulation of Hawaiians derived from the sample survey. The discrepancy between U.S. census figures and the count of the Hawaii Health Surveillance Program is explained by State Statistician Robert C. Schmitt:

> The growing number of Hawaii residents with one-eighth, one-sixteenth, or even less Hawaiian blood suggests the possibility that many such persons, technically classified as Part Hawaiians, may be reporting themselves as non-Hawaiians to census enumerators. Evidence supporting such a notion appears in migration estimates, which show a heavy net out-migration for Hawaiians and Part Hawaiians. These estimates, computed by the residual method, may in fact reflect "passing" of Part Hawaiians as non-Hawaiians as much as they mirror a true out-migration. A Part Hawaiian child, correctly classified on its birth certificate but thought of as non-Hawaiian by the census-taker, would appear as an out-migrant in computations of intercensal components of population change.[21]

Evidence of this loss appears in the Part Hawaiian population pyramids (Figure 3–2). From a relatively small population with a balanced sex ratio in 1900, the Part Hawaiian population expanded steadily until 1960, indicating high birth rates from the increased number of persons in the lower age groups. The abrupt reduction in numbers of persons up to the age of twenty in 1970 and 1980 reflects U.S. census definitional changes, in which children of Part Hawaiian blood were tabulated with parents in another racial group (usually White, Part Hawaiian, or Chinese Part Hawaiian). The inflated pyramid for 1980 indicates increased numbers of people in all age groups.

The population pyramids for the pure Hawaiian graphically portray the loss of that group in the sequence from 1900 to 1960 (Figure 3–2). Tabulations for pure Hawaiians by age and sex were not recorded by the U.S. census after 1960.

The 1980 Hawaiian sex ratio of 101.9 gives a balanced group of 57,205 males and 58,295 females (Table 3–3.d; Table 3–3.e). The largest number of Hawaiians reside in Honolulu County on Oʻahu, although their number represents only 10.5 percent of that county's population in contrast to 18.8 percent in Hawaii County and 17.4 percent in Maui County (Table 3–4).

By 1985 Hawaiians registered about 5,500 births and 1,000 deaths each year (Table 3–5). Fertility rates that use 1980 U.S. census figures as the denominator for the population of Hawaiians present disproportionately high figures when contrasted to rates that use 1980 Hawaii Health Surveillance Program population estimates (Table 3–7). For example:

HAWAIIAN

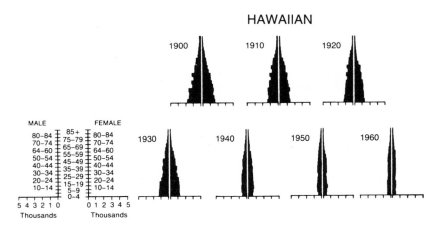

PART HAWAIIAN

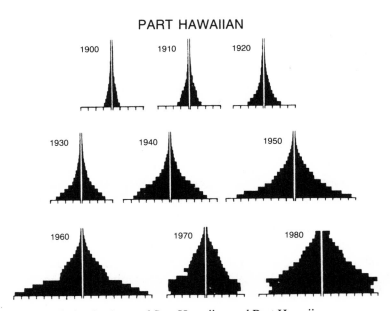

Figure 3-2. Population by Age and Sex: Hawaiian and Part Hawaiian

Note: These pyramids are based on U.S. census definition of race and are not comparable to Hawaii Health Surveillance Program tabulations of Part Hawaiians. Changing definitions in 1970 and 1980 resulted in a loss of Part Hawaiians, especially among ages 0–19, to Chinese, White, and other racial groups.

Source: See Table 3–3.d.

Fertility of Hawaiians

Hawaiians, 1980	U.S. Census	Health Survey
Crude Birth Rate	34.7	22.7
General Fertility Rate	142.7	91.9
Total Fertility Rate	3.8	2.5

Fertility rates for Hawaiians appear slightly higher than the state average; this may be explained by the comparatively young age of the Hawaiian population, by social change with high rates of intermarriage, and by cultural practice that favors childbearing. The child-woman ratio of Hawaiians has dropped from 913.1 in 1960 to 463.6 in 1980, a significant reduction in numbers of children under 5 years old per 1,000 Hawaiian women age 15 to 44 and only slightly above the state average of 339 children per 1,000 women of that age group (Table 3–6). The largest percentage of Hawaiian births occurs to women below age 25, and this racial group has the highest rate of births among all ethnic categories in the state for girls age 15 to 19 (Table 3–8).

Hawaiians have a comparatively high level of births to unmarried mothers, a general acceptance of the practice of adoption, and a low level of abortion (Table 3–9), reflecting cultural values.[22] According to psychocultural observer Dr. Benjamin B. C. Young: "If viewed from strict observational and epidemiological data, there are exceptionally high rates of adoption and illegitimacy among Hawaiians. This does not necessarily suggest a negative connotation. In fact, quite often the opposite is true. It matters not that the parents of a child are unmarried. What matters is that a child has been brought into the world and must be cared for. . . . With this understanding of the Hawaiians' love for children, regardless of legitimacy or illegitimacy, it is easy to comprehend the concept of *hānai* (adoption)."[23]

The Hawaiian family *'ohana* relationship is explained by Mary Kawena Pukui, E. W. Haertig, and Catherine A. Lee in their extensive discussion of Hawaiian cultural knowledge, *Nānā I Ke Kumu*, Volumes 1 and 2: "The child knew both cousins and siblings as brothers and sisters; parents, aunts, and uncles, all as mothers and fathers; grandaunts and granduncles, all as grandparents. From babyhood, the Hawaiian *keiki* was part of a close-knit social structure of many persons."[24]

Miscegenation of ethnic groups in Hawai'i occurred in three stages: first, there was extensive admixture between foreign men (primarily White and Chinese) and Hawaiian women; second, as immigrant groups brought their wives and picture brides, out-marriage was discouraged; and finally, after World War II, intermarriage became increasingly accepted and widespread.[25] Extremely high rates of interracial marriages for pure Hawaiians contributed to their dilution and amalgamation into other racial groups. The Part Hawaiians have also demonstrated high levels of intermarriage, with about 55.8 to 61.3 percent of brides and grooms in 1960 through 1980 selecting spouses of a different ethnicity (Table 3–10).

Since the arrival of foreigners to the Islands, Hawaiians have suffered high rates of morbidity and mortality. *Ka po'e kahiko,* the ancient Hawaiians, enjoyed general good health. Their high-fiber, low-fat, limited-sugar diets, their physical activity and personal cleanliness, and their freedom from contagious diseases contributed to well-being.[26] Illness was considered an imbalance of spiritual or psychological strength, and healing was effected through chants, pray-

Intermarriage of Hawaiians and Chinese is seen in this family photo of Ualani Kala and husband Keong Lee, with their son, daughter, and Chinese son-in-law. *(On Char photo, Bishop Musuem)*

ers, and medicines.[27,28] The introduction of infectious diseases devastated the native population for over one hundred years, and changes in cultural and social practices altered adaptive abilities for health maintenance.

A study of differential mortality in Honolulu before 1900 shows higher than average death rates among Hawaiians and Part Hawaiians.[29] While immigrant groups, at least during the plantation era, often had the highest death rates for a brief period after their arrival, pure Hawaiians recorded the poorest life expectancy.[30] Mortality rates for pure Hawaiians have been consistently higher than for Part Hawaiians, whose rates were not substantially greater than those of the "all races" group.[31,32] Primary causes of Hawaiian deaths in the period 1980–1985 were diseases of the heart, cancer, cerebrovascular disease, and diabetes mellitus, occurring at a slightly higher rate than the same leading causes of death in the United States' total population.[33,34] The Hawaiians have had the highest or next highest rate for many health indices studies, directing attention to the need for increased medical care.[35]

In measurement of life expectancy, Hawaiians have demonstrated a remarkable extension of life in the past hundred years. In 1883–1886, life expectancy in Honolulu (with over half the population pure Hawaiian) was only 32.0 years.[36] By 1980 the life expectancy for Hawaiians at 74.0 years exceeded that for the U.S. total population at 73.7 years (Table 4–10).[37] Since 1910 Hawaiians have added over 41 years to their life expectancy. Although life expectancy for Hawaiians measures slightly lower than that for other ethnic groups in Hawai'i, this finding probably reflects factors that affect mortality, such as nutrition, medical care, income, education, housing, and lifestyle, which can be expected to change with improved economic and social patterns.

"These are the modern Hawaiians, a vastly different people from their ancient progenitors," says Hawaiian scholar and author George S. Kanahele. "Two centuries of enormous, almost cataclysmic change imposed from within and without have altered their conditions, outlooks, attitudes, and values. Although some traditional practices and beliefs have been retained, even these have been modified. In general, today's Hawaiians have little familiarity with the ancient culture."[38]

Hawaiians in Hawai'i in the last quarter of the twentieth century are a vibrant, proud, rapidly growing, young, heterogeneous group, with only 4.5 percent at age 65 and over (Table 4–12). Hawaiian resurgence is observed in politics, culture, education, and economics, with leading roles taken by highly educated native people.[39] Hawaiian activist, political theorist, and University of Hawai'i professor Haunani-Kay Trask commented in 1982:

> Hawaiians have begun to reveal a new consciousness about their heritage, their subjugation to American imperialism, and their pride in being Hawaiian. Part of the expanding awareness can be seen in the recent movement for cultural and political rights which has erupted in local Hawaiian communities throughout the state, and which includes demands for restitution in both land and money from the American government. Other indications are the flowering of Hawaiian dance, the establishment of societies for Hawaiian artists, and a renewed emphasis on Hawaiian as a living, spoken language. The heart of this Hawaiian revival is the concept and practice of *aloha 'aina*—love for the land.[40]

By the end of the next century the Hawaiians, the most intermingled of all the races in the Islands, may have merged to fuse biological differences, and education and life in Hawai'i may have reduced cultural dissimilarities. By then it may not be necessary to have some blood of the ancient Polynesians to qualify as a Hawaiian. Hawaiiana scholar E. S. C. Handy said: "All of us here in Hawaii, whether we have Hawaiian blood or not, are proud of the fact that we have aloha

A family living in Honolulu, Hawai'i, in 1975 of Hawaiian, Chinese, Japanese, Filipino, and White descent. *(Lynette K. Tong photo)*

for each other and for strangers. It is really impossible for true Hawaiians to draw apart and be a separate group because there are many people who are just as Hawaiian in attitude and point of view as those of Hawaiian blood."[41]

Hawaiian treasure and *kumu* hula teacher Maiki Aiu Lake shared her love of the land and cultural knowledge, joining together *kama'āina* (oldtimers) and *malihini* (newcomers) by her advice: "Take off your shoes and walk barefoot in the sand and feel the *'āina* [land] and the sea between your toes. Breathe the sweet air. Look up at the mountains. Savor it all. And if you love these things, you love Hawai'i."[42]

Whites

White people reached Hawai'i's shores as early explorers, seafarers, tradesmen, missionaries, plantation laborers, merchants, members of the armed forces, and in-migrants from the mainland United States. After two hundred years of immigration and intermarriage, the White population is counted in the 1980s at about a quarter of the state population and by miscegenation is represented among all ethnic groups in Hawai'i (Table 3–1; Table 3–3.j).

It is possible that late pre-contact Hawaiian culture was influenced by the accidental arrival of White people. Sometime after A.D. 1500 voyagers are reported to have landed on the island of Hawai'i, and the feathered helmets and cloaks of the ancient Hawaiians may have been designed according to instructions from castaways. (See discussion on possible early Spanish influence, Chapter 2.)[43]

The exploration voyage of Captain James Cook in 1778 opened the Islands to White habitation and intermarriage. A few seamen deserted ship to remain in the Hawaiian chain. Archibald Campbell, who visited the Sandwich Islands in 1809, wrote:

> At one time during my stay, there were nearly sixty white people upon Wahoo [O'ahu] alone; but the number was constantly varying, and was considerably diminished before my departure. Although the great majority had been left by American vessels, not above one third of them belonged to that nation; the rest were almost all English, and of these six or eight were convicts who had made their escape from New South Wales.
>
> Many inducements are held out to sailors to remain here. If they conduct themselves with propriety, they rank as chiefs, and are entitled to all the privileges of the order; at all events, they are certain of being main-

tained by some of the chiefs, who are always anxious to have white people about them. The king has a considerable number in his service, chiefly carpenters, joiners, masons, blacksmiths, and bricklayers; these he rewards liberally with grants of land. . . . [44]

White persons became known as *haole,* from the Hawaiian words *ha* or "breath" and *'ole* "without," a term originally used by Hawaiians for persons who could not speak the Hawaiian language and did not understand the native culture.[45] *Haole* did not indicate skin color in its early usage—the term was applied in reference to a stranger. In the early nineteenth century the Hawaiian words *ha'ole 'ele 'ele* were used in speaking about Black foreigners.[46] *Haole* was applied to foreign residents from America, the British Empire, France, and Russia.[47]

Today there is some ambiguity in interpreting which persons are *haole.* This term usually refers to people of light-complexioned skin, yet often their mixed ancestry traces origins from many regions of the world. According to sociologist Bernhard Hormann: "Haole today has connotations of 'upper class' or 'upper middle class'. It may also connote 'outsider' or 'person who is not quite local'."[48] The expressions "mainland haole," "military haole," and "local haole" usually refer to persons who associate primarily with others of the same group and do not integrate into the total population.

The number of Whites remained small in the kingdom of Hawai'i in the first half of the nineteenth century. Protestant missionaries listed fewer than two hundred arrivals between 1820 and 1847.[49] Although there was a sharp increase in the number of merchant, whaling, and military vessels stopping in the Islands, few persons remained to establish permanent homes.

Immigrants who were brought from Europe as plantation laborers, including Portuguese, Germans, Norwegians, Spaniards, and Puerto Ricans, were classified in the censuses of the Hawaiian Kingdom and the United States by their countries of origin until they were included in the broader definition "Caucasian," or "White" (the latter term has been used by the U.S. census since 1970).

The adoption of the Reciprocity Treaty with the United States in 1876 permitted the exportation of duty-free sugar from the kingdom of Hawai'i to a large American market. This gave impetus to the Hawaiian government to subsidize recruitment of labor. The White population, stimulated by business interests and importation of contract labor from Europe, increased in six years from 3,748 persons in 1878 to 16,579 inhabitants by 1884.

The Hawaiian Sugar Planters' Association (HSPA) was established to coordinate the efforts of planters, plantation agents, and others concerned with agricultural production. Disillusioned by the employment of Polynesians, who had been brought from several Pacific islands for plantation labor but who adapted poorly to field work, and responding to resident community criticism of the rapidly increasing number of Chinese males, the HSPA prepared more liberal contract agreements to bring new employees from Portugal.

Between 1878 and 1887 seventeen ships brought almost twelve thousand Portuguese from the islands of Madeira and the Azores to the Hawaiian Islands.[50] The Portuguese migration was initiated in response to poor economic conditions in the mother country where a blight had crippled the the wine industry, resulting in unemployment and hunger. As standards of living worsened, the people welcomed prospects for a better way to exist. Portuguese workers who moved to Hawai'i were considered sober, thrifty, honest, industrious, and peaceable, and the presence of their wives and families gave them social stability.

Portuguese laborers came to Hawai'i with their women and children, bringing a musical instrument that was adapted by the Hawaiians to become the 'ukulele. *(Hawaii State Archives)*

When the Hawaiian Islands were designated a territory of the United States in 1900, they became subject to U.S. laws. At that time the United States did not permit people from Asia to become naturalized citizens, so the Hawaii Board of Immigration in 1905 adopted a policy to try to bring to Hawai'i persons who would be eligible for U.S. citizenship. Potential immigrant families from Portugal and Spain were offered an acre of land, a house, and improved working conditions. Almost 13,000 persons (4,334 men, 3,169 women, and 5,388 children) responded in the second large wave of Portuguese immigration in 1906 to 1913.

The Portuguese became the *luna* (foremen) on the plantations, and their families settled into Island communities and multiplied. Most of the Spaniards moved on to California, where they joined other Spanish communities.

John Henry Felix and Peter F. Senecal, Portuguese historians, offer a self-portrait of an immigrant from Portugal:

We came with our families to settle down and stay, to build Hawaii, not just to make money and run away. We worked the land hard and kept our

Portuguese *luna* and Chinese laborers working on a Hawaiian sugar plantation in 1896. *(Hawaii State Archives)*

homes well. Our wives stayed at home where they belonged. We loved the outdoors and animals and pets. We had no crazy ideas about becoming lawyers, doctors, or engineers, but were willing to work with the great and good men who settled Hawaii and made it what it is today. We were open and honest with others. We were devout Catholics and instilled in our children respect for the social order. We did not become troublemakers.[51]

The number of persons of Portuguese descent in Hawai'i increased from 9,967 in 1884 to 27,588 residents in 1930, the last census to count this ethnic group as a separate category (Table 3–1). Portuguese have shown high rates of intermarriage and fertility. About 57,500 persons of Portuguese ancestry were estimated to live in Hawai'i in 1980.[52]

Private enterprise initiated the recruitment of several northern European groups. Two vessels in 1881 brought about six hundred Scandinavians—primarily Norwegians, with a few Swedes—including women and children. However, their food preferences, meat and dairy products, and their training as artisans and tradesmen did not

Albert Bechert of Hammerstein, West Prussia, Germany (now Poland) moved with his family to Kaua'i in 1885 for employment with the Lihue Plantation Company. By 1895 five Hawai'i-born children (front row) had joined the three German-born children in the family. *(Edna Bechert collection)*

A Puerto Rican immigrant with newly granted U.S. citizenship poses with his family in 1917 in the military uniform of his country. *(Blaze Camacho Souza collection)*

suit them to plantation life.[53] Only about fifty of the Scandinavian immigrants are estimated to have remained in the Islands; most of them moved to the mainland United States or returned home.[54]

German immigrants were selected by a private commercial firm, H. Hackfeld and Company, with more attention to their adaptability to life in a semitropical climate and to plantation work. Almost 1,400 persons arrived from northwest Germany between 1881 and 1897. Under the paternalistic care of a Kaua'i sugar plantation, they formed a successful community that continued many of their homeland customs.[55] The German community felt the backlash of America's war hysteria in World War I (1914–1918) and sought to de-emphasize their cultural heritage during the period of war between their native and adoptive countries.[56] This group made considerable contributions to the business, religious, literary, medical, and educational life in Hawai'i, and it strongly influenced musical trends by integrating many German and Austrian melodies into Hawaiian music.[57]

Russian vessels brought residents of the imperial domain of Catherine II to Hawai'i in 1804 during the reign of Kamehameha I.[58] The Russians were befriended by Kaumuali'i of Kaua'i and later by King Kamehameha, and food provisions were offered to them in exchange for sea otter skins.[59] Czar Alexander I refused to acknowledge a fort built by Russians at Waimea, Kaua'i, in 1817, and he instructed his representatives to limit their work to peaceful commercial relations with the island kingdom. Without government support, the Russians departed.[60,61] A group of Ukrainian laborers signed contracts in 1897 to serve on sugar plantations in Hawai'i for a three-year term.[62] In the early twentieth century, the Hawaii Board of Immigration recruited 110 Molokans and more than 2,000 Russians from Harbin in Manchuria, but few remained in the Islands after their period of plantation contract.[63]

Puerto Ricans, a Spanish-speaking people, became U.S. nationals when Puerto Rico was named a territory of the United States in 1898 following the Spanish-American War. In 1899 a severe hurricane in Puerto Rico devastated coffee, tobacco, sugar, fruit, and vegetable crops; and homes, schools, and office buildings were destroyed. With the loss of jobs and with a depressed Spanish *peso,* laborers responded positively to prospects of a new life and employment in the Territory of Hawaii.[64,65] In response to promises of free transportation, housing, education, and medical care, 5,203 persons, including 2,869 men and boys age twelve and over, left their homeland in 1900 and 1901 to move to Hawai'i. They drew their diverse ethnic heritage from pre-Columbian Indians, Caucasians of Spanish background, and Blacks of African descent.

Puerto Rican intermarriage with Portuguese, Spaniards, Hawaiians, and Filipinos was common, and the family size was large. In 1950, in the last U.S. census in which Puerto Ricans were counted separately, their number had increased to 9,551 persons (Table 3–1). About 15,000 persons reported Puerto Rican ancestry in Hawai'i in 1980.[66]

Other White groups whose importation costs were subsidized by government or plantations moved to the Islands during the late nine-

Hawai'i residents of Scottish-English-Dutch ancestry play with their dogs at Kawela Bay on the north shore of O'ahu in 1976. *(R. Nordyke family collection)*

teenth and early twentieth centuries. They included 372 Austrians, 84 Italians, a few Scots, and about 100 White Americans.[67]

Some Scots came independently to Hawai'i and made permanent contributions to the culture. Princess Kai'ulani, the last princess of the Hawaiian royalty, was half Scottish—her parents were Princess Miriam Likelike and Archibald Scott Cleghorn. Scottish immigrants were horticulturists, engineers, accountants, and educators. As plantation employees they were admired as "self-reliant, self-sufficient, and responsible."[68] No separate census count of Scot immigrants was taken, since they were identified by the census among persons from the British Islands, but the 1980 U.S. census showed 24,300 persons in Hawai'i reporting Scottish ancestry.

Another group counted among the White population was the Greeks. These people arrived independently from Greece, and many encouraged their relatives and friends to follow. Between 1879 and 1914, about eighty-five male Greeks from Sparta settled in the Islands, followed by twelve Greek women.[69] Several hundred second-

and third-generation Americans of Greek ancestry moved to Hawai'i in the twentieth century. The infusion of Greek culture in Hawai'i contributed new language, music, and foods, as well as business knowledge and Greek Orthodox religious practices.

In 1853 there were 1,687 Whites, which constitututed 2.0 percent of the population; by 1970 they included 301,429 persons, or 39.2 percent; and in 1980 they comprised 318,770 persons, or 33.0 percent of the people in Hawai'i (Table 3-1). The population pyramids for Whites show a steady expansion at all age levels. The presence of White military personnel is observable in the heavy concentration of males aged 20 to 29, especially between 20 and 24 (Figure 3-3). A decline in fertility during the Depression years is apparent in the contraction of numbers of persons born during that period and continues as they age through the decades. Reduced numbers in the 15 to 19 age group in 1950–1960 show out-migration. The comparatively large 1970 and 1980 pyramids mirror the expanded population of Whites through the presence of the armed forces and their dependents who consist primarily of Whites, to in-migration of Whites from the continental United States, and to changed census definitions of race.

The average annual growth rate of 0.56 for Whites in the 1970–1980 decade was significantly less than the state population annual growth rate of 2.3 percent. This reflected large interstate in- and out-migration of Whites, some change of Whites to other classifications, and the growth of population in Hawai'i by other ethnic groups during that period.

While there were only 16,531 males to 12,288 females in the White population in 1900, these numbers swelled to 171,064 males and 147,706 females among that ethnic group in 1980. Much of the excess of White males is found in age groups 20–24 years and is attributed to the military presence (Table 3-3.j). The presence of Whites in Honolulu County dropped from 41.2 percent in 1970 to 33.1 percent in 1980, while Hawaii, Kauai, and Maui counties showed a significant growth of White persons in that period (Table 3-4).

In 1900, Whites had 306 births and 318 deaths in contrast to 4,696 births and 1,749 deaths for this group in 1985; however, about 3,000 of these White births occurred to members of the armed services and their dependents who usually do not remain in Hawai'i as permanent residents (Table 3-6). Fertility in 1980 of civilian Whites was very low. With the inclusion of military population, the White crude birth rate of 18.4 births per 1,000 population, the total fertility rate of 1.9 children per 1,000 women of child-bearing age, the child-woman ratio of

WHITE

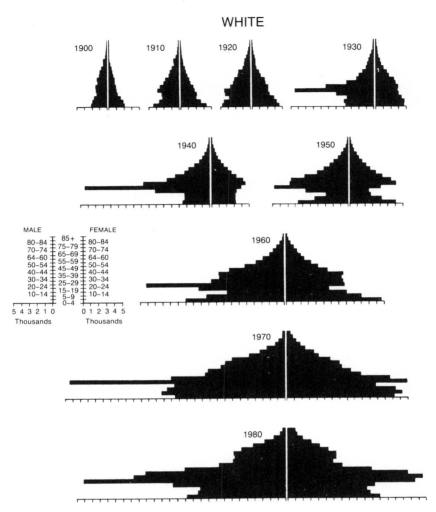

Figure 3-3. Population by Age and Sex: White
Note: See note, Table 3-3.a. These pyramids are based on U.S. census definition of race.
Source: See Table 3-3.j.

314 children per 1,000 women, and the age-specific fertility rates signified fertility levels below state average (Table 3-6, Table 3-8). The use of elective abortions among Whites was slightly lower than the average for the population of Hawai'i (Table 3-9.).

Whites showed the lowest participation in interracial marriage among both brides and grooms (Table 3-10). However, when visitors who marry in Hawai'i (usually White) are excluded from the tabulations, White residents indicate a slightly higher rate of intermarriage.

The White racial group living in Hawai'i added 19 years to life expectancy in the 1920–1980 period. In 1980 White males could expect to live on the average to 74.2 years and females to 79.1 years (Table 4–10). In 1980 the White population in Hawai'i included 6.8 percent in the group age 65 and over; among all persons age 65 and above in the state, 28.3 percent were White (Table 4–12).

The White population has become one of the largest ethnic groups in the state. At present, when the Whites in the military population and in the daily visitor population are added to the resident Whites, this group represents more than one-third of the people of Hawai'i.

Chinese

Chinese were the first Asians to come to Hawai'i. After the opening of the Hawaiian Islands to Western seafarers by Captain Cook's expedition in 1778, merchant ships with Chinese crewmen stopped at these semitropical mid-Pacific islands for water, rest, refreshment, and provisions before making their journey across the Pacific to the northwest region of America.[70]

In 1788 Captain John Meares sailed from China, commanding two vessels with crews of Europeans and fifty Chinese, including artisans and carpenters. The next year Captain Simon Metcalfe on the schooner *Eleanora* reached Maui from Macao with a crew of ten Americans and forty-five Chinese.[71] Some of the crewmembers of these British and American ships remained in the Hawaiian Islands and married native women.[72,73] Captain George Vancouver reported a Chinese resident upon his visit to the Sandwich Islands in 1794.[74] By 1838 there were between thirty and forty Chinese counted among the four hundred foreigners residing in Honolulu.[75]

The accidental discovery of sandalwood among firewood obtained by early fur traders established a commercial relationship with China. During the period from 1790 to 1840, Hawai'i's sandalwood and labor were exploited in exchange for economic growth.[76] People of China came to know Hawai'i as Tan Heung Shan, or the Sandalwood Mountains.[77]

The Chinese are credited with developing the first sugar mill in Hawai'i. Although sugar cane was present in Hawai'i upon Cook's arrival, its use was limited. In 1802 a Chinese, Wong Tze-Chun, brought a mill and boilers aboard a sandalwood trading ship and set up the first venture in sugar production on Lana'i.[78] Another mill was developed by two Chinese men, Ahung and Atai, on Maui in 1828, and Chinese participated in the manufacture of sugar on Kaua'i in the mid-1830s and on the island of Hawai'i in the 1840s. A visitor to the Sandwich Islands in 1856 reported: "Whalers and other vessels touching at the islands had occasionally left some Chinese behind them; and it was soon discovered that not only were these men better laborers, generally, than the natives, but that they were so superior in industry and steadier, that they could be employed with the greatest advantage as overseers of estates."[79]

The enterprising Chinese pioneers started numerous businesses, including rice farming, general merchandising, a bakery, restaurants, and the sale of wines and liquors. They formed companies with Island foreigners, and they recruited other Chinese to come to Hawai'i as commercial partners.[80]

One of the first concerns of the Royal Hawaiian Agricultural Society, founded in 1850, was the acute shortage of workers. It commissioned Captain Cass of the barque *Thetis* to obtain a supply of laborers from China for employment on the sugar plantations. He returned

Contract laborers from China arrive in Hawai'i in the 1880s. *(Hawaii State Archives)*

with 175 field hands and 20 domestic servants.[81] The early groups of indentured immigrants to enter Hawaii were from the two southeastern maritime provinces of Kwangtung and Fukien in mainland China.[82] Under provisions authorized by the *Act for the Government of Masters and Servants,* passed in 1850, laborers could be imported to Hawai'i as apprenticed plantation workers to serve for terms not to exceed five years. Chinese men willingly left their homeland, which was at that time in a state of political and economic crisis, to move to the "land of fragrant sandalwood mountains." They were offered free passage, wages of $3 a month, clothing, and room and board in exchange for a promise to work for five years on a sugar plantation.[83]

Their arrival and adaptation to a new life in Hawai'i is described by a Chinese historian:

> When they reached Honolulu, they were kept in the quarantine station for about two weeks. They were made to clean themselves in a tank and have their clothes fumigated. Planters looked them over and picked them for work in much the same way a horse was looked at before he was bought. These Chinese were taken to the plantations. There they lived in grass houses or unpainted wooden buildings with dirt floors. Sometimes as many as forty men were put into one room. They slept on wooden boards about two feet wide and about three feet from the floor. Every morning at five, their bosses, called *lunas,* marched them to the fields. There they cut the sugar cane and hauled it on their backs to ox drawn carts which took the cane to the mill to be made into sugar. While they worked, they were not allowed to talk or smoke. They could rest only at times okayed by the *lunas.* If the men slowed down in their work or showed signs of not working, for whatever reason, the *lunas* whipped them with black snake whips.[84]

The early Chinese arrivals were reported to be quiet, able, and willing workers, but they were criticized by King Kamehameha IV as having "no affinities, attractions, or tendencies to blend with this or any other race."[85] Later they were accused by health authorities of introducing smallpox, leprosy, and opium addiction to the Hawaiian community. As their contracts expired, they moved into the towns, and authorities held them responsible for contributing to unemployment, gambling, and crime, as well as for competing with natives and other foreigners in new business endeavors. Dr. William Hillebrand, royal commissioner to China and India, explained to the Hawaiian Board of Immigration in 1865: "The fault has been in great measure with ourselves, inasmuch as no females were imported at the time, and no organization existed to control and direct the course of those who had served out their time."[86]

In 1864 the Bureau of Immigration was created to control more closely the importation of foreign labor.[87] Both the United States and Great Britain were sensitive to criticisms of "coolie trade" in the kingdom of Hawai'i, because, especially with the U.S. endorsement of human rights at the conclusion of the U.S. Civil War in 1865, any contract system that might resemble serfdom or slavery was objectionable. The Hawaiian government reaffirmed its position that immigration was promoted for the primary purpose of population reinforcement, rather than for obtaining labor for economic growth through expansion of the sugar industry.

The effect of the large numbers of Chinese males on the composition of the population was a continuing concern of the legislators. Commissioner of Immigration William Hillebrand agreed to go to China to secure coolies "of the most respectable and best class of persons" and to try to induce wives and families to accompany the men.[88,89] He returned in 1865 with 473 male laborers and 52 wives.[90]

With the passage in 1876 of the Reciprocity Treaty, which allowed Hawaiian sugar and rice to be imported to the United States free of duty, the demand for plantation labor skyrocketed.[91] To encourage immigration, the legislative assembly appropriated funds to bring more laborers and their families to Hawai'i. Wages for plantation workers increased to $12 to $14 per month, excluding board.[92] Chinese were actively recruited from China and California. During the late nineteenth and early twentieth centuries, a significant number of Chinese immigrants arrived who embraced the Christian faith.[93]

Between 1866 and 1884, the population of Chinese in Hawai'i increased from 1,300 to more than 18,000 persons (Table 3–1; Table 3–3.b). For every 17 Chinese men in 1884, there was only 1 Chinese woman. United States Secretary of State James G. Blaine wrote in 1881:

The steady diminution of the native population of the islands, amounting to some 10 percent between 1872 and 1878, and still continuing, is doubtless a cause of great alarm to the government of the kingdom. . . . The problem, however, is not to be met by a substitution of Mongolian supremacy for native control—as seems at first sight possible through the rapid increase in Chinese immigration to the islands. . . . The Hawaiian

Islands cannot be joined to the Asiatic system. If they drift from their independent station it must be toward assimilation and identification with the American system. . . . [94]

In response to reports of mistreatment and exploitation of the Chinese plantation workers and of abuses in the policies of recruiting and transporting laborers, the government of China in 1881 prohibited emigration to Hawai'i. The colonial office in London also issued a directive that emigration from Hong Kong to the Hawaiian Islands be stopped. On May 6, 1882, the United States adopted the Chinese Exclusion Act in response to anti-Chinese agitation in California, with the result that some Chinese migrated to Hawai'i from the West Coast, and others on their way to California changed their destination to the kingdom of Hawai'i.

In 1883 the Hawaiian Cabinet Council, concerned that the Chinese had glutted the Hawaiian labor market, passed a resolution restricting Chinese immigration to 2,400 persons per year. Hawaiian government regulations in 1885 and 1886 virtually ended Chinese contract labor

The family of a Chinese merchant poses in front of its Honolulu business establishment in the 1920s. *(On Char photo, Bishop Museum)*

immigration by requiring that passports be issued only to residents who had been working in trade or industrial enterprises in Hawaiʻi for at least one year, to Chinese women and children, and to a few residents of China who were invited to the Islands by the minister of foreign affairs. Chinese were permitted to enter Hawaiʻi under conditional work permits that required departure in five years.[95,96]

During the next decade, regulations concerning entry of Chinese laborers were adjusted in an effort to conform to the government policy of restricting their immigration so that Chinese arrivals would not exceed Chinese departures.[97] Many Chinese who settled in Hawaiʻi before the 1885 and 1886 regulations fulfilled their contracts to work on the sugar plantations and moved to other agricultural pursuits, including the cultivation of rice, vegetables, and coffee, while others joined businesses in metropolitan areas. In 1888 there were 5,727 Chinese employed on the sugar plantations, but by 1892 only 2,617 persons participated in that work. Some Chinese laborers returned to their homeland, and between 1884 and 1890 the Chinese population in Hawaiʻi declined from 18,254 to 16,752 persons.

Historian Clarence Glick, discussing Chinese migrants who remained in the Islands and established a resident community that was part of Hawaiʻi's multiethnic society, has written:

> Chinese who entered from the mid-1880's onward in one or another exempt category played a disproportionate role in this process. They included merchants, bankers, newspaper editors, Chinese-language-school teachers, physicians, Christian ministers and priests, priests of Buddhist and Taoist sects, professors, artists. Merchants were the most numerous of the men in these categories; there were probably no more than a few hundred in all the other categories combined. Men in these categories could bring their wives, even after Annexation, and their children born in Hawaii qualified for American citizenship under the principle of *jus soli*. These families helped to reduce the preponderance of males in the Hawaii Chinese population and to provide a broader basis for the perpetuation and ultimate growth of a Chinese ethnic group in Hawaii.[98]

When Hawaiʻi became a territory of the United States in 1900, the U.S. Chinese Exclusion laws were extended to the Islands, virtually discontinuing Chinese immigration apart from those from China who could qualify for an exempt status. These laws remained in effect until their repeal in 1943. Since World War II, Chinese immigration has been expanded by congressional legislation including the War

Brides Act of 1946, the Walter-McCarran Act of 1948, the Immigration and Nationality Act of 1952, the Refugee Relief Act of 1953, the Refugee Escape Act of 1957, and the amended Immigration and Nationality Act of 1965 (See Chapter 4, section on migration).[99,100]

Estimates of the total number of Chinese immigrants arriving in Hawai'i over the past two hundred years have ranged from 40,000 to 50,000 (Table 3-11; Table 4-15). Restrictive laws caused their numbers to decline, and about 27,000 Chinese left the Islands between 1886 and 1903. With the repeal of the United States Chinese Exclusion Act in 1943, the liberalization of immigration quotas, and improved political climate, there has been a significant increase in Chinese migration to Hawai'i from the People's Republic of China, Hong Kong, and Taiwan to about 800 persons annually in the 1980s.

The 1853 census of the Hawaiian Kingdom counted 364 persons from China. By 1980, the U.S. census reported 56,285 Chinese in Hawai'i, or 5.8 percent of the total state population (Table 3-1). About 94 percent of Hawai'i's Chinese resided in Honolulu County; the number of this group living in Hawaii and Maui counties was reduced in the 1970-1980 decade (Table 3-4). The unbalanced sex ratio that occurred in the late nineteenth century owing to disproportionate male immigration was eliminated by 1980, with the presence of 27,871 males and 28,414 females among Hawai'i's Chinese (Table 3-3.b).

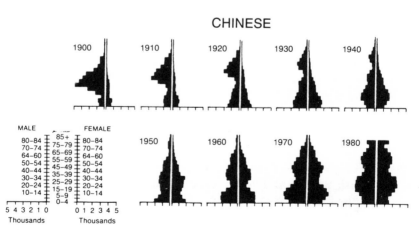

Figure 3-4. Population by Age and Sex: Chinese
Note: These pyramids are based on U.S. census definition of race.
Source: See Table 3-3.b.

The population pyramids for Chinese show the excess of males from 1900 to 1940 and their aging through the decades (Figure 3–4). The sex ratio became more balanced during 1950–1980. Although the number of Chinese in the total population has been comparatively small, the increase in their population during this century is seen in the expansion of the pyramids among persons over age five. The growth in 1970 and 1980 could indicate an in-migration of Chinese (which did not really occur in that volume) or the absorption of persons who had been classified in another ethnic category in previous censuses (the transfer of Part Hawaiians into the Chinese group). The 1980 pyramid clearly demonstrates limitation of fertility and an aging population.

Chinese have participated in a high rate of intermarriage. In 1985, 61.8 percent of Chinese grooms and 66.4 percent of Chinese brides were reported as marrying persons of other races (Table 3–10). Fertility rates were low in 1980, with a crude birth rate of only 12.5 births per 1,000 Chinese, and a general fertility rate of 53.7 children per

Three generations of a professional Chinese family reside in Honolulu in 1988. *(Peter H. P. Ho collection)*

1,000 women of childbearing age (Table 3–6). The child-woman ratio of 240 was far below the state average of 339, and the total fertility rate fell from 8.4 in 1930 to 1.5 in 1980. A review of age-specific fertility rates shows a high fertility level among Chinese women in 1930 that fell to a depressed fertility rate among all ages of this group half a century later. It indicates that Chinese women in Hawai'i in 1980 delayed childbearing to ages 25–34 and used family planning methods including abortion for fertility control (Table 3–8; Table 3–9). This low fertility may relate to problems of racial definitions, since some of the children of Chinese women who out-married were tabulated according to the race of the father.

In 1980 Chinese life expectancy was high at 78.4 years for males and 81.7 years for women, who were the longest-lived group in the Islands. These figures were 15 years longer than life expectancy in mainland China (Table 4–8; Table 4–10).

In the late twentieth century, the Chinese in Hawai'i are a blend of descendants of nineteenth-century immigrants and newly arrived migrants from Taiwan, Hong Kong, the People's Republic of China, and the mainland United States.[101] They represent an older population, with 11.7 percent over age 65 in 1980 (Table 4–12). The largest percentage of Chinese reside in Honolulu as highly educated, cultured, and urbanized members of the Hawaiian community.

Japanese

Probably the earliest migrants to the Hawaiian Islands after Polynesian settlement were the Japanese. In ancient Hawai'i from the thirteenth to the eighteenth centuries, there were several incidents of accidental visits by Japanese (see Chapter 2). Arrivals on O'ahu and Maui of shipwrecked fishermen or of vessels blown off course were reported in Japan long after the situations actually occurred; Hawaiian oral traditions related similar events.[102,103]

The intriguing concept of early alien contact focuses on the theory of inadvertent drifts of fishing junks originating in Japan that were tossed beyond the Kuroshio Current by typhoons or mishaps.[104] When Captain Cook's officers on Maui in 1778 observed two worn pieces of iron shaped like skewers, they concluded that these articles had come from earlier visitors or from shipwrecks.[105] The Hawaiian term for iron, *meki* or *meti,* a word not found in other areas of Polynesia, and the resemblance of the iron blade to a Japanese *deba-*

bocho blade, strengthens the hypothesis of pre-Western Japanese contact.

During the early nineteenth century, rescued Japanese seamen were brought to Hawai'i. "On my arrival at Wahoo [O'ahu] in 1806, I found eight Japanese, who had been taken off a wreck at sea by Captain Cornelius Sole, of Providence, Rhode-Island, who was bound from China across the Pacific ocean to the coast of America," wrote Captain Amaso Delano in a narrative of his voyages.[106] A Japanese crewman from Hiroshima reported the sinking of his ship followed by a rescue and deliverance to Hawai'i. In the fourth year of Bunka (1807), according to the lunar calendar, he was returned to Nagasaki on a Dutch ship.[107]

The shogunate policy of strict isolationism decreed in 1633 was not rescinded until 1853. Ships from Japan were prohibited from leaving Japanese waters and foreign ships were restricted in port entries, so the visits to Hawai'i of Japanese seamen before the mid-nineteenth century were accidental. Sailing vessel mishaps accounted for the presence of a few men of Nihon, and although most of the seamen returned to their homeland, three men from Japan chose to remain in the Islands and became naturalized subjects of the kingdom of Hawai'i before 1850.

The growth of the sugar industry as the base for the Hawaiian economy gave impetus to the search for cheap labor. With the passing of the Masters and Servants Act in 1850, the Hawaiian Kingdom established a legal foundation for a contract labor system. The first foreign mission from Japan at the end of the Tokugawa era in 1860 stopped in Honolulu, en route to the United States, to exchange treaty documents with King Kamehameha IV, who requested consideration of a Hawai'i-Japan treaty to permit recruitment of sugar plantation laborers.[108] Eugene Van Reed, the Hawaiian consul general in Yokohama, solicited the first group of 148 Japanese immigrants, which included 140 men, 6 women, and 2 children.[109] They were called the *Gannen Mono,* the "first-year people," because they came to Hawai'i in Meiji Gannen, the first year of the reign of Emperor Meiji. Despite the refusal of authorization for departure by the new Meiji government, workers lured by offers of good wages were shipped out of Yokohama for Hawai'i in 1868.

"First and nearest to us lies Japan, inhabited by a people generally considered akin to the Hawaiians and who, we all agree, would be desirable immigrants," said Dr. William Hillebrand, commissioner of the Bureau of Immigration in the 1860s. However, it was not long before complaints were received from both employees and employers. The Japanese reported that their contracts had been violated and that they had received brutal treatment and low wages while charged high prices at plantation stores. Plantation employers asserted that some of the immigrants were "unadapted by education or habits for the service at which they were being employed."[110] An arrangement in 1870 with the Meiji government provided for the return of forty of the discontented workers and closed the door to further labor recruitment for over a decade.

The Hawaiian emissaries continued to try to convince officials in Japan to permit workers to leave their homeland. A Treaty of Commerce and Friendship was signed in 1871. In 1872 politician Walter Murray Gibson declared to the Chamber of Commerce in Honolulu:

> You have considered the races that are desirable, not only to supply your needs of labor but to furnish an increase of population that will assimilate with the Hawaiian. . . . We must never forget the desires and privileges of the race among whom we reside and who properly enjoy a political supremacy, owing to birthright and numbers. . . . We must look to races, who, whilst being good workers, will not much affect the identity of the Hawaiian, and whose gradual influx will harmonize with, and strengthen, by the infusion of new blood, the native stock. A moderate portion of the Japanese, of the agricultural class, will not conflict with the view that I present, and if they bring their women with them, and settle permanently in the country, they may be counted upon as likely to become desirable Hawaiian subjects.[111]

In 1876 King Kalākaua entertained Captain Ito of the Japanese naval ship, the *Tsukuba,* and emphasized the continued interest by the Hawaiian government in recruitment of workers from Japan. King Kalākaua's visit to Japan in 1881 provided a personal friendship with Emperor Meiji and smoothed the relationship of the Hawaiian Kingdom with the Japanese government. Earlier contracts that provided a wage of $4 a month, as well as food, housing, and medical care, were replaced by new three-year contracts that offered free steerage passage and work on a sugar plantation at monthly wages of $9 for men and $6 for women, food allowance, lodging, medical care, fuel, no taxes, and rice at not more than five cents a pound. In addition, workers were required to set aside 25 percent of their earnings to guarantee that they would have some savings at the conclusion of their contract period.[112] Mr. R. W. Irwin, agent in Japan for the Hawaiian Board of Immigration, suggested that these people could be led "by the silken thread of kindness," and he requested sugar planters to provide five gallons of hot water for each person daily, since "cleanliness is a strong point in their lives."[113]

Laborers were selected "from the farming class with particular attention given to physical condition, youth, and industrious habits."[114] An emigration fever described as "Hawaii Netsu" swept through the neighboring prefectures in the Chugoku district of southwest Japan, attracting workers from Hiroshima, Yamaguchi, Fukuoka, and Kumamoto. Recruiting agents described Hawai'i as the land of eternal summer where people were "sincere and gentle by nature" and "very kind towards strangers." The *dekasegi,* or laborers who

King Kalākaua (center) and William Armstrong, Commissioner of Immigration for the Kingdom of Hawaii (top right), meet with Japanese officials in Tokyo, Japan, in 1881 to discuss employment of contract laborers for Hawai'i. *(Norman Hill photo, Hawaii State Archives)*

The living quarters for the families of Japanese workers on the island of Hawai'i in 1890 were simple thatched huts. *(R. J. Baker collection, Bishop Museum)*

chose to work for a period of time in a foreign country, expected to save enough money to return to their homeland and purchase land. Japanese scholar Ronald Takaki explained: "Three years of hard labor in faraway cane fields; three years of separation from friends, family, and village seemed to be a small sacrifice to make for the realization of such an ambitious dream."[115,116]

The convention of 1886 signed by Foreign Minister Inouye Kaoru of Japan and R. W. Irwin of Hawai'i delineated the arrangements to assure the well being, happiness, and prosperity of Japanese subjects emigrating to Hawai'i.[117] About 75 percent of the contract laborers arriving in 1885–1890 returned to Japan or moved to the U.S. mainland. After 1894 the government-sponsored emigration was changed by emigrant protection laws that established a legal framework for overseas movement of laborers under the management of private enterprise.[118] Political shifts in the final decade of the nineteenth century changed Hawai'i from a kingdom to a republic that was annexed to the United States as a territory in 1900. Japanese were released from their status as contract laborers with the implementation of the Organic Act of 1900 that specifically prohibited importation of "penal contract" labor.

For more than thirty years the Japanese provided the major source of labor for the sugar plantations. Gradually the workers became disillusioned with the low wages, the limited opportunity for personal growth in the industry, and the lack of social status in plantation employment. Many sought economic security in other work.[119] Japanese moved into the industries of fishing and rice, coffee, and pineapple cultivation.[120]

At the end of the Sino-Japanese War in 1895, Okinawans were urged to emigrate owing to problems of overcrowding in their country and economic depression in postwar Japan. Formosa and Hawai'i were suggested as areas seeking laborers.[121] Twenty-six men arrived in Honolulu in the first group in January, 1900; they were followed by more than 8,000 Okinawan workers over the next eight years, when government regulations curtailed migration.[122] About 20,000 Japanese immigrants arrived from Okinawa between 1900 and 1924, and they have gradually assimilated with Japanese from Japan into the Hawaiian community.[123]

A gradual resentment toward numbers of foreign laborers, especially on the western coast of the United States, precipitated the passage of *The Immigration Act of 1907* that refused issuing passports if they were to be used "for the purpose of enabling the holders to come to the continental territory of the United States to the detriment of labor conditions therein . . ." This first important measure to control Japanese immigration was followed by the "Gentlemen's Agreement," an informal understanding with Japan in which the Japanese government cooperated with the United States by not granting passports to skilled or unskilled laborers other than "settled agriculturists, or farmers owning or having an interest or share in their produce or crops."[124] The issuance of passports to Hawai'i was limited to "former residents" and "parents, wives, and children of residents." The door for further immigration was closed with the passage of the Immigration Act of May 26, 1924, also known as the "Oriental Exclusion Act," which declared aliens ineligible for citizenship (unless they were White or Black aliens) and excluded them from permanent immigration.

The number of Japanese in Hawai'i grew rapidly from 116 persons in 1884 to 61,111 residents in 1900, by which time they had become the largest ethnic group in the Islands, comprising almost 40 percent of the total population (Table 3-1; Table 3-3.f). Between 1868 and 1924, when the Immigration Act of 1924 prevented further immigration, arrivals from Japan totaled 159,288 men, 49,612 women, and 4,852 children.[125]

The period from 1908 to 1920 is commonly called the *Yobiyose Jidai,* or the "period of summoning" of wives, families, and picture brides. Unlike the Chinese, Korean, and some White immigrant workers who intermarried with Hawaiian and Portuguese women, Japanese males seldom intermarried because of the availability of Japanese women willing to come to the Islands as "picture brides." Often these young women, selected from photos, were married by proxy in Japan to men whom they had never met, or were married after meeting their intended husbands upon arrival in the Territory of Hawai'i. Between 1911 and 1919, 9,841 picture brides were admitted to Honolulu, and this improvement of the sex ratio resulted in more Japanese men in 1920 who were married than men of any other ethnic group.[126,127]

The count of the Japanese population in Hawai'i increased from 79,675 persons in 1910 to 109,274 residents in 1920, or 42.7 percent of the total population (Table 3-1). About 40,000 of the emigrants from Japan left the Islands to go to the U.S. mainland or to return to their homeland, but most of the new residents remained in Hawai'i to settle and have large families, to seek improvement in their living and working conditions, and to promote educational achievement for their children.[128]

The first generation immigrants from Japan, known as issei, and the second generation (nisei) moved to Honolulu and neighbor island urban centers. They became independent wage earners, merchants, shopkeepers, and tradesmen. The nisei were American citizens by birth, and they became molded by democratic principles taught in the American public school system. The bravery of their volunteer 100th Battalion and the 442nd Regimental Combat team during World War II displayed the loyalty of the Japanese of Hawai'i to their adopted country and instilled pride in this group by all residents of the Islands.[129]

At first the Japanese were predominantly alien or too young to vote, but as this group matured their votes had greater strength. Whereas in 1920 the Japanese represented only 2.5 percent of the total registered voters, the proportion rose to 31 percent in 1940.[130] The voting strength of this group has continued to influence political power in the Islands throughout the twentieth century.[131]

The upward mobility of Japanese was demonstrated by their educational achievements and contributions to the community.[132] Economist Thomas K. Hitch reported on the prominence of the Americans of Japanese ancestry: "During the 50 year period from 1915 to 1965,

A family of Japanese ancestry, Ted T. Tsukiyama, his wife Fuku Yokoyama Tsukiyama, and their children Sandra, Timothy, and Paul, pose with their boxer and
eight puppies in Honolulu in 1966. *(Tsukiyama family photo)*

the percentage of practitioners of Japanese ancestry in certain professions in Hawaii increased dramatically: from 2 percent to 24 percent
among attorneys, from zero percent to 25 percent among architects,
from 6 percent to 62 percent among dentists, and from zero percent
to 60 percent among optometrists."[133]

Okinawans, who represented about 14 percent of all Japanese
immigrants, were first viewed as strangers and not accepted by others
from mainland Japan.[134] They followed the pattern of persons of
Japanese ancestry and became highly successful in such fields as den-
tistry, insurance, and real estate, and made important contributions
to the Hawaiian community as financial, political, and cultural leaders. Sociologist Y. Scott Matsumoto reported in 1982: "The Okinawans have worked diligently to attain the status of a thriving group,

at a social and economic level equal to others of the Japanese community."[135]

The population of Japanese in Hawai'i increased in one hundred years to 239,748 residents according to the 1980 U.S. census, or 24.9 percent of the total state population (Table 3-1). During the early years of subsidized and voluntary immigration, there was a disproportion of males to females, but by 1950 the groups were evenly balanced, and in 1980 the sex ratio of 93.6 showed a slight excess of females (Table 3-3.f; Figure 3-5). The Japanese population pyramids demonstrate the aging of the early immigrants and the expanding of the population; the high birth rates of the years from 1920-1930 and 1940-1960 contrast with a sharp reduction of births and numbers of young people in the years 1930-1940 and 1960-1980. About 79 percent of the Japanese lived in Honolulu County in 1980, with the remainder representing about a quarter of the population on each neighbor island (Table 3-4).

In the 1920-1930 decade, high birth rates accompanied high marriage rates, and mortality levels dropped with improved provisions of health care. After World War II the Japanese in Hawai'i experienced better economic conditions and improved social status, which were accompanied by a reduction in family size. In 1980 this group showed a crude birth rate of only 11.1 children per 1,000 population (Table 3-6). Their total fertility rate, a more specific measurement of the number of children the average woman bears, was only 1.4, a figure far below the 2.1 rate necessary for replacement level and lowest among all ethnic groups in the Islands. Japanese age-specific fertility rates in 1980 were markedly depressed at all age groups when compared to earlier decades, and Japanese women showed a tendency to delay reproduction to ages 25-34 (Table 3-8).

The number of interracial marriages of Japanese was low in comparison with other groups in 1912 to 1916 with only 0.5 percent outmarriage among grooms and 0.2 percent among brides. Through the decades the pattern toward intermarriage became more acceptable to the varied cultures in Hawai'i, so that by 1985 among Japanese 41.0 percent of the grooms and 50.0 percent of the brides married persons of other races (Table 3-10).

Life expectancy of 77.7 years for males and 81.5 years for females of Japanese ancestry was among the longest of all ethnic groups in Hawai'i (Table 4-10). The Japanese had the largest representation— 35.6 percent—of Hawai'i's population of persons age 65 and above in 1980 (Table 4-12). Despite liberalization of immigration laws in 1965,

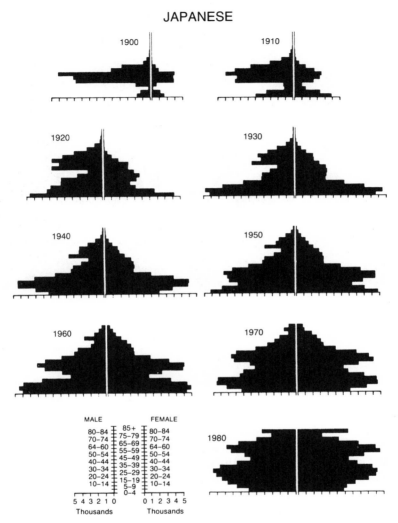

Figure 3-5. Population by Age and Sex: Japanese
Note: These pyramids are based on U.S. census definition of race.
Source: See Table 3-3.f.

movement of Japanese to Hawai'i has remained at a low level, with fewer than 300 annual immigrants from Japan seeking permanent residence in the Islands in 1980–1985 (Table 4–15).[136]

Toward the end of the twentieth century the Japanese in Hawai'i as issei, nisei, sansei (third generation), and yonsei (fourth generation)

The strength of the political contribution to Hawai'i of persons of Japanese ancestry has been exemplified by the contribution of Senator Daniel K. Inouye, shown here with his wife and son in the 1980s. Senator Inouye has received national recognition for his many years of service as Hawai'i's congressional representative. *(Benny's Studio photo)*

identify first with the Hawaiian-American lifestyle and only secondarily with ancestral traditions. Dorothy Hazama and Jane Komeiji wrote in 1986: "[The Japanese in Hawai'i] have learned the lessons of liberty, equality, and justice. They have learned to live with and to respect peoples of backgrounds different from theirs. They have had the taste of success as they progressed from being the lowest outsiders in the Hawaiian hierarchy to mainstream members and even to leaders. The story does not end here, but will continue with the passage of time."[137]

Blacks

Blacks first came to Hawai'i as crew members of merchant ships in the early nineteenth century. A Black businessman named Anthony Allen from Schenectady, New York, landed in the Islands in 1810 and established a boarding house, a "dram shop" (saloon), and an infor-

Betsey Stockton, a member of missionary Charles Stewart's household in 1823, became a teacher of Hawaiians on Maui. This photo is dated about 1863. *(Hawaiian Mission Children's Society)*

mal hospital for both sailors and Hawaiians.[138,139] Betsey Stockton was a Black member of the missionary Charles Stewart's household in 1823 and served as a schoolteacher on Maui.[140]

A small number of Black Portuguese arrived aboard whaling ships from the Cape Verde Islands between 1820 and 1880, and history records their contributions as cooks, barbers, and members of musical groups. Many of them married Hawaiians, and they were classified in censuses as Portuguese or Part Hawaiian.[141]

Blacks were deliberately excluded from a list of potential contract labor immigrant groups in the 1860s. Responding to Civil War sentiment that equated work on sugar plantations with the slavery of the southern U.S. cotton and tobacco plantations, sugar planters rejected proposals to bring Blacks from the United States to work in the kingdom of Hawai'i.

In 1881 U.S. Secretary of State James G. Blaine discussed how entirely Hawai'i was a part of the productive and commercial system of the American states, and he urged importing Blacks instead of Orientals for the cultivation of sugar and rice. He said that the problem of replenishment of the vital forces of Hawai'i presented itself for intelligent solution in an American and "not an Asiatic or British sense."[142] However, J. E. Bush, president of the kingdom of Hawaii's

Children of Black ancestry in Hawai'i in the 1920s. *(On Char photo, Bishop Museum)*

Board of Immigration, reported in 1882, "The Legislature was decidedly averse to Negro immigrants, even to opposing people from New Hebrides."[143]

In 1907 the Hawaiian Sugar Planters' Association recruited about thirty Black families to Maui from Tennessee, Mississippi, and Alabama. However, these people did not establish a separate homogeneous community, and many returned to their home regions or became amalgamated by intermarriage and association with local groups.

Puerto Ricans brought to Hawai'i in 1901 were of Black African, American Indian, and Spanish descent. Although the U.S. census in the early twentieth century usually classified persons of Black descent as "Negro," Puerto Rican Blacks were tabulated as Puerto Ricans, who were later absorbed in the Caucasian, or White, totals. According to Romanzo C. Adams, pioneer sociologist in Hawai'i, "In 1940 another change in the classification of part Puerto Ricans reduced the Negro population from 563 to 255 at a time when the American Negro population was in all probability growing."[144]

The military establishment in Hawai'i brought a small number of American Blacks to the Islands after annexation of Hawai'i to the United States in 1900. The 25th Infantry Regiment of all-Black males served in Hawai'i in 1913. By 1930, there were 322 males and 241 females of Black ancestry living in the Islands (Table 3-3.a). Since 1950 the number of Blacks in the Islands has almost doubled each decade (Table 3-1). The majority of Black persons who have come to Hawai'i has been associated with the military as members of the armed forces or their dependents, and, in 1980, 84.1 percent of Hawai'i's Blacks were in this category.[145]

The slow settling of Blacks in the civilian population in early twentieth century Hawai'i was explained by sociologist Shirley Abe:

> If things had gone on naturally, without any introduction of the Mainland pattern of race relations, the Negroes would very likely have been gradually accepted and absorbed into the community, just as the Portuguese, Chinese, Japanese and Filipinos have become a part of the community, each one starting towards the bottom of the social scale and working its way up. Among the tremendous number of Mainland servicemen and war workers, there were a good many men who assumed that the discrimination practiced at home was present wherever they went. The refusal of the local people to accept the Negroes as social equals is thus in large part due to this importation of patterns from the Mainland.[146]

In 1980 the U.S. census counted the Black population at 17,364

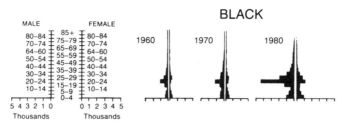

Figure 3–6. Population by Age and Sex: Black
Note: These pyramids are based on U.S. census definition of race.
Source: See Table 3–3.a.

persons, or 1.8 percent of the total state population. The 1983 Health Survey reported 16,179 Blacks, of whom only 2,568 were civilian residents.[147] The imbalanced sex ratio of 212 males for every 100 females in this ethnic group was attributed to the presence of a large number of Black military men of ages 18–29 (Table 3–3.a). This disproportion is clearly observed in the Black population pyramids, especially for 1980 (Figure 3–6).

About 97 percent of the Black population lived in Honolulu County in 1980. The unequal sex distribution among Blacks in Hawai'i distorted some demographic measurements. Women in this group in 1980 showed the lowest rate of intermarriage (Table 3–10). Only 19.3 percent of Black women who married in that year selected mates outside their race, whereas 51 percent of Black men chose women of other ethnic backgrounds.

Black women had the highest child-woman ratio—621 children compared to a state average of 339 children per 1,000 women of child-bearing age (Table 3–6, Table 3–7). The crude birth rate fell from 41.0 in 1960 to 23.4 births per 1,000 Blacks in 1980, reflecting national trends. The total fertility rate, which measures the number of children the average woman bears, was 2.6 children, a figure significantly higher than the state total fertility count of 1.8 children. In 1980 Black women showed high age-specific fertility rates for the age group 15–24 (Table 3–8). They had one of the lowest levels of abortion among all ethnic groups, with about 20 abortions per 100 live births (Table 3–9). The high level of fertility among Black women in Hawai'i in 1980 was related to the high proportion of military wives of child-bearing age.

The number of deaths among Blacks was small, reflecting the young age of this racial group in Hawai'i. Life expectancy figures were not computed owing to the unreliability of information from the distorted age and sex composition of the small Black population.

Four generations of a professional family of Black heritage residing in Honolulu in 1987. *(Dr. and Mrs. John W. Edwards, Jr. collection)*

Less than 1 percent of Blacks in Hawai'i are counted in the elderly category of age 65 and over (Table 4–12). There is no tabulation of migration by American Blacks. It is probable that this population, most of which is associated with the military on short assignments to the Islands, contributes disproportionately to the high rate of inter-state migration from and to the U.S. mainland.

Although their civilian population has been small, Blacks have made a significant contribution to Hawai'i's community life.[148] As attorneys and lawyers they have served as advisers to the kingdom and to the territorial and state legislatures. They have been active in medical and educational professions, and they are recognized for their musical and athletic competence.

According to University of Hawaii ethnic studies educator Kathryn Takara in 1986: ". . . . the Black [in Hawai'i] as a group has still not been fully accepted, although there is much lip-service given to the practice of racial harmony. As an individual, however, the Black person can easily assimilate into the island community according to his or her personal merit. . . ."[149]

Filipinos

Hawai'i became a part of the United States with the signing of a joint resolution of Congress approved by President McKinley on August 12, 1898.[150] On December 10 of the same year, at the conclusion of the Spanish-American War, the Philippine Islands were ceded by Spain to the United States.[151] The relationship of these two groups of islands in social, economic, and historical events during the succeeding century was closely related to the political changes that took place at that time.

The passage of Hawai'i's Organic Act on June 13, 1900, provided that citizens of the Republic of Hawai'i in 1898 would automatically become citizens of the new Territory of Hawai'i and of the United States, and it made Hawai'i subject to national labor laws. This closed the era of contract labor that had brought workers to the Islands since 1852.[152] With the passage of laws forbidding recruitment of Chinese labor, with the increasing limitations on immigration in agreements with Japan and Korea, and with the end of the Spanish-American War, planters focused on the U.S.-controlled Philippine Islands as a new source of inexpensive labor that could enter Hawai'i as nationals.[153]

Hawai'i's U.S. consul general, William Haywood, was sent by the sugar planters to Washington, D.C., in 1901 to obtain permission for the recruitment of workers for the territory. In 1906 Honolulu attorney Albert F. Judd went to Manila as an agent of the Hawaiian Sugar Planters' Association (HSPA) to persuade 300 Filipino laborers to emigrate to the territory. However, he returned with an experimental group of only 15 men, who were given an introductory tour of work and life on Hawai'i's plantations and then returned to the Philippines to encourage more laborers to move to the Hawaiian Islands.[154] The next year 150 Filipinos were recruited, and by 1909 there was large-scale importation of workers from the Philippines.[155]

The people of the Philippines were descendants of Indochinese, Chinese, Malayan, and Spanish ancestry. Owing to vast distances between the inhabited islands, several subgroups developed with distinct socio-cultural characteristics and dialects.[156] The Tagalog, the dialect group considered of the highest social prestige in the Philippines, were from central and southern Luzon and supplied a small percentage of the laborers for Hawai'i; the Visayan, who lived in the central islands of Cebu, Siquijor, and Leyte, were mostly agriculturists and among the first to be recruited; a small number migrated from Mindanao and other areas of the Philippines; and the Ilocanos, a rural peasant group from the northern regions of Luzon, provided the largest response to offers of work in Hawai'i.[157,158] Their willingness to leave their *barrios* (village communities) to move across the Pacific is explained by Hawai'i Filipino historian Luis V. Teodoro, Jr.:

> There is no doubt that the aggressive recruiting policies of the HSPA, as well as exaggerated reports by friends and relatives in Hawaii, convinced many Filipinos to leave their homeland. But it must also be realized that a no less compelling factor was the difficult situation of the peasantry in the Philippines, even—perhaps especially—during the period of American colonization. . . . The frustration of the Revolution of 1896 and American conquest at the turn of the century had arrested the movement for agrarian revolution in the Philippines. It is no accident that, as peasant exploitation intensified with the tying of the Philippine agricultural system to the world capitalist system, the lure of Hawaii became more and more

A family of Filipino heritage pose for a picture in Hawai'i in the 1920s. *(On Char photo, Bishop Museum)*

irresistible to those Filipinos who had only a bleak future to look forward to in the Philippines.[159]

Homeland regions of Filipino migrants to Hawai'i have been characterized as areas with problems of imbalance of land ownership, low agricultural productivity, and high population densities, as well as locations of natural disasters, famine, pestilence, and disease.[160,161] Low wage levels and unfair tenant-landlord relationships were major reasons given by recruits for moving to the Hawaiian Islands.

The HSPA brought waves of laborers at different times for different reasons. In addition to the need to replace workers who had moved into the cities to accept other forms of employment, a numerical balance of ethnic groups on the plantations was considered by sugar management to be a safeguard against labor strikes. Filipino immigration was encouraged to counteract the increasing power of organized Japanese workers, to prevent laborers from organizing, and to break strikes.[162,163] Filipino workers were offered free transportation to Hawai'i, three years employment for the laborer, his wife, and any grown children who wished to work, a free home, fuel, water, and health care.[164] They were expected to work ten hours in the field or twelve hours in the mill each day for twenty-six days per month at a pay rate of $16 a month for the men, $12 for boys of ages 15 to 18, and $10 for women.

By 1930 about 100,000 persons—mostly males—had come to Hawai'i (Table 3–1; Table 4–15). In the period between 1916 and 1928, 56 percent of the workers moved from the four Ilokano provinces of Abra, Ilokos Norte, Ilokos Sur, and La Union; 27 percent migrated from Bohol, Cebu, Leyte, and Negros Oriental in the Visayas; 13 percent originated from Pangasinan and Tarlac provinces in central Luzon; and 4 percent represented thirty-five other provinces.[165] This pattern of migration remained the same throughout Filipino immigration until 1934.

The Filipinos were slow to urbanize. Most of the new recruits were young males without families who took jobs as unskilled laborers on rural plantations. In 1930 more than 30 percent of the immigrants were illiterate, and Filipino children had poor school attendance records. Economic constraints in the Depression of the 1930s and the ratio of five men to every Filipino woman contributed to an outmigration from Hawai'i of approximately half of the Filipino alien residents, of whom two-thirds returned to the Philippines and one-third moved to the mainland United States (Table 3–3.c).[166]

The Tydings and McDuffie legislative bill of 1934 introduced a provision for the independence of the Philippine Islands and placed immigration restrictions on Filipino labor, with the exception that the Secretary of the Interior would be allowed to specify exemptions based on a determination of need for labor in Hawai'i. Although this exception guaranteed continued access to Philippine labor during the 1930s, economic and political restraints of the Depression years severely reduced further movement. After World War II there was renewed interest among the sugar planters to recruit inexpensive labor from the Philippines. A wave of immigration from the Philippines occurred in early 1946. Six thousand men, 446 women, and 915 children were brought to Hawai'i before Philippine independence on July 4, 1946, which restricted Filipinos to U.S. immigration quotas.[167]

The term *sakada* identifies the Filipinos who came to Hawai'i during the years of labor recruitment between 1906 and 1946 (Table 3–

A Filipino immigrant family in Hawai'i in the 1970s. *(Hawaii State Department of Health photo)*

12). It refers to a laborer-recruit as well as to the process of recruiting for temporary labor migration.[168] The *sakada* was the foundation for Filipino life in Hawai'i, representing primarily males from a broad spectrum of islands in the Philippines who shared their *barrio* culture and responded to the opportunities for educational and economic growth. In 1946 this group was granted naturalization privileges by the United States.[169]

The United States Immigration and Nationality Act of 1965 abolished the national origin quota system and permitted a larger number of immigrants to enter from Asia. The quota for the Philippines was increased from the 1946 allowance of 100 immigrants per year to the per-country annual allotment of 20,000 persons plus exempt classes such as close relatives of U.S. citizens.[170] This law enabled many Filipino families to be reunited, and it promoted marriage by bringing brides from the homeland.

The adaptation of recent immigrant Filipinos to patterns of living in Hawai'i has varied from the social and cultural lifestyles of the *at-at* Filipino children of the *sakada* first-generation immigrants.[171] *At-ats* were expected to keep filial obligations and to remain close to home; recent immigrants are urbanized, display a more cosmopolitan orientation, and may be less reserved. Reports of increased levels of crime among post-1965 male arrivals was attributed to frustrations in employment, communication, and housing, and to social mobility blocked by immigrant status.[172] Social interaction between first generation and recent Filipino immigrants was sometimes strained.

In the United States Filipinos have become the second-largest Asian group, and, with over 40,000 immigration admissions per year, they are expected to exceed the number of Chinese or Japanese residents in the nation by the late twentieth century.[173] Since the passage of the U.S. 1965 Immigration and Nationality Act, the number of Filipinos moving to Hawai'i increased to about 3,000 to 5,000 annually (Table 4–15). In addition to allowing family members to enter the United States, preference is given to members of professions or to persons of exceptional ability in the sciences and arts and to skilled and unskilled workers in short supply. This law has had a disproportionate effect upon Hawai'i, to which more immigrants have come in relation to the size of the resident population than to any other state.[174] Among ethnic groups in Hawai'i with alien immigrants in the 1970s and 1980s, Filipinos have by far the largest number, of whom about 75 to 80 percent originated in the Ilocos region.[175] These immigrants have created a new image for this ethnic group.

Juan C. Dionesio wrote about this "new breed" of Filipinos:

They are respected for their accomplishments and admired for "enhancing" the Filipino image. At the same time, they are resented by some of the older immigrants and local-born Filipinos for their "pushiness." Unburdened by feelings of inferiority built into the psyche of the descendents of first-generation labor-immigrants who had been cowed by years of abuse and discriminatory treatment, they are better educated and motivated, aggressive in the pursuit of their goals. They are forging ahead fast; they are go-getters.[176]

The Filipino population in Hawai'i has grown from 2,361 persons in 1910 and 95,354 residents recorded in 1970, to 133,940 members of this group in 1980. The U.S. census showed a high 3.4 percent average annual growth rate for Filipinos in the 1970–1980 decade, representing the third-largest ethnic group in Hawaii with 13.9 percent of the total population (Table 3–1).

About three-quarters of all Filipinos live on the island of O'ahu, while the rest are evenly distributed among the counties of Hawaii (10 percent), Maui (10 percent), and Kauai (8 percent). On the neighbor islands in 1980 Filipinos had a disproportionately high representation, at 26.2 percent of the population of Kaua'i and 18.9 percent of Maui's people, reflecting early sugar plantation settlement patterns (Table 3–4). Within each county, Filipino ethnic groups are often concentrated in specific residential areas. Almost half of all Filipinos on O'ahu in 1975 lived in just four districts: Kalihi-Palama and Upper Kalihi in central Honolulu, and Waipahu and 'Ewa-Makakilo in the outskirts of the city. These concentrations are related to economic factors as well as to the closeness of ethnic and kinship ties among Hawai'i Filipinos.[177]

The abnormalities of age and sex distribution resulting from an excess of male immigration to Hawai'i in 1910–1930 is gradually diminishing, and this group of early immigrants can be observed in successive population pyramids as they age through the decades (Figure 3–7). The distorted sex ratio of five Filipino men per Filipino woman in 1930 has been reduced to 1.09 in 1980. The expanded population of persons of Philippine Island ancestry who live in Hawai'i in the late twentieth century is young, with a larger proportion of children under the age of fifteen than other racial groups in the state (Table 3–3.c; Table 4–3).

In the 1975–1985 period Filipinos have recorded annually about 2,800 births (Table 3–5). The 1980 crude birth rate of 22.7 births per

FILIPINO

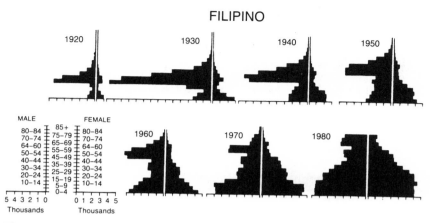

Figure 3-7. Population by Age and Sex: Filipino
Note: These pyramids are based on U.S. census definition of race.
Source: See Table 3-3.c.

1,000 Filipinos, the general fertility rate of 94.9 births per 1,000 women of childbearing age, and the child-woman ratio of 395 are slightly above the state average (Table 3-6). The total fertility rate dropped from 8.4 in 1930 and 5.9 in 1970 to 2.6 in 1980, indicating practice of fertility control and changing perceptions toward smaller family size. Age-specific fertility rates show a higher rate of births occurring among young mothers of ages 20-24 (Table 3-8). In the 1980s, Filipinos recorded a low ratio of about 25 abortions per 100 live births (Table 3-9).

Intermarriage is a common practice for persons from the Philippines, and since the 1950s Filipinos have kept pace with the state pattern for out-marriage. Among Filipino residents in 1985, 42 percent of the grooms and 56 percent of the brides married a person of another race (Table 3-10). Some older men take young wives.[178] Over 700 babies born in Hawai'i in 1970-1980 were fathered by Filipino men of age 65 and over.

Mortality figures for Filipinos in Hawai'i reveal a low crude death rate of 4.6 deaths per 1,000 population and a long life expectancy— 77.3 years for men and 81.0 years for women in 1980 (Table 3-5; Table 4-10). This contrasts sharply to the life expectancy in the Philippines in 1975-1980 of only 60.9 years for men and 64.3 years for women (Table 4-8). The Filipino population of Hawai'i includes 9.5 percent elderly persons age 65 and over, a figure slightly higher than the state average of 7.9 percent in 1980 (Table 4-12).

Benjamin J. Cayetano was elected in 1986 to serve as lieutenant governor of the state of Hawaii. *(R. Wiley—Honolulu photo, Courtesy of the Office of the Lieutenant Governor)*

A detailed 1985 survey of Ilokano adults who immigrated to Hawai'i since 1965 showed an average male Filipino having 41 years of age, married with more than three children, a 30 percent chance of college attendance and a 50 percent chance of high school graduation, and employment as a service or construction worker.[179] Women reported a higher than average labor participation rate; Ilokanos, with more working adults than most households in Hawai'i, indicated a slightly higher median income. Hawai'i was accepted as a desirable place to live for reasons of better economic opportunities, jobs, recreation, and educational advantages.

The Filipino immigrants and their families have played an important role in the economic development of Hawaii.[180] In addition to their contributions to the sugar and pineapple industries, they have participated in construction, the hotel and tourist industry, individual businesses, the health and legal professions, and politics. Their rapid growth in numbers has provided a collective identity, and it is expected that they will have an increasing impact on the economic, social, and political life of Hawai'i in the future.

Koreans

Korea, also known as Chosen—the Land of the Morning Calm—was the last of the large Asian coastal nations to open its door to Western visitors and to permit the departure of its citizens to serve as laborers in a foreign country. Korea was a tributary state of China and isolated from the Western world until 1876, when the Japanese Meiji government forced a treaty upon the Koreans and initiated diplomatic relations with other governments.[181]

In 1882 the United States was the first Western nation to conclude a treaty with Korea. With the defeat of China in the Sino-Japanese War of 1894–1895, the peasant life in ancestral villages was uprooted and workers moved to the larger cities. Political unrest, calamities of war and famine, and oppressive taxes set the stage for the Yi dynasty to accept the request by U.S. government representatives to permit recruitment of workers for Hawai'i.

At least 35 Koreans came to Hawai'i to engage in business in the 1896–1902 period prior to an official agreement by Emperor Yi on November 15, 1902, that permitted "the control of laborers of Great Korea to be employed abroad."[182,183] The emperor was pleased that his people were permitted to go abroad after workers from China had been excluded from further U.S. immigration, and he anticipated better job opportunities for Koreans who suffered from poverty, economic inflation, and disease. U.S. diplomat to Korea, Horace S. Allen, sought emigration concessions in order to increase America's economic interests in that country. He aided Honolulu businessmen and planters in their efforts to secure new laborers from Korea to replace Chinese immigration and to offset the preponderance of Japanese plantation workers.

Posters displayed in urban centers and port cities of Seoul, Inchon, Pusan, Wonsan, Chinnampo, and Mokpo painted attractive pictures of life in Hawai'i.[184] Theodore F. Lansing, immigration commissioner and advertising agent for the U.S. Territory of Hawaiʻi sent placards distributed by the East-West Development Company that declared:

> The Government of Hawaii in Great America has designated the following proclamation:
> 1. Conveniences will be given to those who eagerly want to come to Hawaii and live there either alone or with their family.
> 2. The climate is suitable for everyone as there is no severe heat or cold.
> 3. There are schools on every island. English is taught and tuition is free.
> 4. Jobs for farmers are available all year around. They will be protected by law.
> 5. Monthly payment is $15.
> 6. Housing, fuel, water, and hospital expenses will be payed [*sic*] by the employer.
> 7. Posting of this advertisement is permitted by the Korean government.[185]

The first boatload of Korean workers arrived in Honolulu on January 13, 1903, with 56 men, 21 women, and 25 children. In 1905, Korean emigration closed in response to reports of mistreatment of Korean laborers in Mexico and in compliance with the pressure of the Japanese government in Korea, which had developed a policy to prohibit Korean emigration to Hawaiʻi because it did not want Korean workers competing against its own laborers already in those islands.[186] A total of 7,843 persons—6,701 males, 677 females, and 465 children under the age of fourteen—were brought to the Islands from Korea in the 1903–1905 period.[187]

The first Korean immigrants to Hawaiʻi were a heterogeneous group of mostly young men between the ages of 25–30 years who had been port coolies, exsoldiers of the Korean army who opposed control by Japan, political refugees, students, household servants, and minor government clerks. Less than 15 percent had been employed as farmers prior to emigration, although many had lived in a rural setting before moving to urban areas during periods of political unrest.[188] The majority of the immigrants were Christians associated with foreign missions. They came from the northern Korean provinces of Hwanghae and P'yongyang where Catholicism took its first Korean roots in the eighteenth century followed by American missions in the late nineteenth century.[189]

Methodist ministers often persuaded members of their congregation to take advantage of the prospects for social and economic improvement by accepting work in Hawai'i.[190] Religious leaders often accompanied these recruits on the transporting vessels, causing the unusual situation where, according to Bernice Kim, "an entire Oriental immigrant group discarded their time-honored beliefs and embraced Christianity."[191] Many persons from Korea have remained active in the Protestant church movement in Hawai'i. Women came as wives and daughters of laborers, and a few sought escape from bad marriages in which they opposed their husband's practice of keeping *kisaeng* concubines.[192] Some of the Methodist women were ministers, called "Bible women," who accompanied the emigrants on the ships and served as quasi-ministers, teachers, public health assistants, and social workers.

The Korean employees were known to be patient, hard-working, and eager to learn and succeed. They were not indentured laborers, because the United States Organic Act of 1900 specifically prohibited the importation of "penal contract" labor, but they were free to work

A Korean family of Hilo, Hawai'i, about 1910. *(G. Akau collection, Hawaii State Archives)*

on plantations or elsewhere. Some left the Islands for higher wages in the California rice fields. By 1910 Koreans in Hawai'i numbered only 3,931 males and 602 females (Table 3–3.g).

The inequality of the sex ratio contributed to interracial marriages, which were sanctioned by law and public opinion. Plantation managers hoped that the presence of Korean wives would increase the stability of the labor force. Almost 1,000 picture brides ages 18–24 were brought to Hawai'i from the densely populated and poor province of Kyung Song between 1910 and 1923.

Korean historians recount tragicomic situations that arose from misunderstandings and differences between the young women and older men in social and personal backgrounds, regional origins, and goals.[193] Some of the apprehensions of seeking a picture bride were described by R. Kim upon the 75th anniversary of Korean immigration to Hawai'i: "What if she doesn't like our new 'home'? Boy, she's going to be sweating with this year-round heat, doing the laundry, tailoring, cleaning, and working. What if she can't cook? What's going to happen to me? . . . I'm glad that she decided to come out here! I guess I'm pretty lucky, that is, if she stays to live with me. I know we can learn to love each other."[194]

The presence of wives brought stability and economic gain, and they provided a continuity to the ethnic stock that resulted in third- and fourth-generation Koreans living in Hawai'i in the 1980s. The Korean women instilled Korean traditional family values, including filial piety requiring respect for elders and superiors, and they emphasized learning and scholarship.[195]

Between 1910 and 1916, 1,168 Koreans moved to the continental United States and 1,246 returned to the Orient. Most of those who arrived in Hawai'i in 1903–1905 left employment on sugar plantations within a few years to seek higher paying jobs in the cities.[196,197] They took jobs as carpenters, tailors, laundry workers, and growers of rice and vegetables. Compared to other immigrant groups, Koreans had a higher level of literacy, and their ability with the English language facilitated scholastic advancement.[198] They differed significantly from other Oriental immigrants, owing to their urban origin, relatively higher educational attainment, nonfarming occupations, and Christian influences that permitted a more liberal and nontraditional value structure.[199]

Largely because of their small male population, and despite a feeling that "to marry out is to desert the cause," Koreans intermarried at a faster rate than most other ethnic groups in Hawai'i.[200] In 1960–

1969, 75.1 percent of males and 82.1 percent of females married partners of another race (Table 3–10). After the passage of the liberalized Immigration Act of 1965, which permitted wives, children, parents, married children, and unmarried and married siblings of American citizens to enter the United States, Korean intermarriage of males dropped in 1985 to 44.1 percent, although 77.7 percent of females continued to marry outside their race.

A demographic profile of the Korean population in Hawai'i reflects the gradual increase from 4,533 persons in 1910, 9,625 in 1970, and almost a doubled number of 17,962 residents in 1980 (Table 3–1). A high annual growth rate for Koreans of 6.2 percent in 1970–1980 indicated the rapid expansion of this group by immigration. In 1980 Koreans represented 1.9 percent of the state population; although, with a possible census undercount of persons who resided in low-socioeconomic and high density areas, this figure may understate the actual number of Koreans present in Hawai'i at that time.[201]

The 1910 sex ratio for Koreans of 652 males per 100 females dropped to only 71.6 males per 100 females by 1980, indicating a balancing of the sex ratio by births and by a high level of female immigration. This excess of males aged 20 to 39 and their gradual aging is observed in the Korean population pyramids for 1910–1930 (Figure 3–8). Inconsistent U.S. census tabulations over the decades counted Koreans with "Others" for 1940, 1950, and 1960. The pyramids for 1970 and 1980 reflect fertility control, an aging of the population, and a greater number of women. The number of Korean females doubled in 1970–1980 from 5,111 to 10,467 women, giving a distorted sex ratio of 48 men per 100 women for ages 25–34 years, or about 2 women for each man in that age group (Table 3–3.g). Ninety-four percent of Koreans in the Islands in 1980 live in Honolulu, where they represent 2.2 percent of that county's residents (Table 3–4).

The fertility level in 1980 of Koreans was low, with a general fertility rate of 69.3 live births per 1,000 Korean women of childbearing age, a total fertility rate of 1.8, and a child-woman ratio of 201 that registered the lowest among all ethnic groups in Hawai'i (Table 3–6). The number of annual Korean births doubled from less than 150 per year in 1970 to more than 300 births in 1985; this increase can be attributed to the larger population of women of childbearing age (Table 3–5.). Koreans had the highest ratio of elective abortions among all racial groups, reporting 70 per 100 Korean live births compared to the state average of 32 abortions per 100 live births (Table 3–9); that may reflect changing lifestyles and emphasis on upward

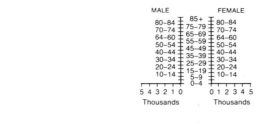

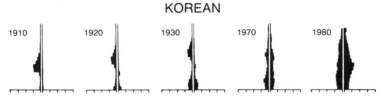

Figure 3–8. Population by Age and Sex: Korean
Note: These pyramids are based on U.S. census definition of race.
Source: See Table 3–3.g.

mobility and economic improvement. Age-specific fertility rates for Korean women in 1980 demonstrated delayed childbearing to ages 25–29 years (Table 3–8).

Deaths of Koreans numbered fewer than 100 per year in 1980, with a crude death rate of only 4.3 annual deaths per 100 Korean population (Table 3–5). Life expectancy of Koreans in Hawai'i is not calculated separately owing to small population size. This group is included with "Total Population," which shows 75.0 years for males and 81.5 years for females—figures that far exceed the life expectancy in the Republic of Korea of 62.7 years for males and 69.1 years for females (Table 4–8). The Korean population in Hawai'i is young with only 5.8 percent of persons aged 65 and over in 1980 (Table 4–12).

In the last half of the twentieth century, Koreans have become the second-largest foreign immigrant group to move to Hawai'i, adding over 1,000 persons annually, or about 17,000 residents between 1969 and 1985 (Table 4–15). Most of the recent immigrants were young with college education and professional, technical, and managerial expertise.[202] Since 1965, Korean female immigrants have outnumbered males.[203] Women came to join relatives, for economic improvement for their families, and for educational and occupational advantages for their children. They gave up traditional values to achieve economic gain, adapting to the new culture by accepting a temporary downward mobility in status.[204] Young Korean women have entered the work force at a higher than average labor participation rate, and they have found it easier than men to secure employment in low-paying service industry jobs.[205] According to women's studies scholar Alice Chai:

> Korean women in Hawaii work harder than men both inside and outside of the home, bear a greater burden of child care and domestic tasks in the absence of domestic help and extended family, and experience greater isolation from family members and other women than in Korea. Yet wives prefer life in Hawaii because of better living standards, better educational and occupational opportunities for children, and more autonomy from the husbands' family elders. Moreover, they engage in more husband-wife joint activities. . . .[206]

Although the early and recent Korean immigrants to the Hawaiian Islands share common ancestry, their historical, cultural, and social

Dr. Lee-Jay Cho, shown with his wife and children, serves as director of the Population Institute at the East-West Center in the 1980s. *(Lee-Jay Cho family collection)*

backgrounds offer wide disparity. Both groups emphasized upward mobility and a willingness to relinquish traditional patterns toward adaptation to new lifestyles. They are closely attached to church and family activities and have not become deeply involved in the larger political sphere of public activities.

As a relatively small and nonhomogeneous group in the late twentieth century in Hawai'i, the Koreans have shown a resurgence of ethnic identity as a result of rapid growth by immigration. Higher education has exerted a strong role in their values of social responsibility and achievement, and they have become prominent in Island intellectual, musical, artistic, and professional endeavors.

Samoans

A few Polynesians from the archipelago of Samoa may have come to Hawai'i as seafarers in the days of ancient Hawai'i and aboard merchant ships in the nineteenth century. Large-scale Samoan migration to the Hawaiian Islands is a phenomenon of the twentieth century in response to political shifts, religious influence, and economic incentives.

The Treaty of Berlin with Great Britain and Germany in 1899 established American jurisdiction over the islands of Tutuila and Manu'a in eastern Samoa, enabling the residents of this unincorporated territory of the United States to migrate as American Samoan nationals to Hawai'i and the U.S. mainland.[207] Germany controlled the Western Samoan Islands of Upolu, Savai'i, Manono, and Apolima until a New Zealand expeditionary force occupied that land in 1914; under the mandate of the Versailles Treaty, Western Samoa was an integral part of New Zealand until independence from colonial control was granted on January 1, 1962.[208] Western Samoans who wanted to move to American Samoa applied for work visas, and immigration clearance was necessary if they wanted to migrate to the United States.

Following the construction of a Mormon temple at Lā'ie on O'ahu in 1919, Samoan Mormon families were encouraged to settle in Hawai'i.[209] An agricultural community was established for Samoans in that northshore area.

In the early 1940s World War II had a permanent impact on the population and culture of American Samoa. Government activities created a demand for Samoan labor, and many Western Samoans migrated to American Samoa in response to work opportunities.[210] Increased U.S. military presence expanded contact of Samoans with Americans and offered jobs in communication, shipping, and transportation. Several thousand part-Samoan children were born during that period.[211]

Administrative changes in 1951 caused a sharp reduction in federal funding and jobs, and, with the weakened economic situation, the U.S. Navy offered to transfer Samoan workers and families to Hawai'i.[212] A surge of almost 1,000 Samoans arrived in the Islands in 1952, of whom nearly half were age nine or younger, and the contingent included a substantial majority of females.[213]

In the 1950–1979 period the exact number of Samoans was not precise because no count was taken of the arrival and departure of U.S. nationals, nor were Samoans counted by the census as a separate major racial group in Hawai'i.[214] The U.S. census in 1980 tabulated Samoans as a distinct ethnic group for the first time, making possible a demographic profile of this racial classification and showing migratory patterns to California and Hawai'i.

The Samoan population of Hawai'i in 1980 included 14,073 persons, representing 1.5 percent of the state population and comprising 33.4 percent of the 41,948 Samoans recorded in the United States. The 6,953 males and 7,120 females were evenly balanced with a sex ratio of 97.7 males per 100 females, and 43 percent of this group was under the age of fifteen (Table 3–3.h; Figure 3–9). Ninety-eight percent of Samoans resided in Honolulu County, with large concentrations in the neighborhoods of Kalihi-Palama, Lā'ie-Hauula, and Pearl City-Waipahu (Table 3–4).

Samoan birth rates recorded by the State Department of Health have been high, which may be explained by the large percentage of

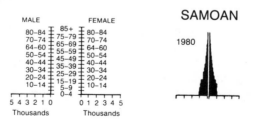

Figure 3–9. Population by Age and Sex: Samoan
Note: This pyramid is based on U.S. census definition of race.
Source: See Table 3–3.h.

young women of reproductive age and by a Samoan cultural tendency to large families. Their 1980 crude birth rate of 34.8 births per 1,000 population was above that for all other ethnic groups in the Islands, the Samoan general fertility rate was 150.9, and their child-woman ratio of 664 (in contrast to the state average of 339 children under age 5 per 1,000 women age 15–44) showed an elevated level of fertility (Table 3–6). For age groups 20–34, Samoan women had the highest rates for age-specific fertility among all ethnic groups in Hawai'i (Table 3–8). Samoans have had fewer elective abortions than other racial groups since 1971 (Table 3–9). Their 1980 total fertility rate of 4.1 dropped from a 1975 figure of 4.9, which may suggest a trend toward fertility reduction.[215]

In 1980 a Samoan average household contained 5.0 persons compared to the state average household size of 3.15. About one Samoan family in four was without a male head. According to demographer

A Samoan family at the Samoan Church Village at Nānākuli, O'ahu, in 1972. *(Courtesy of the General Assistance Center for the Pacific, Department of Educational Foundations, University of Hawaii)*

Robert W. Franco: "These Samoan males might have been in Samoa or on the mainland, looking for employment opportunities or conducting family business, or they might have been in the U.S. armed forces and stationed outside Hawaii. Samoan families headed by females qualify more easily for public housing, and this probably contributes to the relatively high percentage of families headed by females."[216]

Intermarriage is commonly practiced by Samoans in Hawai'i, with 55 percent of males and 47 percent of females marrying persons of other races in 1985 (Table 3-10). Samoan females who intermarried in 1975-1984 were more likely to choose Hawaiian, White, or Black partners, while males selected Hawaiians or Whites; there was little intermarriage of Samoans with persons of Asian ancestry.

Mortality figures for Samoans in Hawai'i recorded about 55-60 annual deaths for 1980-1985, or a low crude death rate of 4.3 deaths per 1,000 Samoans in 1980 (Table 3-5). No life expectancy tables have been tabulated for this young and relatively small population.

As one of the newest immigrant groups, Samoans have had problems of adjustment to life in Hawai'i.[217,218] Samoans in the civilian labor force showed the highest level of unemployment among all racial groups in Hawai'i, and Samoan women have the lowest level of participation in the labor force.[219] They contributed disproportionately to law enforcement, health, and social welfare workloads.[220]

In the twenty-first century, higher levels of education, employment, and occupations will alter the role of Samoans in the Hawaiian community. With an increased number of second- and third-generation U.S.-born Samoans residing in the Islands, this group of voters (in contrast to Samoan nationals, who are unable to vote unless they become U.S. citizens) will become a stronger political voice. The Samoan population will grow through continued in-migration and by natural increase, resulting in the intermixing, assimilating, and strengthening of this new Polynesian blood in Hawai'i.

Other Ethnic Groups

During the nineteenth century most immigrants to the Islands were members of national groups brought as laborers for economic expansion of the kingdom of Hawai'i, representatives of religious groups, or business entrepreneurs. These people were Blacks, Chinese, Filipinos, Japanese, Koreans, Samoans, and Whites (including Spanish,

Portuguese, Puerto Ricans, Mexicans, as well as northern Europeans such as Scotch, Irish, Germans, Scandinavians, Russians, and others).

The term "Other" in this review refers to persons of smaller count such as American Indians and those classified in the 1980 decennial census as Eskimo, Aleut, Asian Indian, Guamanian, Vietnamese, and "Other Asian and Pacific Islanders," which includes persons from Thailand, Laos, Cambodia, Pakistan, Tonga, Fiji, Micronesia, and other areas (Table 3–1).

King Kamehameha IV suggested to his legislature in 1855 that people from other Pacific islands should be invited to work in Hawai'i to provide a continuity to the Polynesian stock.[221] However, government funds were not made available for this project during his reign, and a proposal to bring the Pitcairn Island population to Hawai'i was not carried out. In 1859 ten islanders from Rarotonga were solicited by private businessmen to work on a plantation on Kaua'i. A few years later a more active recruitment of inhabitants of the Pacific succeeded in engaging about 2,500 persons. According to sociologist Andrew Lind: "Reports by ship captains indicate they had to travel vast distances through all three major ethnic areas of the Pacific and visit countless islands to obtain even that limited number over a period of seven years. Natives were recruited from Rotumah in the Marquesas, from Manihiki in the Cook Islands, from the Gilberts and Carolines of Micronesia, and from the New Hebrides and Solomons of Melanesia, among others."[222]

Missionary groups in Micronesia disapproved of the taking of members of their congregations to meet labor needs for Hawai'i's economic growth. Although women and children were included in the movement, the immigrant Polynesian, Melanesian, and Micronesian workers did not adapt well to life on plantations, and the families failed to adjust to the cultural changes in lifestyle. By 1900 the U.S. census reported the presence of only 415 Pacific islanders in Hawai'i; most of those recruited had died or returned to their homelands.

Plans to bring workers from Indonesia and India did not materialize. The royal commissioner of immigration, W. N. Armstrong, decided in 1881 that cultural and governmental obstacles precluded efforts to bring Indonesians to Hawai'i.[223] Several attempts were made to recruit East Indians, but Commissioner Henry A. P. Carter wrote from London that Hawai'i "could not expect any active assistance from local authorities in India who were inclined to passively resist any efforts to induce the people to emigrate."[224] He said the

British government would "throw every obstacle" in the way of Indian emigration to Hawai'i because Indians had already been sent to Mauritius, and the British Empire did not wish to lose more people to work in other parts of the world.

In an attempt to learn more about the American Indians, the U.S. census in 1960 added the racial category "Indian." The classification was ambiguous, as the term could include American Indians, persons of mixed ancestry who claimed to be native Americans, and East Indians.[225] Persons listed in this category increased from 472 in 1960 to 2,655 in 1980, when they represented 0.3 percent of the total popula-

Hue Cao, a Vietnamese immigrant to Hawai'i, won a national award in 1986 for her essay "What the Statue of Liberty Means to Me." (*Bruce Asato photo, Courtesy of* The Honolulu Advertiser)

tion. Most American Indians in Hawai'i in 1980 were members of the armed forces with their dependents living in Honolulu in census tracts near military bases or on shipboard.[226]

Recent immigrant groups to Hawai'i have included refugees from Indochina. At the conclusion of the Vietnamese War in April 1975 the United States permitted large-scale entrance of evacuees. Refugees in the late twentieth century continue their exodus and movement to resettlement camps in the Philippines, Malaysia, and Thailand, with some absorption into the United States and movement to Hawai'i.

The 1980 census based on a 100 percent count reported 3,463 Vietnamese living in Hawai'i (Table 3-1; Table 3-3.i). A later 15.7 percent census sample identified 3,403 Vietnamese, 1,369 Laotians, 58 Cambodians, and 52 Hmong (Table 4-2).[227,228] These numbers may understate the actual figures, since this transient group may have been undercounted by the census as they shifted residences and moved to and from the U.S. mainland. Ethnically, the Indochinese refugees are Vietnamese, Chinese from Vietnam, and Lao and Hmong from Laos.[229] As a young population, Vietnamese recorded a high crude birth rate of 28.8 births per 1,000 population in 1980. These recent

A Tongan immigrant family residing in Honolulu in 1988. *(Deacon Ritterbush photo)*

refugee residents were making gradual adjustments in linguistic, economic, educational, and social and cultural relationships.[230,231]

A few small clusters of persons of other ethnic groups live in the Islands. Among the Asian population in 1980 were 708 Asian Indians, 153 Indonesians, 59 Malayans, 59 Pakistani, and 765 Thai. Pacific islander Polynesian population included 1,482 Tongans and 269 Tahitians; Micronesians counted 1,630 Guamanians, 56 Northern Mariana Islanders, 78 Marshallese, and 305 Palauans; and of the 355 Melanesians, 260 were Fijians.

Population figures for the category "Other Ethnic Groups" (or "Others") were inconsistently defined and recorded by the U.S. censuses over the decades (Table 3-3.k). Statistical findings for this group are not strictly comparable through the years owing to classification changes.

Population pyramids of "Others" demonstrate an excess of males aged 15–29 in 1910 that is attributed to Filipino male immigrants (Figure 3–10). The expansion in the 1940–1960 pyramids is explained by the inclusion of Koreans. The 1970 pyramid, which represents primarily Samoans, shows balanced sex ratios and a steadily growing population. The 1980 pyramid uses figures from the 100 percent census count; a subsequent tabulation based on a sample reclassified some respondents to Whites or other Asian and Pacific islander groups, resulting in the reduction in size of this group from 42,537 to 21,444 persons.[232]

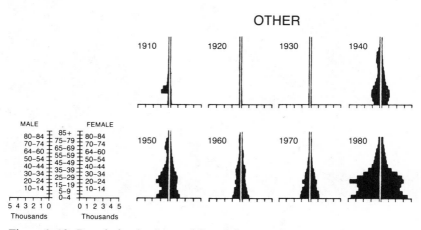

Figure 3–10. Population by Age and Sex: Other
Note: These pyramids are based on U.S. census definition of race.
Source: See Table 3–3.k.

CHAPTER 4

The Demographic Situation

The demographic history of Hawai'i for the past two centuries reflects the dramatic depopulation of native Hawaiians upon exposure to Western man, the gradual repopulation by immigrant national groups in response to deliberate government policy, the intermarriage and development of a multiethnic society, and the recent state emphasis on economic growth in the labor-intensive visitor industry that causes rapid expansion of the population by foreign immigrants and by in-migrants from the continental United States (Figure 2-1).[1]

Hawai'i's population has grown steadily since the 1870s, with patterns of high fertility in the first part of the 1900s and high migration levels since statehood. Studies by the State Department of Planning and Economic Development (DPED) show the direct relationship of population growth to economic conditions.[2] In their 1984 economic-population forecasting model, the DPED illustrated how population increased with demand for labor by Hawai'i's visitor industry (see Chapter 5). Migration was used as the forecasting variable to adjust the demand and supply of labor, and net migration became the number of new residents required to provide the labor force that, when added to the surviving labor force, equaled the demand for labor.

State economic growth policies in the 1980s endorsed high rates of economic expansion. To achieve these goals visitor industry development was encouraged, and the number of new jobs exceeded the potential resident labor pool. This resulted in a shortage of labor that invited migration into Hawai'i and promoted expansion of population to fill the expected labor needs.

The 1980 resident population of 964,691 was more than six times as large as the 1900 population of 154,001, having increased at an average annual growth rate of 2.3 percent; in contrast, the U.S. average

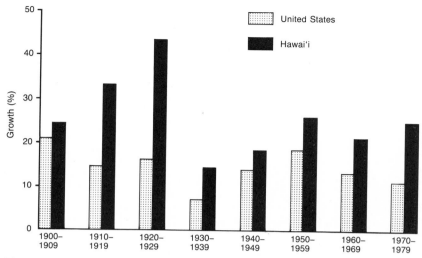

Figure 4-1. Resident Population Growth by Decade, Hawai'i and the United States, 1900–1980
Sources: See Table 2-1 and U.S. Bureau of the Census 1986, Table 2.

annual population growth rate during the same period was less than 1.4 percent (Figure 4-1). A 1987 estimate of the resident population of Hawai'i counted 1,082,500 persons, indicating that the annual rate of resident growth had slowed to 1.5 percent. The de facto population, which included all persons physically present in the Islands in 1987, was estimated at 1,198,800 residents and visitors, over 10 percent higher than the resident population.[3,4]

Size and Growth of Population

The eight major islands of Hawai'i include a total of 6,425 square miles (16,641 square kilometers), ranking forty-seventh among the states in land area. In 1985 the density of estimated de facto population of 179 persons per square mile (69 per square kilometer) was more than double the average U.S. density of 67 per square mile (26 per square kilometer) (Table 4-1; Figure 4-2). The population was unevenly distributed, with a de facto density on the island of O'ahu of 1,451 (560 per square kilometer). Hundreds of square miles in the higher regions of the larger islands are uninhabited, owing to the steep grade, and those areas are reserved for forests and watersheds.

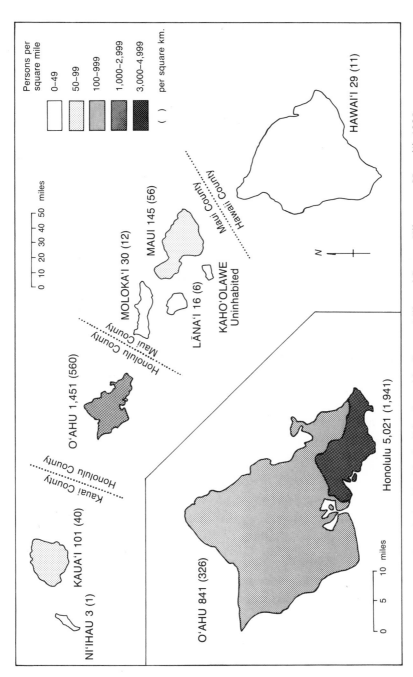

Figure 4–2. De Facto Population Density by Island, and by Square Mile and Square Kilometer, Hawai'i, 1985

Source: See Table 4–1.

The state of Hawaii is divided into four counties: Honolulu (the island of Oʻahu); Kauai (the islands of Kauaʻi and Niʻihau); Maui (the islands of Maui, Molokaʻi [including Kalawao County], Lānaʻi, and the uninhabited island of Kahoʻolawe); and Hawaii (the island of Hawaiʻi) (Table 2–1; Table 5–3).

Honolulu County (with the city of Honolulu) on Oʻahu is the industrial, business, and political center of the state. Oʻahu, the third-largest island (593 square miles; see Table 4–1), has been the major center for growth since 1900, and its 1985 population was almost 14 times as large as its number at the beginning of the twentieth century. It contained 814,611 persons, or over 75 percent of the state's inhabitants in 1985. Some areas of urban Oʻahu are among the most densely populated in the world (for example, Kuhio Park Terrace with 71,067 persons per square mile and the Ena Road census tract in Waikīkī with 62,976 persons per square mile).[5]

The population of the county of Honolulu declined from 81.9 percent of the state total to 79.0 percent in 1970–1980, and to about 77.3 percent by July 1, 1985. However, the actual number of persons in Honolulu was higher, growing by 184,000 resident population in 1970–1985 or an increase of 214,400 de facto population. These figures exceeded the 99,915 new residents or the de facto growth of 141,000 persons on the neighbor islands during that time.

Between 1930 and 1960 the population on the neighbor islands (the counties of Kauai, Maui, and Hawaii) dropped from 165,400 to 132,400, partly because of job losses related to mechanization of the sugar and pineapple industries that resulted in out-migration of young people looking for work in Honolulu and on the U.S. mainland. With the rapid development of the visitor industry since 1970, the average annual population growth rate for Maui, Hawaiʻi, and Kauaʻi exceeded that for Honolulu.

Kauaʻi, located 63 miles northeast of Oʻahu, has a population that ranged in number between 20,000 and 35,000 until the mid-1980s, when the county grew rapidly to an estimated 44,600 residents, or 55,600 de facto population.[6] Niʻihau, a small, privately owned island of 70 square miles that lies east of Kauaʻi, is a part of the county of Kauai. In 1985 Niʻihau had 180 residents, of whom 95 percent were full or Part Hawaiians; its population density was only 3 persons per square mile.

The population of Maui, the second-largest island, has grown rapidly since 1970. In that year the resident population for the county was 46,156 and the de facto population was 48,400 persons. With the expansion of the visitor industry, the estimated resident total for 1985 almost doubled at 85,300 people, and the de facto population reached 115,500, or 139 percent higher than the 1970 de facto population.[7] The estimated 1985 average de facto density was 98 persons per square mile.

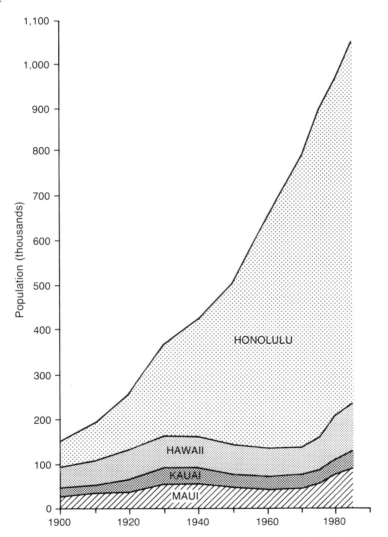

Figure 4-3. Resident Population Growth by Counties, Hawai'i, 1900–1985
Source: See Table 2-1.

Included in the county of Maui is Moloka'i, an island 40 miles long and 7 miles wide, which held a relatively constant population of about 5,000 residents in the 1930–1970 period. It experienced a 30 percent growth in 1970–1985 to 6,500 persons. One census tract in Maui County, known as Kalawao County, is the Kalaupapa leprosy settlement, administered by the State Department of Health; its population decreased from 172 persons in 1970 to 144 residents in 1980. Lāna'i, an agricultural island in Maui county, has maintained population stability for over fifty years of about 2,200 people. Kaho'olawe is a small island near Maui unoccupied with the exception of short-term stays by military personnel since 1940.[8]

Hawai'i is the largest island, and two hundred years ago it was probably the most populous, containing perhaps 40 percent of the inhabitants of the Hawaiian chain. At the time of the first missionary census in 1831–1832, 35 percent of the population of the Islands resided on Hawai'i, but this percentage dropped steadily to a low of 8 percent in 1970. Since that time, dramatic population growth occurred with the expansion of the visitor industry and with the development of new agricultural crops. The Hawai'i Island 1970 resident population of 63,468 increased to 109,200 by 1985, and the de facto population of 65,700 jumped to 115,800 persons in the same time period, or a growth of 76.3 percent in fifteen years. The island is sparsely inhabited, with an estimated 1985 Hawaii County de facto density of 29 persons per square mile (Figure 4–3).

Ethnicity

Because the population of Hawai'i emerged from a culturally and racially diverse stock, an analysis of its ethnic composition offers one of the most interesting and complex statistical problems in the study of the demography of Hawai'i. Race has been defined, interpreted, and redefined anew by succeeding censuses and by state, county, and private agencies.[9] Inconsistency in definition has resulted in incomparability when data are reviewed over a period of time, with findings that may be considered either questionable or almost meaningless. Changing racial definitions have seriously clouded trends of growth by ethnic groups, especially among Hawaiians, Chinese, and Whites (Figure 2–1; Figure 4–4).

Users of ethnic data should be aware of significant discrepancies that occur in figures from different compilations of racial data, and

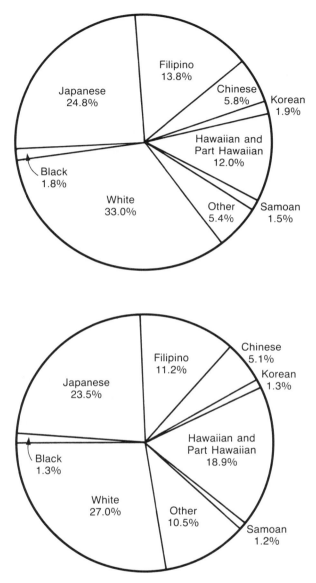

Figure 4–4. Ethnicity (percent) by U.S. Census and Hawaii Health Surveillance Program, Hawai'i, 1980
Sources: See Table 3–1 and Table 3–2.

source of data should be cited for clarification of analysis. The two most common sources of figures on race are the statistics from the Hawaii Health Surveillance Program (HHSP) and those from the U.S. census. The Hawaii State Department of Business and Economic Development (in 1987 the name was changed from the Hawaii State Department of Planning and Economic Development) and the Hawaii State Department of Health usually cite ethnic figures derived from the HHSP, an ongoing sample survey of about 18,000 persons, excluding persons in institutions or military barracks, on Niʻihau, or at Kalawao on Molokaʻi. In response to the questions "Of what race or combination of races is: Your father? Your mother?," state publications included statistical detail on ten unmixed groups (Black, Caucasian, Chinese, Filipino, Hawaiian, Japanese, Korean, Puerto Rican, Samoan, and "other unmixed or unknown") and two mixed groups (Part Hawaiian and non-Hawaiian).

The State Department of Health in 1980 provided categories of American Indian, Guamanian, and Vietnamese, and they further refined their figures for tabulations of births, deaths, fetal deaths, marriages, and divorces, using 1978 criteria developed in cooperation with the National Center for Health Statistics.[10] The coding specifications were:

a. If a mixture is of Hawaiian and any other race, code as Part Hawaiian.
b. If a mixture is of White races (White, Caucasian, Puerto Rican, Portuguese, Cuban, or Mexican), code to the first race listed.
c. If a mixture is of White (White, Caucasian, Puerto Rican, Portuguese, Cuban, or Mexican) and any other race, code to the non-White race.
d. If a mixture is of non-White races (except Hawaiian and Part Hawaiian), code to the first race listed.

The State Health Department determines a child's race from the parents' ethnic group following 1978 coding procedures:

a. If both parents are of the same race, child's race is parents' race.
b. If either parent is of unknown race, child's race is that of the parent with the known race.
c. If either parent is Hawaiian or Part Hawaiian, child's race is Part Hawaiian.
d. If either parent is Black, child's race is Black (except Hawaiian and Part Hawaiian).
e. If parents' races are White but not the same, (Caucasian, Puerto Rican, Portuguese, Cuban, or Mexican), the child's race is that of the father's race.

f. If one parent is White and the other parent is non-White, child's race is that of the non-White parent.
g. If both parents are non-White but not the same race, child's race is that of the father.

In this book most of the data on ethnic populations in Hawai'i are taken from official census counts and presented in chronological continuity. Ethnicity information on vital events is recorded from vital registration statistics. Despite specified definitions, racial data in Hawai'i remain ambiguous (see Glossary for Blacks and Whites). An increasing proportion of persons are without knowledge of their father's race; a large number are a "mixed" blend of numerous races.

The U.S. census has released three sets of statistics bearing on race from the 1980 census: a full count; a one-in-six sample; and the five-percent Public Use Microdata Sample, with extensive editing and shifts in figures (Table 3–2, Figure 4–4).[11] A comparison of these three sets of figures with the 1980 HHSP estimates indicated broad differences: according to the U.S. census, Hawaiians numbered between 115,500 to 122,660 persons, while the HHSP tabulated 9,366 Hawaiians and 166,087 Part Hawaiians. Whites, on the other hand, varied in number from the U.S. census figures of 318,770–327,640 to the HHSP count of 244,832. These discrepancies illustrate difficulties in analyzing racial patterns with any degree of accuracy.

The earliest censuses were taken by missionaries and by government officials in the kingdom and in the republic.[12,13,14,15] Ethnicity for non-Hawaiians was first recorded in 1890, although estimates of race based on place-of-birth data had been recorded since 1849. Race was determined by biological criteria similar to categories suggested above by the HHSP, with preference to Hawaiian and Part Hawaiian; non-Hawaiian mixtures were classified according to the race of father except for part Whites who were counted with the non-White parent.

In 1970 the U.S. census utilized a method of self-identification by respondents without denoting any clear-cut scientific definition of biological stock. Data represented self-classification by people according to the race with which they identified. For persons who could not provide a single response to the race question, the race of the person's father was used in 1970 and that of the person's mother in 1980.[16] This method of self-identification resulted in data that were not comparable, and it was partially responsible for an increase in the percentages of persons recorded as Whites, Filipinos, and Chinese and for a decrease in percentages recorded as Japanese and Part Hawaiians.

Preferential tabulation has been given to persons of Hawaiian blood. Through the 1960 U.S. census, the term "Hawaiian" referred to full-blooded descendants of ancient Polynesian inhabitants of the Islands. All other persons with any Hawaiian blood were Part Hawaiian. Members of this latter group were first called half-native or Part Hawaiian in 1890; later they were classified as Caucasian-Hawaiian and Asiatic Hawaiian; in 1940 they again became Part Hawaiian.

By 1970 full Hawaiians were no longer counted by the U.S. census as a separate group, and they probably numbered only between 1,000 and 10,000 persons (in 1985 the HHSP suggested a tabulation of 6,824 for this group).[17] The Part Hawaiian category was abandoned by the U.S. census, and persons of Hawaiian ancestry were tabulated under the general term of "Hawaiian" or reclassified with Chinese, White, or other groups.

Hawaiians, often undercounted by the U.S. census, may be over-counted by the HHSP. According to State Statistician Robert C. Schmitt:

> The Part Hawaiian category has historically been subject to shifting net undercounts. In past years, Part Hawaiians were often misclassified as unmixed Hawaiians, and this practice obviously continues in the present. More recently, however, a growing number of persons with one-eighth, 1/16th, or even smaller fractions of Hawaiian blood have classified themselves as non-Hawaiians. Even when the classification is accurate, however, analysts may question the value of a category which combines such disparate groups as 1/16th- and 15/16th-Hawaiians."[18]

Caucasians (called "White" by the U.S. census since 1970) were first defined as persons of American and European ancestry, including Britons, Germans, Norwegians, Swedes, and other northern Europeans. Portuguese, Spaniards, and Puerto Ricans were absorbed gradually in this classification, and in 1980 the White category in the U.S. census included responses such as Canadian, German, Italian, Lebanese, Polish, Cuban, Mexican, and Dominican.

Early Blacks in Hawai'i were descended from the Black Portuguese seamen who came on whaling vessels in the 1820–1880 period. Most of these men married Hawaiians; their descendants, estimated in 1940 between 7,000 and 8,000, were classified for census purposes as Part Hawaiian.[19] Since 1950 the small number of Blacks has doubled each decade, but only 15 percent of the 17,364 Blacks in Hawai'i in 1980 were civilian residents; the majority of this group were counted as members of the armed forces and their dependents.

Persons with ancestors from China, the Philippines, Japan, Korea, and Samoa were classified as Chinese, Filipinos, Japanese, Koreans, and Samoans by the 1980 U.S. census. The 1980 data also provided 100 percent tabulations on American Indians, Asian Indians, Guamanians, Vietnamese, and Eskimos and Aleuts from Alaska and Canada. Other groups counted in a 15.7 percent sample included Polynesian, Micronesian, Melanesian, and Other (Table 4–2).

Early Hawai'i demographer Romanzo Adams suggested that the full assimilation of Hawai'i's minorities resulting in a stable racial mixture of a culturally homogeneous people may take two or three hundred years.[20] While cultural traits may be retained through social practices, the high rates of intermarriage and of births of babies of multiple ancestry in the 1980s clouded distinct ethnic classifications and suggested a gradual miscegenation of subgroups in Hawai'i in the twenty-first century.

Age and Sex Composition

Two of the most useful pieces of demographic information about a population are its age and sex composition. Knowledge of the age composition helps government planners determine needs for transportation and housing; information on the number of women of childbearing age gives an indication of how many babies may be born and how many teachers, classrooms, and schools may be needed in the near future. The number of young and older persons influences the birth and death rates.

Age and sex figures are used to plan for employment and for the economics of a community—how many persons will be a part of the labor force and pay taxes, and how many will be dependent and need to be supported, for example. Economists classify people who are between 15 and 64 years old as the economically productive population; those persons younger than 15 and older than 64 are considered dependent, although there are many exceptions to this breakdown. Projections for the future are not based on total populations but are developed from the numbers of persons at specific ages in the present population.

The age and sex composition of a group may be seen on a graph called a population pyramid, in which the numbers of males in various age groups are represented on the left and those of females are shown on the right (Figure 4–5). The youngest group appears at the base and the oldest is at the top.

The Demographic Situation

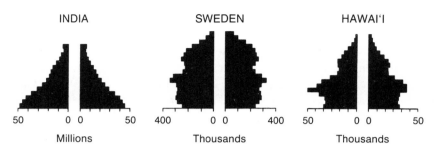

Figure 4–5. Population Pyramid Shapes
Sources: Hawaii, DPED, *Statistical Report,* No. 163 (1983, Table 4); United Nations, DIESA, *Demographic Yearbook* (1983, Table 7); United States, BOC (1982, Table 19).

A population pyramid that resembles a triangle (as in India, 1980, in Figure 4–5) shows a growing population of a developing country, with high fertility rates indicative of large numbers of young children and fewer persons in each higher age bracket. (Age pyramids are usually constructed for five-year intervals.) If a population pyramid is shaped in a figure similar to a rectangle (as in Sweden, 1980), it shows almost as many people in the older age groups as there are children, a situation characteristic of a developed country with low fertility and an older population that is not increasing in size (a stable population). A pyramid that bulges out in one place (as in Hawai'i, 1980) indicates a relatively large number of persons in one age group. This is true of Hawai'i's 1980 pyramid owing to the disproportionate number of residents who are members of the armed forces and their dependents in the 20–24 year age category. The contraction at the base of Hawaii's pyramid reflects recently lowered numbers of births in the state.

Over the past eighty years, the age and sex composition of Hawaii changed markedly (Table 4–3; Figure 4–6). At the start of the century the age distribution, especially that of males, was distorted by immigrants who were primarily young male laborers without families. As time passed, the population grew and aged, and the pyramids assumed a more balanced and expanded shape. Recent pyramids, however, have indicated some irregularities:

1. The 1980 pyramid appears inflated, in contrast to the 1970 graph, reflecting a resident population increase of 196,130 persons.
2. Indentations and bulges in the pyramids may be the result of fluctuating numbers of births. The low birth rates of the Depres-

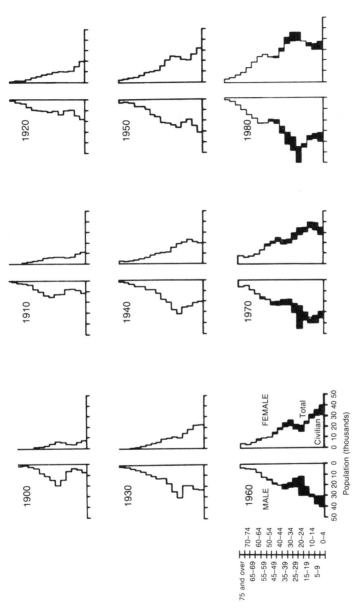

Figure 4–6. Population by Age and Sex, Hawai'i, 1900–1980
Source: United States, BOC 1953, Table 11; 1961, Table 16; 1971b, Table 20; 1982a, Tables 19 and 22. See Table 4–3.

sion years of the 1930s are observed in the contraction of the
pyramids at ages 10–19 in 1950, ages 20–29 in 1960, ages 30–39
in 1970, and ages 40–49 in 1980. The contraction for ages 0–14
in the 1980 pyramid is a reflection of reduced numbers of births
from earlier small cohorts as well as low birth rates in response
to the use of family planning methods.

3. The sex ratio (the number of males per 100 females) historically
favored males in the Islands, as may be seen in the larger left
halves of the pyramids. While a "closed" population would
show a sex ratio at birth of about 106 that decreases slowly in
accordance with higher male mortality rates, Hawai'i's population has reflected male dominance from migration. From a ratio
of 223 males to 100 females in 1900, the ratio dropped to 105
males per 100 females in 1980, well above the 1980 U.S. sex ratio
level of 94.5.[21] Male-dominant military residents (shown in Figure 4–6 in black for easy identification) distort the sex ratio for
ages 18–35, and the effect is dramatically evident in the 20–24
year level with a sex ratio of 115.4. For persons age 75 and over,
the sex ratio in Hawai'i of 81 males per 100 females far exceeds
the U.S. sex ratio of 55 for that age group.

4. The young average age of immigrants (44 percent of Hawai'i's
immigrants in 1980 and 1981 were aged 18–34) contributes to the
bulge of the mid-section of the pyramids.[22] All age levels are
affected by migration movement to the Islands.

5. The aging of the population is apparent with the progressive
expansion of the pyramid at each age level. In 1900 the median
age of 28.3 for males was much higher than 22.3 for females, the
result of immigration of males (Table 4–3). With the balancing
of the numbers of each sex, a closer alignment in median age
occurred over the decades. In 1980 the median age was 29.1
years for females and 27.7 for males, with an average of 28.4
years. This is expected to rise to 33.7 years by the year 2000 with
increasing longevity and a greater proportion of elderly population.

The population pyramids of ethnic groups depict changes in the
population of each racial category in Hawai'i since 1900, based upon
U.S. census definition and count. The pyramids reflect migration histories, demographic shifts in cultural trends of fertility, and mortality
patterns. A review of these pyramids is presented in the discussions on
each ethnic group in Chapter 3.[23]

Military Population

The demography of Hawai'i has been significantly influenced by the presence of the military (defined in this volume to include members of the armed forces and their dependents). Since the early nineteenth century, warships and other national vessels have stopped in the Islands for supplies, rest, recuperation, and diplomatic relationships.[24] The acquisition of Pearl Harbor by the United States in the 1887 amendment to the Reciprocity Treaty with the kingdom of Hawai'i gave exclusive use of the harbor to the United States as a naval station.[25] With the annexation of Hawai'i to the United States in 1898 followed by the establishment of the Territory of Hawai'i in 1900, new army and navy installations opened jobs and economic growth for the Islands.

Defense expenditures have been a leading source of outside income for Hawai'i. Defense spending ranked first from 1941 until 1972, when it was displaced by the visitor industry. In 1985 defense spending still ranked second and accounted for $1.95 billion, or between 15

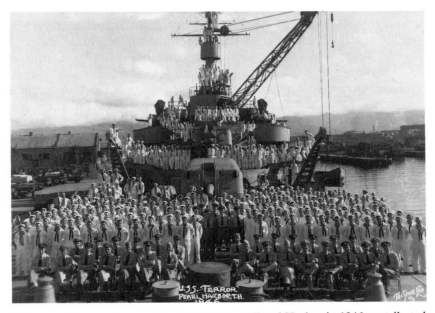

Military officers and crew of the USS *Terror* at Pearl Harbor in 1946 contributed to the imbalanced sex ratio that has favored males for a century in the population of Hawai'i. *(Tai Sing Loo photo, Bishop Museum)*

to 20 percent of the total direct income from major export industries.[26]

As Hawai'i became a military center of major importance, the numbers in the military increased from about 4,370 in 1920 to 29,830 persons in 1940.[27] During World War II in 1944 the number of active-duty military peaked at 442,160 personnel, but these figures reduced sharply at the end of the war to a level of about 110,000–125,000 armed forces and their families. In 1986 there were 58,584 officers and enlisted men and 66,210 dependents, of whom 99.5 percent resided in Honolulu County (Figure 4–6).[28] The number of female members of the armed forces has increased from about 600 in 1960 to over 4,000 women in 1980 (Table 4–4).

The ethnic composition of the military population showed a disproportionate number of Whites and Blacks (Table 4–5). In contrast to Hawai'i's resident population of 34.4 percent White, 1.8 percent Black, and 61.3 percent Asiatic, the military population in 1980 had 73.8 percent White, 13.3 percent Black, and only 8.1 percent Asiatic.

Military residents are usually temporary, but they influence the demographic analysis of the total population. They have a disproportionate number of males. High fertility rates are recorded among the armed forces wives. In 1985 the armed forces and dependents, representing about 12 percent of Hawai'i's population, produced about 22 percent of the state's births; their crude birth rate was 33.5 in contrast to 13.9 births per 1,000 civilian population.[29] The death rate of military members is low owing to their youthful age composition. Since the armed forces assignment to Hawai'i is of short term, there is a large in- and out-migration. Military dependents show a heavy net out-migration owing to the departure of their babies born while on duty in the Islands.

To determine more accurately the birth, death, and migration trends of Hawai'i's civilian resident population, members of the armed forces and their dependents, as well as visitors, are often removed from total population tabulations. The military population data is observed independently whenever possible to identify the different characteristics of this important population group in Hawai'i.

Births, Births to Unmarried Mothers, and Abortion Rates

Although statistics on vital events were recorded in the Hawaiian Islands since the days of the early missionaries, the data were considered neither complete nor fairly reliable until the second or third decade of the twentieth century. While crude rates were calculated from 1900, analysis of early reports is complicated by underregistration of births and deaths and by the rapidly changing age and sex composition of the population during the 1900–1924 period of heavy immigration (Table 3–5; Table 4–6).

The rise in the crude birth rate between 1912 and 1924 (Figure 4–7), with a peak at 42 births per 1,000 population, was the result of increasingly complete birth records, the presence of a greater number of women of childbearing age, and the actual rise in fertility. During the Depression years in the 1930s, the birth rate fell; after World War II ended in 1945, the "baby boom" generation contributed to a rise in the crude birth rate; and since 1954 there has been a gradual decline to between 17.3 and 18.0 births per 1,000 resident population (including military dependents) in the 1975–1985 period. A higher rate that might have been expected with the rise in the total number of women of childbearing ages 15–44 years (from 134,000 in 1960 to over 230,000 females in 1980) has not occurred. That births have remained at a fairly constant level suggests changes in cultural and social practices that relate to economic constraints and use of family planning measures.

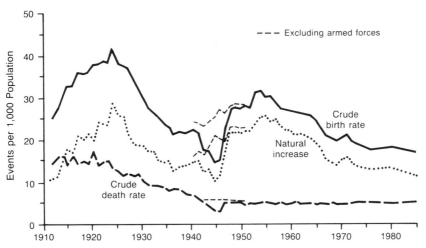

Figure 4–7. Crude Birth Rates, Crude Death Rates, and Rates of Natural Increase, Hawai'i, 1912–1985
Source: See Table 4–6.

Numerous refined measures (in contrast to the crude birth rate) analyze fertility, including the age-specific birth rate, the general fertility rate, the total fertility rate, and the gross and net reproduction rates (see Glossary).[30] The general fertility rate, which removes the effects of the age and sex distribution, dropped over 62 percent in the 1960–1980 decades; similarly, the total fertility rate and the gross reproductive rate fell by about 70 percent in the 1920–1980 period (Table 3–6).

Ethnic birth rates, which indicate the number of births per 1,000 population by specific racial groups, show marked reduction of reproduction since 1960 by Chinese, Japanese, Koreans, and civilian Whites. The child-woman ratio among ethnic groups confirmed that Samoans and Blacks had the highest fertility, followed by Hawaiians, Filipinos, and military Whites.

Some of the problems related to ethnic fertility analysis may be attributed to racial definitions in source data (see Chapter 4, section on ethnicity). Significant differences in rates occur when the population denominator is derived from the U.S. census in contrast to figures from the Hawaii Health Surveillance Program (HHSP). When population from the U.S. census was used, Hawaiians showed high fertility rates (a crude birth rate of 50.9 in 1970 and 34.4 births per 1,000 Hawaiians in 1980), while rates calculated with HHSP population estimates resulted in lower fertility (a crude birth rate for Hawaiians of 26.8 in 1970 and 22.7 in 1980; Table 3–7).

In part, the high tabulations for Hawaiians and "Others" were an overstatement reflecting problems of classification. Babies were recorded in the vital statistics as Hawaiian, although their parents were counted by the census as non-Hawaiian; this inconsistency resulted in a spuriously high birth rate for Hawaiians. (See Chapter 3 for additional information on fertility by ethnic group.)

Age-specific fertility measurement focuses on the number of births per 1,000 women in a specific age group. Since 1960 the fertility of women in Hawai'i between the ages of 25 and 29 declined in comparison to that of women aged 20 through 24, and before 1960 women had a higher percentage of their children at younger ages (Table 3–8; Figure 4–8). The sharp peak in the curve in 1960 at ages 20 through 24 reflected the baby boom of that period. Between 1960 and 1980 a steep drop in fertility was noted at all ages, with an especially sharp reduction among persons over age 30. The large discrepancy in fertility patterns of the civilian and military populations of Hawai'i was apparent in this age-specific fertility measurement, with especially

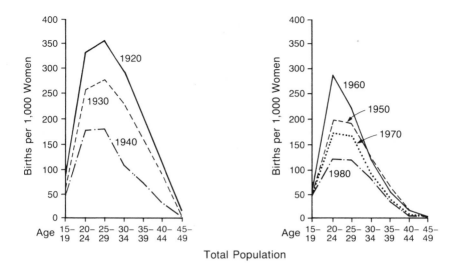

Total Population

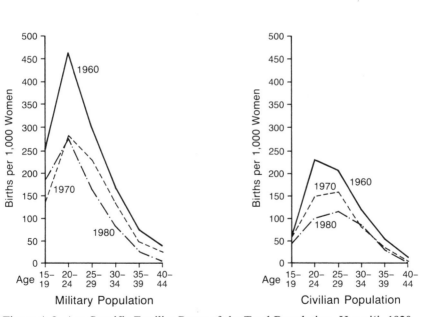

Military Population   Civilian Population

Figure 4–8. Age-Specific Fertility Rates of the Total Population, Hawai'i, 1920–
1980, and of the Military and Civilian Populations, 1960–1980
Source: See Table 3–8.

high rates for military women under age 30. Chinese, Japanese, and Koreans demonstrated lowered fertility at all ages, and childbearing occurred at a higher rate in the 25–29 year age group. The fertility pattern of recent migrants such as Samoans, Vietnamese, and Filipinos showed high fertility, although Filipino birth rates declined significantly at all age levels in the 1970–1980 decade.

Changing social attitudes toward births to unmarried mothers (illegitimacy) and abortion is observed in the statistical review of these practices. The number of births reported as occurring outside of marriage increased sharply from 317 in 1930 to 882 in 1960, 1,936 in 1975, and 3,650 in 1985, growing from a rate of 29 per 1,000 live births in 1930 to 200 in 1985 (Table 4–7). While the median age for all births in Hawai'i in 1980 was 26.0, that for births to unmarried mothers was somewhat younger at 21.8 years.[31,32] Samoans and Hawaiians had highest ratios of births to unmarried mothers, while Japanese, Chinese, and Koreans showed the lowest rates.

Since legal restrictions for elective abortions were removed by State Law of Hawaii, Act 1, on March 11, 1970, the number of abortions annually recorded by the State Department of Health increased from 4,135 in 1970 to between 5,000–6,000 in 1976–1985 (Table 4–7). About one-fourth of the pregnancies in Hawai'i since 1970 were terminated by elective abortion. The availability of this procedure since 1970 has contributed to lowered state birth rates. Striking differences occurred in the practice of abortion among Hawai'i's ethnic groups, with Koreans showing the highest participation and Blacks, Hawaiians, and Samoans having the lowest ratio of abortions to live births in 1980 (Table 3–9).

Marriage and Divorce

The recording of marriages in Hawai'i was initiated by the protestant missionaries in 1828 and recorded by the kingdom of Hawai'i in 1845.[33,34] The publication of marriage statistics was suspended in 1863 and not resumed until 1902 after Hawai'i had become a territory of the United States. Divorce cases tried in the Superior Court were reported in annual and biennial statistics released by the Chief Justice of the Supreme Court.[35]

Since the end of World War II in 1945, marriage rates have remained at a level between 8 and 11 marriages per 1,000 resident population (Table 4–6). Highest rates of marriage of 10 to 13 marriages per 1,000 population occurred during the Vietnam war R and R (rest and recuperation) program; however many of these marriages occurred among military personnel and did not represent state trends.

In 1980 about 57 percent of males and 58 percent of females age 14 and above in Hawai'i were married, with about 2 percent of males and 8 percent of females widowed, and 5 percent of males and 7 percent of females divorced.[36] The median age at marriage rose steadily, paralleling U.S. trends for delayed marriage, with the 1985 median age (including remarriage) for grooms at 29.9 years and 27.8 years for brides.[37]

While the number of divorces in Hawai'i each year has risen slightly, the divorce rate stood between 4.6 and 5.3 divorces per 1,000 resident population in the 1971–1985 period (Table 4–6). In 1985, median years married was about 6 years, and median age of divorce for husbands was 34.3 years and 32 years for wives.

One of the most unique aspects of marital statistics in Hawai'i is intermarriage. Miscegenation of ethnic groups has occurred in three stages: first, there was extensive admixture in the late nineteenth century between foreign men (primarily White and Chinese) and Hawaiian women; second, as immigrant groups brought their wives and picture brides to the Islands, out-marriage was discouraged; and, finally, after World War II, intermarriage became increasingly accepted and widespread.[38] Between 1912 and 1916 only 11.5 percent of Hawai'i's marriages were interracial, but since 1951 out-marriages have ranged between 32.8 and 45 percent of all marriages recorded in the state (Table 3–10). Such factors as length of residence in Hawai'i, size of racial group, sex ratio within each ethnic category, and religious, economic, and cultural traits have contributed to the rate of intermarriage.

State statistical reports in the 1980s separated annual resident marriages among Hawai'i's inhabitants from total marriages, which included inhabitants and visitors to the Islands. In 1985 the resident population intermarriage rate was 45 percent compared to 35.5 percent for the total population, indicating a higher miscegenation among Hawai'i residents than previously reported.

The out-marriage rate among Hawaiians has been consistently high during the twentieth century, reaching 89.2 percent for grooms and 90.1 percent for brides of unmixed Hawaiian ancestry, and 56.1 percent for grooms and 57.3 percent for brides of Part Hawaiian background in 1985. High rates of intermarriage were recorded in 1985 for Puerto Rican and Chinese grooms and brides, for Korean, Vietnamese, and Filipino brides, and for Black grooms.

Death Rates and Life Expectancy

From a crude death rate of 19.5 deaths per 1,000 population in 1901, Hawai'i's death rate dropped in the 1940s and has been sustained at a level between 4.8 and 5.3 in the 1975–1985 decade, compared with a mid-1980 U.S. death rate of 8.9 (Table 4–6; Figure 4–7).[39,40] Infant mortality, which in 1910 accounted for 226.5 deaths per 1,000 live births, fell below 10 in the 1980s and showed a low figure of 8.7 deaths per 1,000 live births in 1985 (Table 4–7).

These low mortality figures are attributed to improved health care through the introduction of antibiotics, the control of communicable diseases, sanitation, and the provision of health services; they are also explained by the young median age of the population (28.3 years in 1980), because death rates are low among young people. With low birth rates and fewer children per adult, the average age of the population is expected to rise. Because mortality rates are higher among older people, this "aging" of the population may result in a higher crude death rate in the future. Of the 5,751 deaths in Hawai'i in 1985, the leading causes of death were diseases of the heart, malignant neoplasms, cerebrovascular disease, and influenza and pneumonia.

Hawai'i in 1980 had the distinction of claiming the longest life expectancy in the United States and in many areas of the world (Table 4–8).[41] At that time life expectancy in Hawai'i for males was 75.0 years (U.S. males—70.1 years) and for females 81.5 years (U.S. females—77.6 years).[42] Since 1920, life expectancy has increased steadily in the Islands (Table 4–9; Figure 4–9).[43,44] During the early twentieth century many lives were lost prematurely by infant mortality, maternal mortality, and disease. As death rates fell with improved health care measures and rising standards of living, longevity was extended. A female baby born in 1980 could expect to live almost thirty-five years longer than one born in 1920; for males the corresponding improvement in life expectancy was more than twenty-seven years.

Over the past half century Hawai'i's ethnic groups have experienced a dramatic extension of life expectancy (Table 4–10). In 1920, Whites, Chinese, and Japanese had life expectancies of about 50–55 years, while Hawaiians and Filipinos showed expected life figures of 30–35 years.[45] Over the decades the range of life expectancy has narrowed among racial groups to about 10 years in 1980 (the longest expectancy is for Chinese females at 81.7 years and the shortest is for

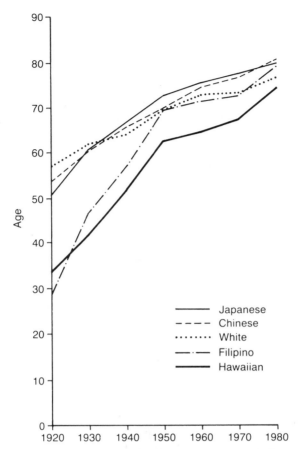

Figure 4-9. Life Expectancy at Birth by Ethnic
Group, Hawai'i, 1920–1980
Source: See Table 4-10.

Hawaiian males at 70.9 years). The convergence of life expectancy
among Hawai'i's ethnic groups resulted in an extension of life in the
1920–1980 period by 45.9 years for Filipinos, 39 years for Hawaiians,
28.5 years for Japanese, 25.4 years for Chinese, and 19.4 years for
Whites.[46] Female life expectancy has exceeded that of males among
all the ethnic groups; these variations are attributed to genetic and
social differences, including factors such as occupation, stress, diet,
smoking, accidents, and other lifestyle patterns.

The Elderly Population

The population of Hawaiʻi is gradually aging. The percentage of the population aged 65 and older increased from 1.7 in 1900 to 7.9 in 1980, and it is projected to grow to 12.6 by the year 2000. The number of persons known as "elderly" in the Islands in 1970–1980 expanded by 72.6 percent, from 44,116 to 76,150 persons, while the total population increased by 25.5 percent.

The "elderly," persons of ages 65 and over, are categorized by varying definitions. This group spans more than a 35-year range, and it is subdivided into the "young-old" (ages 65–74), the "old" (ages 75–84), and the "old-old" (ages 85 and above).[47]

These groupings of the elderly can be identified with birth cohorts that reflect the political, economic, and social history of the state. In 1980, individuals of ages 65–74 were the survivors of those who were born in 1906–1915, the period of the young Territory of Hawaiʻi. Some of those persons were not born in Hawaiʻi but migrated here from Asia, Europe, and other parts of the United States. Those who were 75–84 years of age in 1980 were born in 1896–1905, during the time of government transition when the new Hawaiian Republic was annexed to the United States. Persons aged 85 and above in 1980 were born in 1895 or before as citizens of the kingdom of Hawaiʻi or during the era of political upheaval under a provisional government.[48]

The size of Hawaiʻi's elderly population has increased steadily during the twentieth century (Table 4-11). Their average growth rate of 4.2 percent annually exceeded that of the total population growth rate of 2.3 percent, and consequently its proportion of the total population has been constantly rising. According to figures used by the State M-F series population projections (see Chapter 5, Population Projections, and Table 5-1), the total population is expected to reach 1,267,800 in the year 2000, of which 159,000 persons, or 12.9 percent of the total (13.9 percent if the military population is excluded) will be counted with the elderly group.[49]

Median age measurements also indicate aging of the population. In 1900 in Hawaiʻi the median age for the total population was 26.9 years. During the 1920–1929 period of high fertility, median age dropped to 21.7 years in 1930. Since that time lowered fertility and rising life expectancy have contributed to a higher median age for every decade except one, reaching the 1980 level of 28.4 years and a projected median age level of 34 years by the year 2000.

Although the Islands' population has been aging, its people are younger than those in most of the United States, and Hawai'i in 1980 ranked forty-ninth out of the fifty states for proportion of population in the elderly classification. The explanation for the larger percentage of younger population present in this state was the presence of the military population and the relatively high levels of migration to the state by persons of young adult ages.

Many factors are associated with the past and projected growth of the elderly population. Falling mortality rates reflected higher levels of health care and advancement in medical science. The life expectancy in Hawai'i in 1980 measured among the highest in the world.[50] If the population of Hawai'i residents age 65 and above were to experience the average mortality of 1980 in the future, then the group as a whole could expect to live an average of 19.2 years (males—17.2 years, and females—21.1 years).

Lower levels of fertility contributed to an increased proportion of older people. With the aging of the native-born and of the early migrant populations, the survivors of births that occurred 65 or more years earlier entered the "elderly" classification. This number of elderly people was expected to rise in the coming years to parallel the increasing number of Island births since 1915.

The influence of migration as a growth factor among the elderly is more difficult to determine owing to incomplete recording of interstate and international migration. When survival ratios to the population of ages 55 and above in 1970 are compared with the *expected* 1980 elderly population as contrasted with the *actual* numbers, approximately 9,000 of the 76,150 elderly in Hawai'i in 1980, or about 1 in 8, were survivors of migrants to the state during the previous ten years. While migration contributed to about half of the growth of the total population during the 1970–1980 decade, it accounted for only about 12 percent of the increase in the number of persons 65 years old and over.[51]

According to the 1980 U.S. census, some 7.4 percent of the elderly in Hawai'i were living outside the state five years earlier.[52] A slightly higher percentage of older women than men were recent migrants, and the "young-old" exceeded the number of "old" and "old-old" persons who changed residence to the Islands in that period of time.

An analysis of recent migration based on place of birth of Hawai'i's residents and on place of residence of Hawai'i-born persons showed that 5.7 percent of in-migrants and 2.5 percent of out-migrants between 1975 and 1980 were age 65 and over.[53] There was a distinct net inflow of older persons, but the numbers were small and most of Hawai'i's growth of persons age 65 or older was the result of aging of long-term residents.

Aging of the population through the decades can be observed in Hawai'i's population pyramids (Figure 4–6). Early in the century the sex ratio for elderly persons was extremely high, rising from 187 males per 100 females in 1900 to 242 by 1930, and then dropping to 102 males per 100 females by 1980. These changes reflect the movement of male laborers to Hawai'i; the immigration of female "picture brides," workers, and wives; and the birth of new generations and immigration of new groups, resulting in the expansion and balancing of both sexes in the higher age levels. The 1980 sex ratio of 81 males per 100 females for persons age 75 and over contrasted sharply with the U.S. sex ratio of 55 for that age group. The effect of early heavy immigration of males is seen to pass upward through the pyramids. The aging of male immigrant groups is especially evident in the population pyramids of the Chinese and Filipino groups (Table 4–12; Figure 3–4; Figure 3–7).

The racial composition of the elderly differs somewhat from that of the total population in Hawai'i, owing primarily to the different ethnic migration histories. For persons age 65 and over in 1980, Japanese accounted for 35.6 percent and Whites 28.3 percent of those age 65 and over. Filipinos and Chinese represented a slightly higher proportion of the elderly than of the state total population, while Hawaiians as a growing intermingled group included only 6.9 percent of persons age 65 and over. The Chinese and Japanese have the highest proportions of older persons, while Samoans as recent immigrants with higher fertility and Blacks with a high percent of young military have very low proportions of elderly.[54]

By geographic distribution, Honolulu County had the largest number of elderly (55,368 persons) in 1980 (Table 4–13). A few regions, such as the residential areas of Waikīkī, Diamond Head, Kapi'olani Park, and Ala Moana, showed exceptionally high concentrations of older persons. This disproportion may be related to the presence of residential condominium and cooperative apartments that had regulations restricting young children and favoring older occupants. While Kauai, Maui, and Hawaii counties recorded higher percentages of older persons, Honolulu's figures were more closely aligned if the young military population were excluded. With the migration of younger persons to the neighbor islands to accept employment in the expanding job market, the proportion of elderly may be lowered on the outer islands in the future.

Socioeconomic analysis of the elderly in Hawai'i in 1980 indicates some unique features. A vast majority (77.6 percent) of Island persons age 65 and over lived with family members or friends, in contrast to an estimated 28.2 percent of older persons living with relatives or friends in the United States as a whole. Only 16.3 percent of Hawai'i's older persons lived alone, and 4.9 percent lived in institutions or group quarters.[55] A high proportion (78 percent) of males and 50 percent of females were married, and 42 percent of the elderly married men had wives under age 65.

The 1980 census counted 113 centenarians, of whom 15 claimed to be 110 years old or over.[56] Analysis of this group by sex showed 62 females and 51 males, and by race the count gave 87 Pacific islanders and Asians (there was no breakdown for number of Hawaiians), 24 Whites, and 2 in the "Others" category. Demographer Robert C. Schmitt commented: "The foregoing record, both statistical and individual, suggests a truly remarkable picture of human longevity in Hawaii . . ."

Educational levels of Hawai'i's elderly have been rising, although some older persons who migrated to the Islands with a minimum of

Elderly residents of Hawai'i are honored at the Mayor's Annual Senior Citizens' Recognition Program in Honolulu in 1984. *(Elderly Affairs Division photo, Office of Human Resources, City and County of Honolulu)*

formal education have a low level of educational attainment. In 1980 persons aged 25 and over had finished a median of 11.7 years of school in contrast to those age 65 and over who reported 7.7 median years of school completed.

Many elderly choose to remain actively employed. Nearly 15 percent of those aged 65 and over in Hawai'i participated in the labor force in 1980; this figure is expected to rise with legal action that has extended retirement age. Over 23 percent of the 65–69 year group, 13.4 percent of those aged 70–74, and 6.1 percent of persons aged 75 and over were counted among those employed in 1980. Earnings of the employed elderly were lower than that for the total population, but many older persons were partially subsidized by relatives and had incomes supplemented by pension, retirement, and other sources.

Hawai'i's elderly enjoyed better health than the national average, according to figures measured by U.S. health indices. There were fewer acute and chronic illnesses, lower rates of hospitalization, and comparatively lower rates of mortality at all ages. The elderly in Hawai'i who were unable to continue major activities ranged from 13.2 percent of those 65–69 years old to 22.1 percent of those 75 and over, contrasted with 37 percent of persons 65 and over in the United States who were limited in working or keeping house.[57]

The population of the elderly in Hawai'i is an increasingly expanding and important component of the total population. While this group represented about 8 percent of the 1980 state residents, it is projected that, when the military population is excluded, they will include about 14 percent of the civilian resident population by the year 2000.

Most of the growth of the elderly population is related to aging and general improvement in levels of mortality; migration accounted for only about 12 percent of the increase among the elderly in 1980. While the Islands attract many older visitors for extended vacations, especially during the winter season, Hawai'i has not become a retirement mecca like Florida or Arizona, largely because of the relatively high cost of living and the distance across the sea from immediate family and relatives.

Some unique qualities characterized older persons in the Islands in 1980: life expectancy exceeded that of other regions of the United States and nations of the world, with an increasing number of centenarians; males and females showed a sex ratio that was fairly evenly balanced (although there were wide variations by ethnic group); and about 80 percent of the men and almost 50 percent of the women aged

The life expectancy of residents of Hawai'i increased more than thirty years in the half century between 1930 and 1980. *(R. Kuba photo)*

65 or over were married. While income levels of the elderly were relatively low and Hawai'i's cost of living was high, a large percentage of elderly were financially aided by living with family or friends.

In the final quarter of the twentieth century, Hawai'i's elderly population experienced demographic, social, and environmental advantages that indicated continued rapid growth. The state shared the challenge facing many developed nations of the world to meet the needs of this senior segment of the population, which is becoming an increasingly important economic, political, and social force.

Migration

All of the inhabitants of Hawai'i or their forefathers established their residence in the Islands by migration. Polynesian ancestors of Hawaiians arrived from the South Pacific more than a thousand years ago (see Chapter 1). In the past two hundred years, Hawai'i has been peopled by representatives of Asia, America, Europe, and the South Pacific.

The majority of persons of Chinese, Japanese, and Korean heritage arrived from Asia between 1852 and 1924 (see Chapters 2 and 3 for immigration information by racial group; Table 4–14; Table 4–15). Most persons of White and Black descent came in the nineteenth and early twentieth century as missionaries, seamen, laborers, and businessmen from America, the British Isles, the Madeira and Azores Islands of Portugal, and Puerto Rico. Since the establishment of military bases in Hawai'i in the early 1900s and with statehood in 1959, Whites and Blacks from the United States increased in number. American Samoans have migrated to Hawai'i as nationals since 1952. With liberalization of immigration laws in 1965, Filipinos and Koreans have been the largest groups of immigrants to move to the Islands, and some Vietnamese, Laotian, and Cambodian refugees have settled in Hawai'i since the end of the Vietnam war in April 1975.

Migration, the third major demographic factor of growth, is more difficult to record than fertility and mortality. Hawaiian migration statistics have been kept since 1823, although a regular series on migration was established by the Hawaiian government in 1850.[58] Few statistics were compiled on departures; hence net migration (the balance of migration into and out of the state) can only be estimated from successive census counts. However, this information does not tell whether the migrants came from abroad or the mainland, nor does it tell how many left or arrived. To understand the impact of migration, it is important to determine age and sex, ethnicity, occupation, education, health, and other characteristics of migrants that significantly influence the demographic situation in Hawai'i.

The principal sources of migration data in the 1980s are the U.S. decennial population censuses; records of births, deaths, and military inductions and separations; the ongoing series on visitors present and residents absent from a sample survey maintained by the Hawaii Visitors Bureau (HVB); and the U.S. Immigration and Naturalization Service (INS) tabulations on immigration.[59,60] These data are summarized in annual reports published by the Hawaii State Department of Business and Economic Development [DBED] (formerly the Hawaii State Department of Planning and Economic Development [DPED]): *Hawaii's In-Migrants,* which presents gross migration estimates; *The Population of Hawaii,* with estimates of net migration; and the *State Data Book.*[61]

The problem of inaccurate migration counts was addressed in 1977 by State Statistician Robert C. Schmitt:

Most statistics on migration are in fact subject to incomplete coverage, misreporting, and other deficiencies. Census tabulations on state or country of birth and residence five years earlier have been marred by high non-response rates. Trend data were affected by the treatment of Filipinos as native born before 1946 and foreign born thereafter. The alien address reports program of the INS apparently misses not only many aliens illegally in Hawaii but also some of those legally present. Annual immigration totals published by the INS similarly fail to catch illegal movements, the extent of which is unknown. The HVB survey omits intended residents arriving from Asia and the South Pacific or aboard military ships and aircraft, and is moreover subject to considerable nonresponse. Combining data from the HVB and INS migration surveys overcomes some of these problems, but at the cost of occasional double-counting, and with the continuous omission of persons from American Samoa and other Pacific areas outside the statistical reporting system. The annual estimates of net migration are at best rough approximations, and data on out-migration are extremely limited. All of these series are, moreover, subject to serious distortion because of the inclusion of large numbers of military personnel and dependents, whose presence often swamps the totals for civilian migrants.[62]

Migration laws have been changed by the U.S. federal government several times during this century. Implicit in the U.S. Constitution is a fundamental freedom for citizens to migrate and establish residence in any state in the country.[63] This constitutional right has constrained efforts of advocates of population control to limit interstate migration to Hawai'i.

Immigration from abroad is controlled by congressional acts. The Immigration Act of 1924 favored immigration from Europe by basing the entry quotas on the nationality and number of foreign-born residents already living in the United States in 1890. It also prohibited immigration by aliens ineligible for citizenship, including all Asians except persons from the Philippines.

The Immigration and Nationality Act of 1952 introduced selective immigration for skilled aliens and for relatives of residents of the United States; it also made all races eligible for immigration and naturalization, but quotas for Asians were small. The Immigration and Nationality Act of 1965 abolished the quota system based on national origin and set up an annual limit of 170,000 immigrants from the Eastern Hemisphere. It established a new preference system and redefined immediate relatives of citizens as nonquota immigrants. This policy had the effect of changing the racial profile of immigration.[64] In 1975 the United States permitted Indochinese refugees to enter the country, and some of these people have chosen Hawai'i as their new home.

Data for recent immigration to Hawai'i show the profound impact of 1965 changes in immigration laws. While the number of immigrants from abroad increased slowly at 1,700 persons per year in 1960–1964, they averaged between 8,000 and 9,000 by 1980–1985, arriving at the high annual rate of about 8 aliens per 1,000 resident population (compared to a lower U.S. rate in 1985 of 2.2 foreign

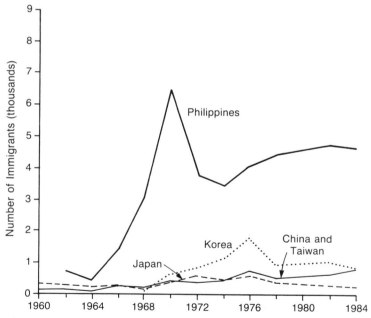

Figure 4–10. Migration to Hawai'i from Selected Asian Countries, 1960–1984
Source: See Table 4–15.

immigrants per 1,000 U.S. residents) (Figure 4–10; Table 4–15). Filipinos represented over 50 percent of all recent immigrants to the state, and Koreans ranked second with 20 percent of the alien arrivals. The relatively large size of Filipino families and, to a lesser extent, Korean families implies a multiplier effect from close relatives who may become eligible for migration to the U.S.[65]

Other large groups of foreign residents included persons from Vietnam, Thailand, and Hong Kong. This did not include the large movement of American Samoans who migrated as nationals to and from the Islands without official tabulation.[66] Over 14 percent of Hawai'i's population in 1980 was foreign-born, compared to just over 6 percent of the total U.S. population.

To provide insight into the dynamics of the complex in-migration patterns in Hawai'i and to offer factual basis for population policy, a study of lifetime and recent migration to and from Hawai'i in 1980 was prepared by the DPED.[67] Using material tabulated from the 1980 U.S. census, migration was estimated from statistics on the 1975 place of residence of persons living in Hawai'i in 1980, and from figures on the 1980 residence of persons who lived in Hawai'i in 1975.

This report showed that out of 964,691 Hawai'i residents in 1980, only 557,990 (57.8 percent) were island-born, while the others included 248,752 persons from the U.S. mainland, 20,933 persons born in U.S. territories or possessions, and 137,016 foreign-born residents. At the same time 259,363 Hawai'i-born persons were living on the U.S. mainland, but a significant proportion of this group was born to Hawai'i military families (about 118,000 births occurred to military couples between 1950 and 1980) who moved back to the U.S. mainland. Of the mainlanders living in Hawai'i, military personnel and college students represented 41 percent, a figure disproportionate to the state population count of only 17 percent for this group.

The DPED study concludes: "After deducting persons who moved for military or educational reasons and all those born out of State, not much of the large body of 1975–1980 in- and out-migrants remains."[68] Out-migrants consisted largely of persons born elsewhere who had moved to the Islands before 1975; if the analysis was limited to those born in Hawai'i, the outflow was rather small and offset by return migrants.

While state planners have been concerned at a possible "brain drain" of Hawai'i residents, the evidence in 1975–1980 showed a loss of 24,920 college graduates to other states and, at the same time, a gain of 24,240 college graduates from the mainland (plus 5,840 from abroad). Managerial and professional specialty occupations revealed a similar transposition of workers, indicating that highly educated persons and those in high-status jobs locally and nationally tend to be more mobile in job location. The statistics on place of birth suggested a more pronounced net in-migration of college graduates and professionals. Thus, a "brain gain" has offset any "brain drain."[69]

Only 3.2 percent of the net in-flow of persons to Hawai'i in 1975–1980 were aged 65 and over. In-migration has had little impact on the rapid growth of the elderly population; most of the increase was related to aging of Hawai'i residents. The median age of migrants to Hawai'i in 1985 was 24.1; the sex ratio favored women, with 75 males to every 100 females moving to the Islands.[70]

The estimated net migration to Hawai'i in the decade between 1970 and 1980, excluding military dependents, yielded a civilian population growth by migration of 107,834 persons, or 56.6 percent of the total population increase of 190,702 persons in that period (Table 4–16). In the 1980–1985 years, civilian net migration accounted for 39,049 of the 89,609 new residents, or 43.6 percent of the growth.

Migration, stimulated by government-endorsed economic growth policies through expansion of the visitor industry, has been the major cause of population increase in Hawai'i since 1970. A 1978 DPED study that integrated economic and population forecasting models showed the relationships and tradeoffs between economic growth and population levels.[71,72] The key linkage between the projection of economic activity and population was the matching of the labor force required for new jobs with the available labor force. It demonstrated that increased net civilian immigration was necessary to meet the labor force needs of the visitor industry. Migration to Hawai'i was associated with rapid economic growth and expansion of employment opportunity, with low unemployment rates among the non-migrant resident population.[73]

In 1984 the DPED endorsed their revised M-F population projection series, which encouraged growth of tourism to 106,500 hotel rooms and provided for a population increase to 1,310,000 residents by the year 2005.[74] (See Chapter 5, Population Projections, for higher 1988 M-K projections; and Table 5–1.) In contrast, the DPED projection series M-B, which used the same fertility-mortality figures as the M-F series but held tourism growth to 58,000 hotel rooms in 2005, provided a slow population growth rate of 0.6 percent. This figure matched the 0.6 percent rate proposed as a population objective by the Hawaii State Commission on Population and the Hawaiian

Future, when it suggested that Hawai'i should: "Achieve a statewide population growth rate not to exceed the national growth rate [0.6–0.8] in 10 years, while attaining a zero net migration rate in Hawaii within 15 years and maintaining a total fertility rate not to exceed replacement level."[75]

A review of state planning indicated emphasis on economic growth over population limitation. Despite stated objectives in the Hawaii State Plan toward slowing population growth, economic growth priorities resulted in population growth by migration. In the final quarter of the twentieth century, Hawai'i's civilian population had reached low fertility and mortality levels, but in-migration from the U.S. mainland and from abroad continued to be uncontrolled. If a lower rate of population growth was to be realized, the slowing of economic growth stimulated by the visitor industry—which produced more jobs than residents could fill and thereby promoted migration to the Islands to meet labor demands—looms as the primary focus for planners to attempt to reduce Hawai'i's rapid rate of population increase.

CHAPTER 5

Hawai'i in Transition

Hawai'i's resident population increased at the rate of 2.3 percent annually between 1900 and 1985, implying a doubling of the number of persons living in the Islands in about thirty years. From 154,000 persons in 1900, the population of Hawai'i surpassed 1,082,500 residents by 1987, and the de facto population, which included visitors present, had reached 1,198,800 persons. A twentieth-century wave of humankind has permanently altered the environment and lifestyle of the Islands. The consequences of continued growth are a subject of serious concern.

The implications of growth rates are often not fully understood. The annual rate of population growth is the result of both natural increase (births minus deaths) and net migration. This rate determines the amount of time required for a population to double in size. (The same principle governs the effect of compounded interest.)[1] A population that doubles requires twice the quantity of food, water, education, housing, medical care, transportation, energy, police and fire protection, recreation facilities, public utilities, and other services just to maintain its standard of living, allowing for no improvement. In the absence of measures to reduce present rates of growth in Hawai'i, the number of people is expected to grow rapidly and thereby geometrically increase the problems associated with population needs.

Rates of Growth and Doubling Times

Rate of Growth per Year (percent)	Years It Takes for a Population to Double
0.5	140
1.0	70
1.5	47
2.0	35
2.5	29
3.0	24
3.5	20
4.0	17

Source: Thompson and Lewis 1965, p. 11.

Population Projections

Predictions based on population projections are risky because it is impossible to anticipate precisely the economic, social, medical, and technological changes that may alter the basic growth components of fertility, mortality, and migration. The value of projections is not so much to predict the future as to show the changes that can occur if certain birth, death, and migration rates continue for a period of time.

Population projections for Hawai'i have been prepared during recent decades by federal, state, and county governments, planning consultants, engineers, bank economists, professional organizations, and many other individuals and groups.[2] The results revealed a wide range of future population trends, most of which included rapid growth—although the degree of growth was usually underestimated.

Projections concerning the civilian population (in this volume, civilian population refers to the resident population excluding the members of the armed forces stationed in Hawai'i and their dependents [see Glossary]) were prepared in 1971 by the Population Institute of the East-West Center (EWPI). These projections were based on six possible growth patterns over one hundred years, ranging from immediate achievement of zero growth in Projection VI to a continuance of recent high rates of net migration in Projection I (Figure 5-1).[3] Some major conclusions have been drawn from this study:

1. Expected net migration as a growth factor has a much greater impact on increasing population than the anticipated levels of fertility and mortality. (In 1980, Hawai'i's total fertility rate of 1.9 was below the replacement fertility level of 2.1.)
2. Even if 1970 birth rates were reduced so that each couple had only two children (which actually seems to have happened), and even if net migration were zero (which has not happened), the

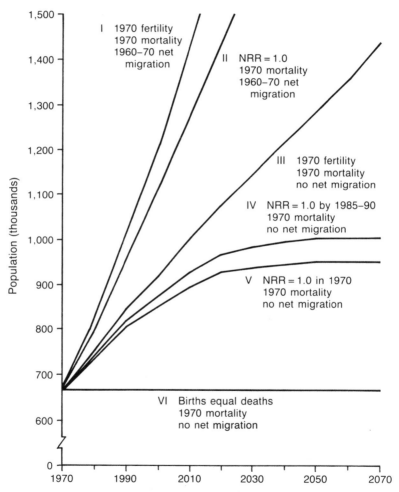

Figure 5-1. Projections of the Civilian Population, Hawai'i, 1970–2070
Source: Gardner and Nordyke 1974, Table 45.

population nevertheless would continue to grow slowly until the middle of the next century owing to the youthful age of Hawai'i's population.

These projections illustrate problems using assumptions for components of growth. In the 1970–1980 decade, fertility rates dropped slightly. Migration rates, on the other hand, surpassed expectations, with a net migration to Hawai'i of 108,000 new civilian residents, compared to 46,000 net in-migrants in the 1960–1970 decade (Table 4–16). This rapid growth by net migration exceeded the highest EWPI assumptions, resulting in actual resident growth at a rate above the steepest projection.

The State Department of Planning and Economic Development (DPED) in 1978 prepared projections of resident and de facto populations that integrated economic and population forecasting models. State economic projections were developed to produce long-range figures of jobs by industry, output, labor force, employment and unemployment, income for twenty industries, gross state product, private capital investment, personal consumption expenditures, per capita personal income, personal income taxes, disposable income, exports, imports, and government spending. This econometric model was linked to a demographic model that used 121 demographic variables, of which the key forces were age and sex composition, net migration, births, and deaths.[4] Projections were generated on an annual basis for a twenty-five year period.

Net migration was based on the interaction of supply and demand for labor. The 1978 DPED "Long Range Population and Economic Simulations and Projections for the State of Hawaii" demonstrated the relationship of population growth to economic conditions.[5] Employment opportunities were assumed to influence in- and out-migration, altering trends in population growth. Migration was used to adjust the available labor force and the population, matching the required labor force to economic forecasts for newly created jobs.

The 1978 DPED economic–population forecasting model presented relationships and tradeoffs between economic growth and population levels. The report showed the effects of different levels of tourism growth rates, and it indicated that the growth of number of jobs required for expansion of the visitor industry was closely correlated to population growth. It declared "If tourism expansion can be controlled, the state has a powerful planning instrument."[6]

In 1984 the State DPED prepared the *Hawaii Population and Eco-*

nomic Projection and Simulation Model, Updated State and County Forecasts, and it endorsed the "M-F" projection to replace the 1978 "II-F" projection for state planning. The 1984 model used 1980 census economic and demographic statistics and extended the projections to 2005. The 1984 projection variables assumed a total fertility rate of 1.91, age-sex-survival rates based on the most recent Hawai'i mortality data, and migration rates determined by projected employment levels and labor force participation rates. The DPED explained the projected in-migration: "The demand for labor in Hawaii is determined by the number of jobs projected by the economic submodel and an assumed long-term unemployment rate. Net migration then becomes the number of new residents required to provide the labor force that when added to the surviving labor force equals the demand for labor."[7]

The demographic input to the model was limited to civilian residents; the 1980 U.S. census count of Hawai'i's 125,000 armed forces members and dependents was added as a final step to the resident population total. De facto population was obtained by adding the projection of the average visitor count (less the projected number of residents absent) to the total resident population.

According to the state DPED's 1984 M-F projection, the demographic profile for Hawai'i in 2005 showed a resident population of 1,310,000 persons and a de facto population of over 1.5 million people. The median age would increase from 28.4 years in 1980 to 34.7 years. The percentage of the population under age 15 would decrease from 23.4 in 1980 to 20.3 percent in 2005, and the number of persons age 65 and over was projected to grow from 7.9 percent to 13.5 percent of Hawai'i's total population in that twenty-five year period. Whereas Honolulu County contained 78 percent of the de facto population in 1980, that county would have only 70.1 percent by 2005, with neighbor island counties of Maui growing to 12.6 percent, Hawaii to 11.2 percent, and Kauai to 6.1 percent.

The use of the 1984 model clearly indicates the apparent sensitivity of population and economic levels to assumptions regarding trends in the growth and distribution of the visitor industry (Table 5-1; Figure 5-2).[8] If the annual visitor count grew slowly for twenty-five years from 3.9 million in 1980 to a level of 4.4 million annual tourists in 2005 (Projection Series M-B), the resident population would be 1,120,000 persons, almost 200,000 fewer than if the state followed the more rapid Series M-F "most likely" visitor growth pattern that increased residents to 1,310,000 and the annual number of visitors to

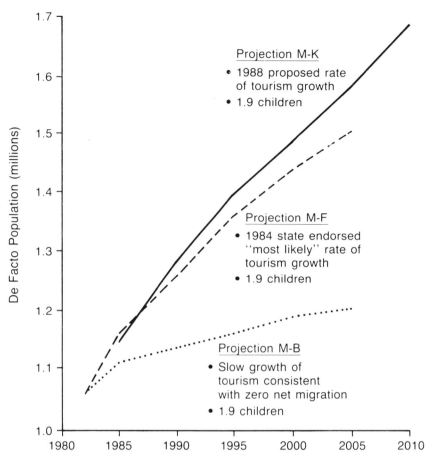

Figure 5-2. Population Projections: The Impact of Visitor Industry Growth on Population Increase, Hawai'i, 1980–2010
Source: See Table 5-1.

8,181,400. The Series M-B "slow tourist growth" projection gave an annual daily visitor count almost 100,000 fewer than the Series M-F figures by the year 2005.

The state requested in 1984 that all federal, state, county, and private agencies adopt the M-F population projection series for planning purposes, stating: "These projections represent expected trends and *not* economic or population goals. They are not to be confused with the State Administrations's broad objective of moderating or stabilizing growth rates through orderly management."[9] Yet the State

Department of Planning and Economic Development urged action toward economic and population growth goals inherent in the higher M-F projection series: "Adoption of these [M-F] projections by interested agencies and individuals will do much to assure consistency and uniformity in planning efforts." This effort suggested a self-fulfilling prophecy to the assumptions in the projections of rapid population and economic growth.

New population and economic projections in preparation in 1988 by the reorganized Hawaii State Department of Business and Economic Development (DBED; formerly DPED) urged acceptance of even higher levels of growth.[10] The M-K projection series ["M" stands for a medium fertility level used in previous projections; "K" is a label for a tourism growth assumption that is higher than that used in earlier projections] raises the projected yearly visitor total to 10.2 million annual tourists by the year 2005 (in contrast to 8.2 million according to the M-F projections) and to 11.6 million visitors in Hawai'i by 2010 (Table 5–1).

Hawai'i's resident population in mid-1986 of 1.06 million was projected in the M-K series to reach 1.44 million residents by the year 2010, with a de facto population of 1.69 million persons. In this scenario, the number of daily visitors present increased from 132,000 tourists in 1986 to 277,100 by the year 2010. The M-K population series, using higher rates of tourism growth, added 524,000 persons to the Islands in 1980–2005. In contrast, the M-B projection series, which maintained a steady visitor level of about 4 million annual tourists, provided a balanced level of migration and a population increase of only 152,800 persons in twenty-five years.

Population projections of the mid-1980s clearly demonstrated the direct relationship of rapid expansion of population in Hawai'i to a state policy endorsing economic growth based upon development of new jobs in the visitor industry. By the year 2000, tourism was expected to represent about 50 percent of Hawai'i's total economy.[11] The state M-K projection showed an average annual population growth rate of 1.32 percent in the 1980–2010 period. This figure is about twice as high as the 0.6–0.8 average annual population growth rate of the United States in the 1980s.

In 1977 the Hawaii State Commission on Population and the Hawaiian Future recommended that Hawai'i should "achieve a statewide population growth rate not to exceed the national growth rate in 10 years."[12] However, there was no legislative implementation of this population objective. State requests for adoption of the 1984 M-F population projection series and the higher 1988 M-K series for state planning implicitly encouraged population growth and counter-manded the intentions of the Hawaii State Plan that set priority directions "to stimulate the economy to provide needed jobs for Hawai'i's people without stimulating unnecessary in-migration."[13]

Visitor Industry Influence on Population Growth

Since August 21, 1959, when Hawai'i was officially admitted into the Union as the fiftieth state of the United States, the visitor industry has been the primary stimulant to population and economic growth in the Islands.[14] According to State DPED assumptions, population growth has been the result of (1) the in-migration of new residents to fill tour-

Increasing numbers of Japanese tourists arrived in Hawai'i in the 1980s to enjoy a holiday in the Islands. *(Commission on Population and the Hawaiian Future, State of Hawaii)*

The Royal Hawaiian Hotel, under construction in Waikīkī in 1927, and the Moana Hotel provided the major facilities for the 17,500 annual tourists visiting Hawai'i at that time.

By the late 1980s, over 65,000 hotel rooms accommodated about six million annual visitors to Hawai'i. *(Department of Planning and Economic Development, State of Hawaii)*

Honolulu Airport, 1955. *(George Bacon photo, Hawaii State Archives)*

Jumbo jets of multinational carriers provide tranportation for millions of travelers to and from Hawai'i in the 1980s. *(Department of Transportation, State of Hawaii)*

ist-related jobs that exceeded the number of workers available in Hawai'i's resident population, and (2) the expansion of the numbers of daily visitors as a part of the de facto population present in the Islands.

The establishment of statehood, the development of large transpacific airplanes, and the infusion of foreign investment capital contributed to a rapid expansion of the visitor industry in Hawai'i. In 1886, annual visitor arrivals numbered only 2,040 travelers; by 1959,

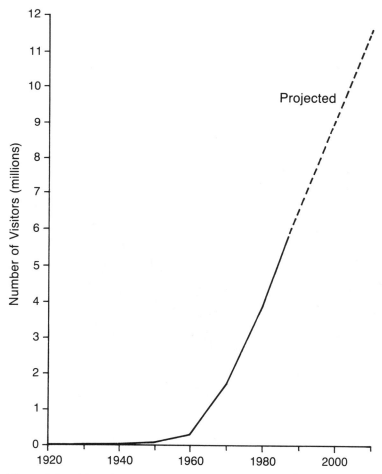

Figure 5-3. Visitors in 1920–1987, with Projections to 2010, Hawai'i
Sources: See Tables 5-1 and 5-2.

243,216 tourists came to the Islands; and in 1987, the Hawaii Visitors Bureau counted 5,799,830 visitors staying overnight or longer (Table 5–2; Figure 5–3).[15] Hotel rooms to accommodate visitors expanded in number from 1,572 in 1946 to 69,012 units in 1987. Annual visitor expenditures increased from $109 million in 1959 to $6.6 billion in 1987. As a percentage of the Gross State Product, visitor expenditures increased from 7 percent in 1959 to 34 percent in 1987.

The economy of the state of Hawai'i has shifted from the territorial agricultural base in sugar and pineapple to a service-based industry of tourism. The Islands have become increasingly dependent on the fragile visitor business, which is vulnerable to external national and international economic and political conditions, as demonstrated in the oil shortage of the early 1970s and in the economic recession in 1980–1982. The research department of the First Hawaiian Bank sounded an alarm in 1984:

> The danger of vulnerability to external economic conditions lies in the exposure of the visitor market, and those industries dependent upon it, to disruptive economic instability. In addition to jobs directly related to tourism such as hotel and travel services, jobs in the construction industry, and tourist-related services such as apparel, transportation services, food services, and trade are also affected when the tourist market contracts. These effects are particularly severe on the Neighbor Islands which have a less diversified employment base."[16]

Population Growth Induced by Visitor Industry Jobs

The expansion of visitor industry jobs has been a major factor in population growth in Hawai'i. The visitor industry created more jobs than Hawai'i's citizens and foreign immigrants needed or could fill. The availability of jobs stimulated in-migration, resulting in population growth of new residents to meet labor force demands (Figure 5–2).[17,18]

Jobs related to tourism (direct, indirect, and induced) grew from 71,000 in 1970 to 175,000 in 1985, representing 36 percent of employment in the mid-1980s in the Islands.[19,20] State economic–population projections, assuming constant labor force participation rates, in 1977 indicated that if tourism grew at a rate of 10 percent in 1980–1985, 114,000 in-migrants would be needed to fill the labor force; if the tourism growth rate was 5 percent in that period, 28,900 new workers would need to come to Hawai'i to meet labor force demands.

In the 1981–1986 period, the visitor industry increased at an annual growth rate of 8.5 percent, necessitating in-migration of over 50,000 workers to fill visitor industry jobs.

In 1984, the M–F economic–population projection series endorsed by the state assumed an annual net migration of about 8,500 persons in 1985–1990 to fill proposed tourist-related jobs, with declining numbers to coincide with reduced rates of visitor industry growth by the year 2005 (Table 5–1). Even this number of new residents was found to be inadequate to provide enough labor to fill jobs in the rapidly expanding tourist industry. The 1988 M–K projections suggested a higher level of 10,000 annual in-migrants to meet expected labor needs.

In September 1988, Hawai'i's jobless rate dipped to a low level at 2.9 percent, compared to the seasonally adjusted rate of 5.2 percent for the nation at that time.[21] Hawai'i, showing an unemployment level well below the 4 to 6 percent jobless rate recognized by economists as a full employment standard, reported among the lowest unemployment levels in the United States.

The number of jobs in Hawai'i has grown more rapidly than the available civilian labor force. Reduced birth rates since the 1960s have lowered civilian labor force growth to 2 percent in the 1980s with a decline to 1 percent in the 1990s and 0.5 percent labor force growth by the year 2000.[22] The 1978 State Tourism Plan recognized that almost three of every five new jobs created between the years 1975–2000 would require migrants to Hawai'i to fill the positions and would contribute to a rapid increase of population in the Islands. Hawai'i does not have enough workers to fill projected tourist industry job expansion; hence in-migration becomes a tool of planning in order to achieve proposed levels of economic growth.

Population Growth Induced by the Presence of Tourists

The second major factor of population growth attributed to the visitor industry is the actual number of tourists present each day in the Islands. Information is collected by the Hawaii Visitors Bureau from figures on the numbers of visitors present and residents absent, which are obtained in a continuing survey of westbound travelers. A questionnaire attached to a state agricultural form provides a demographic profile of age, sex, place of residence, intended length of stay, and other information on arrivals. Less extensive information is available on eastbound, northbound, and southbound arriving passengers.

According to statistics from the Hawaii Visitors Bureau, the average daily visitor census increased from 975 tourists in 1946 to 36,943 in 1970 and to 134,270 visitors in 1987 (Table 5-2).[23] Almost a quarter of Hawai'i's 5.8 million annual visitors in the mid-1980s arrived from Asian or South Pacific countries; in the 1976–1986 decade the number of Japanese visitors doubled, reaching 1,161,000 persons in 1987.[24] Over 41 percent of the westbound tourists came from Pacific and mountain states of the United States, with almost 10 percent from Canada and 1 percent from Europe.

In 1985, summary characteristics of westbound visitors showed that the median age was almost forty years, the number of female tourists exceeded male tourists by 20 percent, over 80 percent of visitors came to the Islands for pleasure with an average stay of about ten days, and about 70 percent of the travelers included a visit to the neighbor islands.[25,26] The average expenditure per visitor day in 1987 was $367 by Japanese and $102 by non-Japanese tourists.[27]

The visitor population is counted in the de facto population, which includes all people physically present in Hawai'i. While the resident population of Hawai'i increased almost 37 percent from 770,000 residents in 1970 to 1,054,000 in 1985, the de facto population rose by 45 percent from 796,000 to 1,152,000 persons in the Islands in the same time interval (Table 5-3). The 216 percent increase in average number of visitors from 37,000 in 1970 to 117,000 by 1985 contributed to the increase in the de facto estimate over the number of residents from 3.5 percent in 1970 to 9.2 percent in 1985.[28] State M-K projections show almost 277,100 daily visitors (11,600,000 annual tourists) present in a de facto population of 1,690,000 persons in Hawai'i by the year 2010.[29]

Tourist-related population growth has been dramatically apparent on the neighbor islands, where an increasing number of tourists are staying and where new residents have moved to accept visitor industry jobs developed since 1970. The Maui County resident population increased 54 percent with an average annual growth rate of 4.3 percent in 1970–1980; the de facto population grew 77 percent with a growth rate of 5.7 percent in that time.

This high rate of growth has also been observed in the counties of Hawaii and Kauai where the increase in jobs and number of tourists has rapidly expanded the population (Tables 2-1 and 5-3, and text table on page 148). An increase in the percentage of Whites residing

Population, Labor Force, and Tourism Projections, Series M-K, Counties of Hawai'i, 1985–2010 (thousands)

	Hawaii		Honolulu		Kauai		Maui		State	
	1985	2010	1985	2010	1985	2010	1985	2010	1985	2010
Resident Population	109.5	189.3	811.1	1,013.0	45.4	86.9	85.5	145.9	1,051.5	1,435.1
De facto Population	116.1	222.8	861.6	1,119.2	56.3	124.5	115.7	220.7	1,149.7	1,687.2
Total Jobs	43.7	83.7	386.0	522.5	20.4	44.1	43.1	78.5	493.0	729.0
Average Daily Visitor Census	8.0	41.6	65.3	119.2	11.5	38.8	31.9	77.6	116.7	277.1

Source: Hawaii (State) DBED 1988, Tables 11, 14.

Note: These figures are presented in a preliminary report of the M-K population projection series; the final report may include some adjustments.

on the neighbor islands between 1970 and 1980 may be related to the growth of visitor industry employment (Table 3–4).

The impact of the presence of tourists is increasingly recognized in statistics on transportation, housing, food supplies, water, sanitation, crime, police and fire protection, recreation, and many other public facilities. De facto population totals have more meaning than resident totals for use in analysis of social and economic trends in Hawai'i.

In summary, the visitor industry has become the major driving force of Hawai'i's population and economic growth. Development of numbers of jobs that exceed resident supply has stimulated in-migration of new residents, and rapidly growing numbers of tourists have contributed to the ballooning de facto population that inhabits the Islands in the last half of the twentieth century.

Evidence of Change

In the late nineteenth century Mark Twain referred to the Hawaiian Islands as "the loveliest fleet of islands that lies anchored in any ocean."[30] While his description may still be appropriate today, the effect of increasing numbers of people on natural resources and quality of life is a subject of increasing concern to residents of Hawai'i who have observed dramatic changes in population density, transpor-

Honolulu harbor in the 1880s. *(Hawaii State Archives)*

Honolulu harbor, 1988. (*T. Umeda photo, courtesy of* The Honolulu Advertiser)

tation, housing, land investment, role of the military, water supply, sources of energy, climate, and other indicators related to population growth.

Honolulu's population density has increased from an average of fewer than 100 persons per square mile in 1900 to an average of 1,451 de facto population per square mile in 1985, with almost 4,400 persons per square mile in urbanized Honolulu city (Table 4–1). In 1980 the gross density of Waikīkī, including over 17,000 residents, 43,000 nonresident visitors, and 32,000 workers employed in the area was about 93,000 persons per square mile—one of the most densely populated regions in the world (Table 5–4).[31]

From a quiet, seaweed-strewn strip of sand where canoeing, swimming, and surfing were favorite local sports, Waikīkī Beach has become a crowded, hotel-lined playground for visitors from around the world. The Hawaiian Islands have only 24.4 miles of sandy shoreline defined as "safe, clean, accessible, and generally suitable for swimming"; yet with population increase, the proportion of beach available to residents and visitors has declined. If all the residents of the Islands (excluding tourists) decided to go to a beach at the same

In 1900 the population density was less than 100 persons per square mile in Honolulu. *(Brother Bertram collection, Hawaii State Archives)*

The density of population in central Honolulu in 1988 is comparable to that of some of the most densely populated areas in the world. *(E. Nordyke photo)*

Waikīkī beach in 1890. *(Brother Bertram collection, Hawaii State Archives)*

Waikīkī beach in the 1980s. (*Carl Viti photo*, The Honolulu Advertiser)

A mule-drawn wagon of the Hawaiian Tramways Company carries passengers through Waikīkī in the 1890s. *(Brother Bertram collection, Hawaii State Archives)*

Buses and automobiles glide bumper to bumper along Kalākaua Avenue in Waikīkī in the 1980s. (*Warren R. Roll photo,* Honolulu Star-Bulletin)

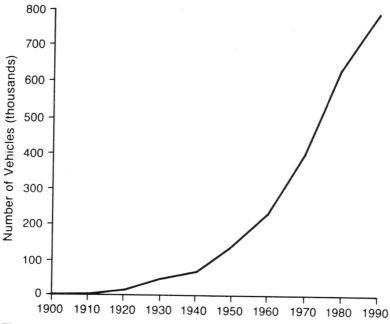

Figure 5-4. Motor Vehicle Registration, Hawai'i, 1900-1986
Sources: Hawaii (State) DPED, 1987 *Data Book* Table 527; Schmitt 1977, Table 17.2.

time, there would be less than two inches of sandy shoreline for each person.[32]

The number of registered cars increased from 4 horseless carriages in 1900 to over 790,000 registered vehicles in 1986 (Figure 5-4).[33] Prime land has been converted to highways to accommodate the increasing number of vehicles, and roads are clogged in peak traffic hours. The state is seeking an integrated multi-modal transportation system including a fixed guideway rapid-transit development through densely populated areas to provide efficient movement of people.[34] In 1987, an editorial in *The Honolulu Advertiser* urged action to alleviate traffic congestion:

> We must have more buses of various sizes. We need widened streets and traffic smoothed by computerized signals and contraflow lanes. We must alter lifestyles with car-pooling, staggered work/school hours and home offices. And we need rail transit through the most congested part of town. We must do everything on the menu, and soon, if our roads are not to become parking lots."[35]

Homeward-bound Pali traffic in 1890. *(Private collection)*

Cars creep along the H-1 freeway through downtown Honolulu during hours of heavy traffic in 1987. (*Courtesy of* Honolulu Star-Bulletin)

A Hawaiian family sits beside a grass shack at Puna, Hawai'i, in the 1890s. *(Brother Bertram collection, Hawaii State Archives)*

Homes blanket the land from the sea to the hillsides at Enchanted Lake, windward O'ahu, in the 1980s. *(Commission on Population and the Hawaiian Future, State of Hawaii)*

By the mid-1980s in Honolulu, over 30 percent of the population resided in high-rise condominiums. *(Commission on Population and the Hawaiian Future, State of Hawaii)*

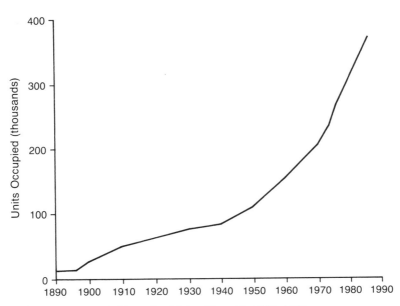

Figure 5-5. Occupied Housing Units, Hawai'i, 1890–1986
Sources: Hawaii (State) DPED, 1974 *Data Book,* Table 260; 1975 *Data Book,* Table 274; 1986 *Data Book,* Table 602.

The number and style of living accommodations in Hawai'i have altered markedly in the past two hundred years. Island residents have shifted from simple grass shacks to modern high-rise structures. In 1970 there were 217,000 dwelling places; by 1980, this number had increased 54 percent to 334,000 housing units with an average of 3.15 persons per occupied unit.[36] In 1986 the number of dwellings had grown to 371,000 including over 100,000 condominium units (Figure 5–5).[37]

Despite continued construction, housing has been in short supply. Assessed real property valuation tripled between 1976 and 1986. The land system in Hawai'i, designed in the mid-nineteenth century to advance interests of large owners, has become the focus of politicians and legislators seeking changes in ownership, taxation, and land use.[38] According to George Cooper and Gavan Daws, authors of *Land and Power in Hawaii*: "In Hawaii, land has always been a political battleground and prize. Those who have held land have generally occupied the high ground in politics." Post World War II Democrats, including many sons and daughters of early Asian and European immigrants, focused on land development as a means of social and economic reform. They followed a "near-absolute dominance of a development ethic and the very small and shifting political base of anti-development sentiment."[39] The intimate web of connections among politicians, landholders, and developers led to extensive real estate investments that changed land values.

Foreign investment in Hawai'i's land in the 1980s has continued to escalate property values. By 1987, foreign interest controlled nearly two-thirds of the major hotel properties, half of the hotel units in Waikīkī and 30 percent of the hotel units in the state, as well as golf course and selected residential properties.[40] The major purchasers were from Japan (71 percent), Hong Kong (9 percent), the United Kingdom (7 percent), and Canada (6 percent). While foreign investment has been sought to finance development of jobs and economic growth, the loss by repatriation of a large annual income to out-of-state investors (over $1.5 billion in 1986) has occurred at the expense of the population of Hawai'i who seek reinvestment of profits in the Hawaiian economy to benefit state tax-paying residents.

Military population representation has changed in Hawai'i in the late twentieth century. Although the number of armed service personnel has remained relatively stable since statehood, their percentage of the total population has dropped: in 1959, this group represented 17.3 percent of the resident population, while in 1986 the estimated 58,100

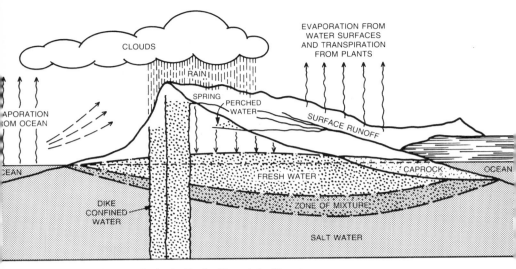

Figure 5-6. The Hydrologic Cycle, Honolulu County

Note: The island of O'ahu (Honolulu County) illustrates a typical island water system in which water from the ocean evaporates and forms clouds that rise over the windward mountains, cool, and condense with rainfall as the result. The naturally purified water filters through dikes and rocks into the freshwater zone beneath the island. With increased population and expanded use of water from this hydrologic cycle, the sustainable yield of groundwater is estimated to be less than groundwater recharge.

Source: University of Hawaii, Department of Geography 1983, p. 49.

armed forces and 66,200 military dependents were 11.7 percent.[41,42] Since the visitor industry replaced defense spending as the major economic source for Hawai'i in the 1980s, the role of the military as the highest contributor to state revenue has declined.[43] The strategic central Pacific position of Hawai'i as a military hub has been lessened by technological developments, including satellite communications, computer networks, and jet aircraft.[44] The armed forces are among the largest landowners in Hawai'i, using about 26 percent of Honolulu County, 4 percent of Hawaii County, and all of Kaho'olawe and Kure Atoll. Population expansion in the Islands has increased competition for land use, resulting in growing political conflicts between the civilian community and military authorities.[45] Native Hawaiians have decried the loss of lands of historical, religious, and archeological value, and voiced open criticism of military control.[46]

Is there enough water to supply an increasing number of residents and visitors? Hawai'i's water cycle involves evaporation from the ocean into clouds that rise over mountains, cool, condense, and drop rainfall on the land (Figure 5–6). Rainwater is dispersed by evapo-transpiration, surface water runoff, and groundwater runoff. Increase in water demand is closely related to population growth. There is concern that water demand in Honolulu County could exceed the total sustainable yield of water sources (Figure 5–7).[47] The State Department of Land and Natural Resources and the State Water Commission recognize that reserves are finite and they have recommended policies to seek alternative water sources, such as use of brackish water, reclaimed or recycled water, and desalinated sea-water.[48] In 1978, the State Constitutional Convention proposed an

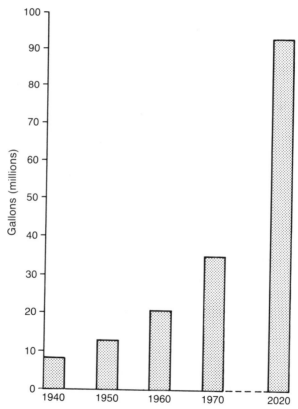

Figure 5–7. Water Usage on O'ahu, 1940–2020
Sources: Hawaii (State) Temporary Commission on Statewide Environmental Planning 1973, p.11; Honolulu (City and County) Board of Water Supply 1971, p. 16.

amendment defining statewide protection and regulation of water resources to be vested in an independent state water agency.[49]

Increasing population has created a serious problem of public sanitation and sewage disposal. In 1987, Honolulu County had 2,400 tons of trash daily; by the year 2000, this is expected to reach 3,300 tons daily. The three landfills on Oʻahu are nearing capacity, and there is a scarcity of suitable land for dump sites. Environmentalists urge use of returnable containers and recycled papers, cans, and other goods to reduce wastage of natural resources. City and county engineers have proposed the conversion of trash into a commodity by H-POWER—Honolulu Program of Waste Energy Recovery—with each ton of garbage equivalent to a barrel of oil, but this energy planning has been confronted by economic, environmental, and political challenge awaiting resolution.

Hawaiʻi is particularly vulnerable to worldwide shortages of energy products. The state depends on imported petroleum for over 90 percent of its fuel.[50] Almost 35 percent of imported oil is used for air transportation while the remaining supply is allocated to ground transportation, production of electricity, and related energy uses. The 1978 Hawaii State Plan with 1986 amendments set primary energy objectives to provide dependable, efficient, and economical statewide energy systems and to increase energy self-sufficiency (Figure 5-8; Figure 5-9).[51] Alternative resources are being developed to lessen the Islands' dependency upon petroleum with its limited global reserves.[52] Wind, ocean thermal energy conversion (OTEC), geothermal, interisland electric transmission cables, biomass, municipal solid waste (H-POWER), coal, hydropower, solar, hydrogen, and fuel cell projects offer research on a number of indigenous renewable natural resources that may meet the technical, environmental, and economic criteria for future energy needs for Hawaiʻi (Figure 5-10).[53]

Despite the quantity of pollutants emitted in the urban metropolis, Honolulu was ranked as one of the cleanest cities in the nation in the late twentieth century, as measured by suspended particulate matter, nitrogen oxides, and carbon monoxide.[54] The prevailing northeast trade winds and frequent rainfall contribute to superior air quality; however, when there are no breezes or if there is a Kona (south) wind, a brown haze may hang over the more densely populated areas of the Islands.

Hawaiʻi enjoys a mild and equable tropical climate. The evenness of temperature is related to its latitude, the thermostatic qualities of the surrounding ocean, its distance from Pacific storm tracks, and the

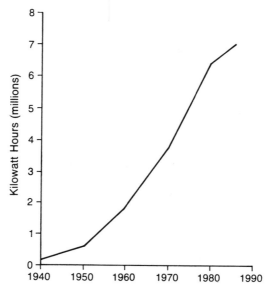

Figure 5–8. Electric Energy Sold, Hawai'i, 1900–
1986

Sources: Hawaii (State) DPED, 1975 *Data Book,* Table
211; 1987 *Data Book,* Table 497.

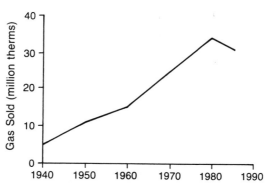

Figure 5–9. Natural Gas Energy Sold, Hawai'i,
1940–1986

Sources: Hawaii (State) DPED, 1975 *Data Book,* Table
213; 1987 *Data Book,* Table 499.

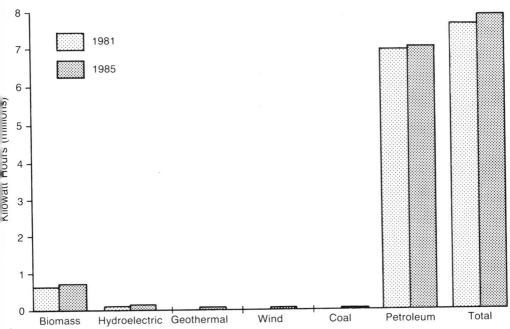

Figure 5-10. Electricity Generation by Source, Hawai'i, 1981-1985
Source: Hawaii (State) DPED, 1986 *Data Book,* Table 469.

variety of volcanic mountain terrain.[55] Higher average temperatures recorded in the 1980s may relate to increased urbanization and population density. World climatic changes, resulting from increased atmospheric carbon dioxide concentrations that reflect escalating world population and the destruction of tropical rain forests, could affect Hawai'i in the next century by contributing to a rise in sea level of nearly three feet by the year 2100.[56] This information is important in future planning for population density on Island shorelines and coastal plains.

Many other indicators of change have been influenced by the increasing numbers of people in Hawai'i, as exemplified by rising social welfare costs (Figure 5-11), elevated noise levels, and a higher incidence of crime; an increase in the latter has been attributed to the expansion of tourism.[57] Other effects have been less tangible, such as levels of health in relation to pollution, the psychological implications of density, and changing habits and lifestyles in adaptation to crowding.

Unusually heavy smog hugged Honolulu on a day in the 1970s when a layer of cold air over the city prevented contaminated air from rising into the upper atmosphere. (*Warren R. Roll photo,* Honolulu Star-Bulletin)

The expansion of population has increased awareness that the natural environment of the state is in danger. The Hawaii State Temporary Commission on Environmental Planning in 1973 identified population as a priority concern and asked the legislature to:

A. Recognize population impact as a major factor in environmental degradation and adopt strategies to alleviate this impact and minimize future degradation.
B. Develop criteria to determine optimum population levels for counties and districts within the state, recognizing that these will change with technology and circumstance, and adopt strategies to limit population to the levels determined.[58]

The adoption of a state environmental policy in 1974 included guidelines for a direct call to action. In 1982 the Office of Environmental Quality Control (OEQC) called attention to Chapter 344–3(2)(A) of the Hawaii Revised Statutes: "It shall be the policy of the State through its programs, authorities, and resources to . . . enhance the quality of life by setting population limits so that the interaction between the natural and man-made environments and the

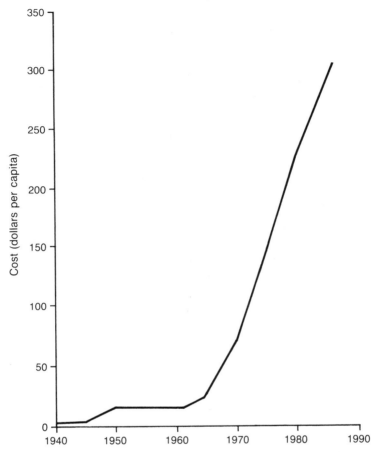

Figure 5-11. Social Welfare Costs per Capita, Hawai'i, 1940–1986
Sources: Hawaii (State) DPED, 1974 *Data Book,* Table 172; 1987 *Data Book,*
Table 3 and Table 348.

population is mutually beneficial"; and it identified population as a
priority concern that still awaited implementation.[59] But by 1986, as
government policies embraced business concerns geared toward economic growth, the revised Hawaii State Plan presented a softer position toward population concerns, as stated in HRS Sec. 226–5(a): "It
shall be the objective in planning for the State's population to guide
population growth to be consistent with the achievement of physical,
economic, and social objectives contained in this chapter."[60]

How many people can Hawaii hold? *(Drawing by Fred N. Domingo, Health Instructional Resources Unit, University of Hawaii)*

In its discussion on the M-K series long-range projections, the State DBED admitted in 1988 that their assumptions of 11.6 million tourists and a de facto population of 1.69 million for Hawaiʻi in 2010 do not represent either a certain or unalterable future. They said: "If the projections suggest future conditions which the community determines to be undesirable, policies can be formulated to help bring about a more desirable future; thus the projections, regardless of their potential accuracy, are not unalterable."[61]

Can the beauty of the natural environment and the charm of the Islands, as found in the expression of "the aloha spirit," be preserved in the relentless increase of Hawaiʻi's economy and population? Legislators, city planners, environmentalists, educators, private agencies, and the general public have become increasingly aware of problems caused by rapid growth, but can they—or will they—take action to check the steep upward trend of more people sharing limited space in Hawaiʻi?

CHAPTER 6
Conclusion

What is the future for the population of Hawai'i? During the twentieth century, Hawai'i has changed from a predominantly rural agrarian community to a service-based urban society increasingly dependent on a visitor industry economy vulnerable to external economic conditions.[1] To what extent will economic growth policies shape the expansion and demographic composition of the people residing in Hawai'i in the twenty-first century?

About 1.7 million people will be present in the Hawaiian Islands by the year 2010, with 11.5 million annual tourists, according to the 1988 State DBED population projection M-K. Honolulu County will have increased population density, more highrise housing, and industrial development along its transit corridors, while rapid growth will continue on the neighbor islands.

The median age of the state population is projected to rise from 28.4 years in 1980 to 35.4 years by 2010. The gradual aging of the population is projected to be characterized by a reduced proportion of children, a larger percentage between ages 20 and 60, and an increase in the percentage of persons aged 65 and over—from 7.9 percent in 1980 to 13.1 percent in 2010. The life expectancy at birth in 2005 is expected to be 76.9 years for males and 82.4 years for females.[2]

The concept of ethnicity may become clouded by high rates of intermarriage and mixed births. Filipino and Korean residents will increase in number by immigration to the state, and the percentage of Whites will grow on the neighbor islands of Hawai'i, Kaua'i, and Maui. Low birth rates of Japanese and Chinese in Hawai'i mean that the proportion of these groups in the Islands is expected to decline.[3]

The future population of Hawai'i will reflect present demographic patterns. Fertility rates in the late twentieth century paralleled those of developed countries that have controlled growth by lower birth rates (Table 6-1). The total fertility rate of the civilian population (1.9 in 1980) was below replacement level (2.1) (Table 3-6). Because low fertility implies an older age structure that would exert an upward pressure on the crude death rate, it is expected that Hawai'i's low crude death rate will gradually rise from the 1985 level of 5.5 to the U.S. average of 9.0 or higher. In 1980, Hawai'i recorded the longest life expectancy for the nation, as well as for most areas of the world, at 75.0 years for males and 81.5 years for females.[4] In the absence of high mortality conditions—such as widespread prevalence of AIDS or nuclear disaster—and with further control of major causes of death, life expectancy in the Islands is expected to continue to rise.

Thus, the rate of natural increase (births minus deaths) may eventually decline to 0.6 percent or less—a slow rate that implies a doubling of population in over one hundred years and one that a finite island state might tolerate for a century or two. On the other hand, net migration, from a high rate of foreign immigration and from a large movement of persons to and from the mainland United States, has been the principal source of Hawai'i's rapid population increase. In the 1970–1980 decade, 56.6 percent of Hawai'i's civilian population growth was attributable to net migration; by 2005–2010 net migration is projected to account for 60.5 percent of net change of the resident population.

The growth of the visitor industry constituted the major driving force to the migratory expansion of population in Hawai'i since 1970. Population projections that used the same fertility and mortality levels but changed rates of tourist growth clearly defined the potential in-migration impact of the visitor industry on population growth. The State Projection M-K (11.6 million tourists by the year 2010, increasing the resident population to 1.44 million persons and the de facto population to 1.7 million inhabitants) showed an annual average population growth rate of 1.32 percent in Hawai'i between the years 1980 and 2010, a rate that would add 470,400 people, representing a 48.8 percent growth to the resident population and a 60.3 percent increase in de facto population. In contrast, a restraint in the number of tourists to the 1982 level of 4.3 million annual visitors (Projection M-B) would provide a population increase of 151,000 residents by the year 2005 at a tolerable growth rate of 0.6 percent (Table 5-1). The visitor industry, by providing jobs that attract in-migration and by promoting an expanding number of daily visitors, was expected to stimulate a large population increase in the Islands in the 1980–2010 period.

Despite recommendations by the Governor's Commission on Population and the Hawaiian Future for legislative policies and action to reduce the rate of population growth, Hawai'i in the 1970–1986 period continued to expand at a 2.4 percent annual de facto population growth rate, or almost three times as fast as the United States as a whole.[5] The State Department of Business and Economic Development in 1988 presented its M-K projections as a guide for long-range planning by the private and public sectors to promote economic growth with accommodation to the increasing density of population in the 1980–2010 period.

A government ethic toward economic growth has implicitly encouraged in-migration with rapid population increase. This has occurred at the cost of environmental deterioration: land, water, air and noise pollution; water supply and sewage overload; urbanization of agricultural, conservation, and beachfront lands; high housing costs; destruction of cultural, historic, and archeological sites; disruption of native ecosystems with loss of land and marine flora and fauna; increased traffic congestion and parking problems; rising crime rates; and social stress.[6,7]

"We are an island community gone mad, behaving like a limitless continent in a world that has already turned into a crowded, strained island," said Hawai'i historian Gavan Daws in 1974.[8]

Thomas Creighton, architect and member of the Honolulu Planning Commission, wrote about misuse of land for speculation that meant large profits for a few and the loss of natural resources for the many. He identified the problem of uncontrolled population growth: "There is the prescription, then: set limits to the population, allow this populace to plan the best ways to use its lands, then give it the power to carry out its plan through its own trust."[9]

The natural laws of the physical world warn that rapid growth cannot continue indefinitely. Even if a balanced in- and out-migration were immediately to be attained and fertility were to remain at replacement level (two children for two adults), Hawai'i's age structure ensures continued growth until the middle of the twenty-first century. At that time it is probable that stabilization or a very slow growth (0.3 percent) would offer a rate of population change that could be tolerated for generations. But the 1970–1986 de facto population growth rate of 2.4 percent, the 2.0 percent resident growth rate in that period, and the 1.32 percent "most likely" resident growth rate proposed in the 1980–2010 state endorsed M-K projections all result in rapid population increase that a finite environment cannot long endure.

If the M-K projection is realized, the de facto population of 1,687,200 persons in the year 2010 will more than double Hawai'i's 1970 population of 796,500 residents.[10] The labor force of 728,800 in 2010 would be over twice the 346,859 persons employed in 1970.[11] Most of the added positions would be filled by new migrants to the Islands. A population of over 2 million projected by 2020 implies 600,000 dwelling units encroaching on agricultural lands, plus over a million cars. But what happens then? Will planners continue to give priority to economic growth rate goals without concern for population growth implications? Will Hawai'i continue to "accommodate" or "manage" population growth as it doubles to 4 million, 8 million, or 16 million people?

Some planners for the future of Hawai'i have suggested a major reevaluation of state policies affecting the rate, type, and location of economic and population growth. The insularity of Hawai'i offers a rare possibility for long-range creative planning and action. "The physical isolation and small scale give it a unique sense of identity and provide an unusual opportunity for measuring, projecting, and evaluating the processes of a total society," wrote George Chaplin, chairman of the Governor's Conference on the Year 2000.[12] Hawai'i's population has continued to increase rapidly as a trade-off in policies for economic growth despite the intellectual adventure of futuristic conference discussions, statements of population concerns in the Hawaii State Plan, an Oahu General Plan policy objective to promote a balance between the rate of in-migration and the rate of out-migration, the establishment of commissions on population and on environment, and proposals to establish a population policy for the state.[13]

There are many ways in which population growth can be slowed. The most direct measure would be to alter state economic growth perceptions and limit the expansion of tourism. The focus of Hawai'i's visitor industry in the 1980s is beginning to change. Bermuda, which has contained the number of annual tourists to about half a million visitors and which has curtailed in-migration by strictly limiting jobs to local residents and controlling the sale and use of land, exemplifies innovative policy directions. Hawai'i's tourism planners are shifting from perceptions of quantity volume to quality growth in order to attract tourists with higher per capita spending, maintaining economic growth without stimulating an increase in the number of jobs and population.[14]

State government policies that have been supportive toward foreign investment in Hawai'i are being reconsidered because foreign funds have been used to increase Hawai'i's overdependency on tourism. In 1986, annual income to out-of-state investors was $1.5 billion, equivalent to the size of Hawai'i's entire construction industry, and a sum that could pay most of the combined local sales taxes, corporate income taxes, individual income taxes, and real estate taxes.[15] While some of the profits were reinvested in Hawai'i, most of the income was repatriated out of state or out of country.[16]

The Gross State Product is expected to increase 105.3 percent, from $15.1 billion in 1985 to $31.0 billion (in 1982 dollars) in the year 2010. Per capita income, however, is projected to rise only 40.3 percent from $12,400 in 1985 to $17,400 (in 1982 dollars) in those twenty-five years (Table 5–1).[17] Hawai'i's open-door policy toward outside investment has resulted in the economy tripling in size accompanied by a falling in average real wages, a widened gap between rich and non-rich, a squeezing of local small businesses, and a rising supremacy of non-resident big businesses. University of Hawaii Professor Robert H. Stauffer reported in 1984: "It is non-resident big businesses, their owners, and associated speculators who have benefited since 1959 from the maturing of Hawai'i's economy. The vast majority of Hawai'i's people, on the other hand, have seen a deterioration in their living standards."[18] Population projections confirmed that per capita income would be higher if there was a lower rate of growth of the visitor industry, and population growth would be slowed (Table 5–1).

Despite government pressures to promote Hawai'i's business climate for out-of-state investors, the research department of the First Hawaiian Bank sounded a gentle alarm in 1987: "More attention could be given to developing more discriminating policies, such as encouraging more reinvestment of profits back into Hawai'i to increase the benefits of foreign investment to Hawai'i residents."[19] The report suggested a need to diversify investments in science, educational, manufacturing, and agricultural programs.

Some local government measures, such as strict limitation of land use, water use, and constraints on construction, could lead to a reduced movement of people to Hawai'i. State support of diversification through new technologies would offer the economy a broader base and greater stability. The creation of scientific and technical jobs in microelectronics, software products, a space port, astronomy, biotechnology, renewable energy, telecommunications, ocean and marine sciences, earth sciences, aquaculture, and tropical agriculture offer diverse high-tech employment opportunities for local residents.

This could reduce economic dependency on the visitor industry, which attracts in-migrants to low-paying service sector jobs, and thereby it could reduce the rate of population growth.[20]

Federal action on immigration policies could amend the U.S. Immigration and Nationality Act to alleviate Hawai'i's disproportionate percentage of alien immigrants. But it is questionable whether the objective of balanced migration is attainable without stronger state policy and action supported by state and national legislation.

Dr. Garrett Hardin, author of the population treatise "Tragedy of the Commons," suggested that constitutional principles may need to be challenged to reduce the rate of immigration to Hawai'i. "The residents of a land of beauty have a responsibility to be its trustees. If you broadly share your wealth, you will probably lose it, and if you are fair to everyone, you are fair to no one."[21]

Federal action has been suggested to preserve areas of natural beauty from overcommercialization and overpopulation. Should the state of Hawai'i, or a section of it, seek protection as a national park?

An industrialized system geared to economic growth and to consumption of nonrenewable resources opposes the natural biological and physical system of which Hawai'i is a part. A planned economy of conservation and an ethic toward population stabilization could offer hope for the future. There is a space-age awareness of limits to growth and increasing recognition of the need to cast off goals of private economic gain in order to preserve the environment and quality of life.[22]

Hawai'i, as a microcosm of the world, reflects the heterogeneous composition of mankind's global civilization. The once-barren volcanic islands, invaded by people about 1,500 years ago, have been inundated in the past 100 years at an increasing growth rate. While the world grapples with problems of rapid population growth related to high birth rates and low death rates, Hawai'i has reduced its rate of natural increase by adoption of social measures and economic attitudes toward small families; however, population growth by migration, stimulated by economic growth policies that attract in-migrants, continues unchecked and threatens environmental overload. Reducing the rate of population and economic growth in the future will entail modifications in government economic policies, but it may be the only way of providing a balance of mankind and nature that could assure harmonious evolution for Hawai'i's people in the generations to come.

APPENDIX

Demographic Tables

Table 1–1. Estimated Population of Hawai'i, A.D. 500 to A.D. 1778

Year	Population	Historic Activity
500	100	Era of La'ila'i (peace): early
600	190	settlement, cooperative;
700	350	leadership by senior family
800	650	members
900	1,200	
1000	2,300	
1100	4,300	
1200	8,000	
1300	15,000	Era of transition: adjustment;
1400	28,000	division of labor and land
1500	53,000	
1600	98,000	Era of strong leadership:
1700	184,000	genealogies connect chiefs with
1778	300,000	gods

Sources: Kelly 1986, p. 17; Schmitt and Zane 1977, p. 4.

Note: These figures are derived from hypothetical calculations.

Table 2-1. Resident Population, Percentage Distribution, and Annual Average Growth Rates, Islands and Counties, Hawai'i, 1778-1985

Estimate or Census Date[a]	State of Hawai'i	Island				
		Hawai'i	O'ahu[b]	Kaua'i	Ni'ihau	Kaho'olawe
1778-1779	250,000	NA	50,000	NA	NA	NA
1823	145,000	NA	34,000	NA	NA	NA
1831-1832	130,313	45,792	29,755	10,977	1,047	80
1835-1836	108,579	39,364	27,809	8,934	993	80
1850: Jan.	84,165	25,864	25,440	6,956	714	0
1853: Dec. 26	73,138	24,450	19,126	6,991	790	0
1860: Dec. 24	69,800	21,481	21,275	6,487	647	0
1866: Dec. 7	62,959	19,808	19,799	6,299	325	0
1872: Dec. 27	56,897	16,001	20,671	4,961	233	0
1878: Dec. 27	57,985	17,034	20,236	5,634	177	0
1884: Dec. 27	80,578	24,991	28,068	8,935[c]	d	0
1890: Dec. 28	89,990	26,754	31,194	11,859[c]	d	0
1896: Sept. 27	109,020	33,285	40,205	15,228	164	0
1900: Jun. 1	154,001	46,843	58,504	20,562	172	0
1910: Apr. 15	191,909	55,382	82,028	23,744	208	2
1920: Jan. 1	255,912	64,895	123,527	29,247	191	3
1930: Apr. 1	368,336	73,325	202,923	35,806	136	2
1940: Apr. 1	423,330	73,276	258,256	35,636	182	1
1950: Apr. 1	499,794	68,350	353,020	29,683	222	0
1960: Apr. 1	632,772	61,332	500,409	27,922	254	0
1970: Apr. 1	769,913[g]	63,468	630,528[g]	29,524	237	0
1980: Apr. 1	964,691	92,053	762,565	38,856	226	0
1985: Jul. 1[h]	1,053,900	109,200	814,600	44,600	180	0

Distribution (percent)

1778	100.0	NA	NA	NA	NA	NA
1823	100.0	NA	NA	NA	NA	NA
1831	100.0	35.1	22.8	8.4	0.8	0.06
1835	100.0	36.3	25.6	8.2	0.9	0.06
1850	100.0	30.7	30.2	8.3	0.8	0
1853	100.0	33.4	26.2	9.6	1.0	0
1860	100.0	30.8	30.5	9.3	0.9	0
1866	100.0	31.5	31.4	10.0	0.5	0
1872	100.0	28.1	36.3	8.7	0.4	0
1878	100.0	29.4	34.9	9.7	0.3	0
1884	100.0	21.0	34.8	11.1	d	0
1890	100.0	29.6	34.6	13.6	d	0
1896	100.0	30.5	36.9	13.9	0.2	0
1900	100.0	30.4	38.0	13.4	0.1	0
1910	100.0	28.9	42.7	12.4	0.1	*
1920	100.0	25.4	48.3	11.4	*	*
1930	100.0	19.9	55.1	9.7	*	*
1940	100.0	17.3	61.0	8.4	*	*
1950	100.0	13.7	70.6	5.9	*	0
1960	100.0	9.7	79.1	4.4	*	0
1970	100.0	8.3	81.9	3.8	*	0
1980	100.0	9.5	79.0	4.1	*	0
1985	100.0	10.4	77.3	4.2	*	0

			County			
Lāna'i	Maui	Moloka'i	Hawai'i	Honolulu	Kaua'i	Maui
NA	NA	NA	NA	NA	NA	NA
NA	NA	NA	NA	NA	NA	NA
1,600	35,062	6,000				
1,200	24,199	6,000				
604	21,047	3,540				
600	17,574	3,607				
646	16,400	2,864		c		
394	14,035	2,299				
348	12,334	2,349				
214	12,109	2,581				
e	15,970	2,614				
e	17,357	2,826				
105	17,726	2,307				
f	25,416[f]	2,504	46,843	58,504	20,734	27,920
131	28,623	1,791	55,382	82,028[c]	23,952	30,547
185	36,080	1,784	64,895	123,527[c]	29,438	38,052
2,356	48,756	5,032	73,325	202,923[c]	35,942	56,146
3,720	46,919	5,340	73,276	258,256[c]	35,818	55,980
3,136	40,103	5,280	68,350	353,020	29,905	48,519
2,115	35,717	5,023	61,332	500,409	28,176	42,855
2,204	38,691	5,261	63,468	630,528[g]	29,761	46,156
2,119	62,823	6,049	92,053	762,565	39,082	70,991
2,200	76,600	6,500	109,200	814,600	44,800	85,300

Distribution (percent)

NA	NA	NA				
NA	NA	NA				
1.2	26.9	4.6				
1.1	22.3	5.5				
0.7	25.0	4.2				
0.9	24.0	4.9		c		
0.9	23.5	4.1				
0.6	22.3	3.7				
0.6	21.7	4.1				
0.4	20.9	4.5				
e	19.8	3.2				
e	19.2	3.0				
0.1	16.3	2.1				
f	16.5[f]	1.6	30.4	38.0	13.5	18.1
0.1	14.9	0.9	28.9	42.7	12.5	15.9
0.1	14.1	0.7	25.4	48.3	11.5	14.9
0.6	13.2	1.4	19.9	55.1	9.8	15.2
0.9	11.1	1.3	17.3	61.0	8.5	13.2
0.6	8.0	1.1	13.7	70.6	6.0	9.7
0.3	5.6	0.8	9.7	79.1	4.5	6.7
0.3	5.0	0.7	8.3	81.9	3.9	6.0
0.2	6.6	0.6	9.5	79.0	4.1	7.4
0.2	7.3	0.6	10.4	77.3	4.2	8.1

continued

175

Table 2–1. *(continued)*

Estimate or Census Date[a]	State of Hawai'i	Island				
		Hawai'i	O'ahu[b]	Kaua'i	Ni'ihau	Kaho'olawe
Average Annual Growth Rate (percent)[i]						
1900–10	2.20	1.67	3.38	1.44	1.90	NA
1910–20	2.95	1.63	4.20	2.14	−0.87	NA
1920–30	3.55	1.19	4.84	1.97	−3.31	NA
1930–40	1.39	−0.01	2.41	−0.05	2.91	NA
1940–50	1.66	−0.70	3.13	−1.83	1.99	NA
1950–60	2.36	−1.08	3.49	−0.61	1.35	NA
1960–70	1.96	0.34	2.31	0.56	−0.69	NA
1970–80	2.26	3.72	1.90	2.75	0.00	NA
1900–80	2.29	0.84	3.21	0.80	0.01	NA
1980–85	1.68	3.25	1.26	2.63	−4.55	NA

Sources: Hawaii (State) DPED, 1985 Data Book, Tables 5, 6; Statistical Memorandum, No. 85-3, Table 1; Statistical Report No. 190, Tables 1, 5, 6, 7; No. 196, Table 1; Schmitt 1968, pp. 42, 70, 84, and 116; 1971, pp. 237-243; 1977, Tables 1.5 and 1.9; United States, BOC 1932, Tables 3, 5; 1953, Table 4; 1961, Table 27; 1971c, Table 35; 1983c, Table P-1.

* Percentage smaller than 0.05.

NA Not available.

[a]Estimates for 1778-1779 and 1823; missionary censuses for 1831-1832 and 1835-1836; official government censuses for 1850-1980.

[b]Includes outlying islands that are legally part of the city and county of Honolulu: Palmyra (32 in 1940, uninhabited in 1950, and detached in 1959) and the northwest Hawaiian Islands from Nihoa to Kure but excluding Midway (14 in 1950, 15 in 1960, 31 in 1970). The figures for 1910-1940 include persons on the Midway Islands, and for 1940 other small outlying islands, not legally part of the territory of Hawai'i (35 in 1910, 31 in 1920, 36 in 1930, and 437 in 1940).

			County			
Lāna'i	Maui	Moloka'i	Hawai'i	Honolulu	Kaua'i	Maui
f	1.23[f]	−3.35	1.67	3.38	1.44	0.90
3.54	2.37	−0.04	1.63	4.20	2.14	2.25
24.82	2.94	10.12	1.19	4.84	1.97	3.80
4.57	−0.38	0.59	−0.01	2.41	−0.03	−0.03
−1.71	−1.57	−0.11	−0.70	3.13	−1.80	−1.43
−3.94	−1.16	−0.50	−1.08	3.49	−0.60	−1.24
0.41	0.78	0.46	0.34	2.29	0.55	0.74
−0.39	4.85	1.10	3.72	1.90	2.72	4.31
3.98[j]	1.13	0.88	0.84	3.21	0.80	1.17
0.75	3.97	1.44	3.25	1.26	2.63	3.50

[c]County governments were not organized until 1905.

[d]Ni'ihau is counted with Kaua'i in 1884 and 1890.

[e]Lana'i included with Moloka'i in 1884 and 1890.

[f]Lana'i included with Maui in 1900.

[g]Final revised totals.

[h]Estimated population.

[i]Calculated by the formula $r = 100 \ \dfrac{\log_e (\frac{P_2}{P_1})}{t}$

[j]1910–1980.

Table 3–1. Ethnic Composition, Percentage Distribution, and Rates of Growth, Hawai'i, 1853–1980

Year	Total	American Indian	Black	Chinese	Filipino	Total Hawaiian	Hawaiian	Part-Hawaiian
Population[b,c]								
1853	73,137	d	—	364	—	71,019	70,036	983
1860	69,800	—	—	816	—	66,984	65,647	1,337
1866	62,959	—	—	1,306	—	58,765	57,125	1,640
1872	56,897	—	—	2,038	—	51,531	49,044	2,487
1878	57,985	—	—	6,045	—	47,508	44,088	3,420
1884	80,578	—	—	18,254	—	44,232	40,014	4,218
1890	89,990	—	—	16,752	—	40,622	34,436	6,186
1896	109,020	—	—	21,616	—	39,504	31,019	8,485
1900	154,001	—	233	25,767	—	37,656	29,799	7,857
1910	191,909	—	695	21,674	2,361	38,547	26,041	12,506
1920	255,912	—	348	23,507	21,031	41,750	23,723	18,027
1930	368,336	—	563	27,179	63,052	50,860	22,636	28,224
1940	423,330	—	255	28,774	52,569	64,310	14,375	49,935
1950[e]	499,769	—	2,651	32,376	61,062	86,090	12,245	73,845
1960	632,772	472	4,943	38,197	69,070	102,403	11,294	91,109
1970–80 using census definitions of ethnicity								
1970[f]	768,559	1,216	7,517	52,375	95,354	71,274	g	71,274
1980[f]	964,691	2,655	17,364	56,285	133,940	115,500	g	115,500
1970–86 using Department of Health definitions of ethnicity[i]								
1970	773,632	NA	5,925	29,966	61,240	132,921	7,697	125,224
1980	930,271	NA	11,799	47,275	104,547	175,453	9,366	166,087
1985	1,015,300	NA	24,215	46,055	112,774	174,818	6,824	167,994
1986	1,022,745	NA	23,032	48,727	115,519	211,448	8,093	203,355
Distribution (percent)								
1853	100.00	NA	NA	0.5	NA	97.1	95.8	1.3
1860	100.00	NA	NA	1.2	NA	96.0	94.1	1.9
1866	100.00	NA	NA	2.1	NA	93.3	90.7	2.6
1872	100.00	NA	NA	3.5	NA	90.6	86.2	4.4
1878	100.00	NA	NA	10.4	NA	81.9	76.0	5.9
1884	100.00	NA	NA	22.7	NA	54.9	49.7	5.2
1890	100.00	NA	NA	18.6	NA	45.2	38.3	6.9
1896	100.00	NA	NA	19.8	NA	36.2	28.4	7.8
1900	100.00	NA	0.2	16.7	NA	24.4	19.3	5.1
1910	100.00	NA	0.4	11.3	1.2	20.1	13.6	6.5
1920	100.00	NA	0.1	9.2	8.2	16.3	9.3	7.0
1930	100.00	NA	0.2	7.4	17.1	13.8	6.1	7.7
1940	100.00	NA	0.1	6.8	12.4	15.2	3.4	11.8
1950	100.00	NA	0.5	6.5	12.2	17.3	2.5	14.8
1960	100.00	0.1	0.8	6.0	10.9	16.1	1.7	14.4
1970–80 using census definitions of ethnicity								
1970	100.00	0.2	1.0	6.8	12.4	9.3	g	9.3
1980	100.00	0.3	1.8	5.8	13.9	12.0	g	12.0
1970–86 using Department of Health definitions of ethnicity[i]								
1970	100.00	NA	0.8	3.9	7.9	17.2	1.0	16.2
1980	100.00	NA	1.3	5.1	11.2	18.9	1.0	17.9
1985	100.00	NA	2.4	4.5	11.1	17.2	0.7	16.5
1986	100.00	NA	2.3	4.8	11.3	20.7	0.8	19.9

| Japanese | Korean | White (Caucasian)[a] | | | | | Other |
		Total White	Puerto Rican	Portuguese	Spanish	Other Caucasian	
—	—	1,687	—d	87	—	1,600	67
—	—	1,900	—	85	—	1,815	100
—	—	2,400	—	90	—	2,310	488
—	—	2,944	—	424	—	2,520	384
—	—	3,748	—	486	—	3,262	684
116	—	16,579	—	9,967	—	6,612	1,397
12,610	—	18,939	—	12,719	—	6,220	1,067
24,407	—	22,438	—	15,191	—	7,247	1,055
61,111	—	28,819	—	18,272	—	10,547	415
79,675	4,533	44,048	4,890	22,301	1,990	14,867	376
109,274	4,950	54,742	5,602	27,002	2,430	19,708	310
139,631	6,461	80,373	6,671	27,588	1,219	44,895	217
157,905	6,851	112,087	8,296	—	—	103,791	579
184,598	7,030	124,344	9,551	—	—	114,793	1,618
203,455	—	202,230	—	—	—	202,230	12,002
217,669	9,625	301,429	—	—	—	301,429	12,100
239,748	17,962	318,770	—	—	—	318,770	62,467h
207,379	7,201	255,437	4,111	—	—	251,326	73,563k
218,176	11,893	244,832	6,649	—	—	238,183	116,386l
232,576	14,636	274,454	5,318	—	—	269,136	135,772m
235,207	13,284	239,294	4,279	—	—	235,015	136,234n
NA	NA	2.3	NA	-0.1	NA	2.2	0.1
NA	NA	2.7	NA	0.1	NA	2.6	0.1
NA	NA	3.8	NA	0.1	NA	3.7	0.8
NA	NA	5.2	NA	0.7	NA	4.4	0.7
NA	NA	6.5	NA	0.8	NA	5.6	1.2
0.1	NA	20.6	NA	12.4	NA	8.2	1.7
14.0	NA	21.0	NA	14.1	NA	6.9	1.2
22.4	NA	20.6	NA	13.9	NA	6.7	1.0
39.7	NA	18.7	NA	11.9	NA	6.8	0.3
41.5	2.4	23.0	2.5	11.7	1.0	7.8	0.1
42.7	1.9	21.4	2.2	10.6	0.9	7.7	0.2
37.9	1.8	21.8	1.8	7.5	0.3	12.2	0.1
37.3	1.6	26.5	2.0	NA	NA	24.5	0.2
36.9	1.4	24.9	1.9	NA	NA	23.0	0.3
32.2	NA	32.0	NA	NA	NA	NA	1.9
28.3	1.3	39.2	NA	NA	NA	NA	1.6
24.9	1.9	33.0	NA	NA	NA	NA	6.4
26.8	1.0	33.0		r			9.5
23.5	1.0	26.3					12.5
22.9	1.4	27.0					13.4
23.0	1.3	23.4					13.3

continued

Table 3-1. *(continued)*

Year	Total	American Indian	Black	Chinese	Filipino	Hawaiian Total Hawaiian	Hawaiian Hawaiian	Hawaiian Part-Hawaiian
Average Annual Growth Rates (× 100)[i]								
1900–10	2.20	NA	10.93	–1.73	NA	0.23	–1.35	4.65
1910–20	2.95	NA	7.09	0.83	22.43	0.80	0.96	3.75
1920–30	3.55	NA	4.69	1.42	10.71	1.97	0.46	4.37
1930–40	1.39	NA	–7.92	0.57	–1.82	2.35	–4.54	5.71
1940–50	1.66	NA	23.41	1.18	1.50	2.92	–1.60	3.91
1950–60	2.36	NA	6.23	1.65	1.23	1.74	–1.54	2.15
1960–70, 1970–80, and 1900–80 using census definitions of ethnicity								
1960–70	1.94	9.46	4.19	3.16	3.22	–3.62	NA	–2.51
1970–80	2.27	3.08	8.37	0.72	3.40	NA	NA	4.83
1900–80	2.29	NA	5.39	0.97	5.05	4.83	–1.21[p]	3.36
1970–80 and 1980–86 using Department of Health definitions of ethnicity[i]								
1970–80	1.84	NA	11.48	4.56	5.35	2.77	1.96	2.82
1980–86	1.58	NA	11.14	0.30	0.17	1.87	–2.43	3.37

Sources: Adams 1925, Table 1; Hawaii (State) DPED, Statistical Report No. 180, Table 2; Data Book, 1972, 1981, 1986, 1987; Lind 1980, Table 3; Schmitt 1968, Table 26; United States, BOC 1961, Table 15; 1972a, Table 139; 1982a, Table 22;1982b, Tables 58 and 59.

Note: See Tables 3–2, 3–3, and 4–2 for additional ethnic population figures. See Chapter 4, Ethnicity, for discussion of racial definitions and problems of incomparability of racial groups.

NA Not available.

[a]Includes Puerto Ricans, Portuguese, Spanish, and "other Caucasians." Portuguese and Spanish were counted as Caucasian after 1930, and most Puerto Ricans were included with this group after 1950. The term "White" replaced "Caucasian" in 1960.

[b]In 1853–1960, persons of unmixed race were classified by race of parents. Persons of mixed background, other than Part Hawaiian, were tabulated by race of non-white parent if part Caucasian or by race of father if non-Caucasian. In 1970 and 1980, the U.S. census classified by self-identification of race or by race of father; in 1980 for persons who could not provide a single response to the race question, the race of the person's mother was used. Many persons who would have been tabulated as Part Hawaiian under the 1960 definition were counted in 1970 and 1980 as White, Chinese, or some other race; therefore figures are not directly comparable with other years because of changed census definitions of race.

[c]U.S. census data are for June 1, 1900; April 15, 1910; January 1, 1920; and April 1 thereafter, except July 1, 1985.

[d]A dash (—) indicates that the population group was either not present or not counted.

[e]Difference between this table and Table 2 reflects differences in the underlying census tables.

[f]Figures for 1970 and 1980 are not directly comparable with other years owing to changed census definitions of race.

[g]Hawaiians are tabulated with Part Hawaiians.

		White (Caucasian)[a]					
Japanese	Korean	Total White	Puerto Rican	Portu-guese	Spanish	Other Caucasian	Other
2.65	NA	4.24					
3.24	0.88	2.23		r			
2.39	2.66	3.75					
1,23	0,58	3.32					
1.56	0.26	1.04					
0.97		4.86					
0.68	1.57o	3.99		r			
0.97	6.23	0.56					
1.71	1.72q	3.00					
0.50	5.02	−0.40		r			
0.13	0.18	−0.38					

[h]The 1980 data are based upon 100% tabulations of the 1980 U.S. census that included 68 Eskimo, 45 Aleut, 604 Asian Indian, 3,463 Vietnamese, 1,677 Guamanian, 14,073 Samoan, and 42,537 "Other." Later 15.7% sample estimates redistributed the "Other" category to 21,444. It increased Blacks to 17,687, Part Hawaiians to 118,251, American Indian to 2,833, Eskimo to 74, Aleuts to 69, and Whites to 331,925. Chinese decreased to 55,916, Japanese to 239,734, Filipinos to 132,075; and Koreans to 17,453. The group known as "Other Asian & Pacific Islanders" numbered 27,230, including estimates of 708 Asian Indian, 3,403 Vietnamese, 1,630 Guamanian, 14,349 Samoan, and 7,140 "Other" (Tongan, Micronesian, Melanesian, and others).

[i]Data based on samples from Hawaii Health Surveillance Program. HHSP definitions do not correspond to census definitions.

[j]Calculated according to the formula: growth rate $= 100\ [(\ln\ \{P_t/P_o\})\ /t]$.

[k]Includes 2,837 "Other and Unknown," 5,846 Samoans, and 60,770 "Mixed, excluding Part Hawaiian." Numbers may not sum to total because of rounding.

[l]Includes 10,723 "Other unmixed or Unknown," 11,173 Samoans, and 87,840 "non-Hawaiian mixed." Numbers may not sum to total because of rounding.

[m]Includes 10,440 "Other unmixed," 5,569 Samoans, and 114,446 "non-Hawaiian mixed." Numbers may not sum to total because of rounding.

[n]Includes 12,729 "Other unmixed or Unknown," 3,825 Samoans, and 115,401 "non-Hawaiian mixed." Numbers may not sum to total because of rounding.

[o]1950–1970.

[p]1900–1960.

[q]1910–1980.

[r]Not calculated.

Table 3–2. Comparison of Ethnic Populations According to U.S. Census and Hawaii Health Surveillance Program (HHSP) Definitions, Hawai'i, 1980

Race	U.S. Census[a]			HHSP[b]
	Full Count	Sample	Public Use Microdata Sample	
Total	964,691	964,691	969,460	930,271
Aleut	45	69	⎫	c
American Indian	2,655	2,833	⎬ 2,680	c
Eskimo	68	74	⎭	c
Asian Indian	604	708	520	c
Black	17,364	17,687	17,580	11,799
Chinese	56,285	55,916	55,780	47,275
Filipino	133,940	132,075	134,960	104,547
Guamanian	1,677	1,630	d	c
Hawaiian	115,500	118,251	122,660	9,366[e]
Japanese	239,748	239,734	241,580	218,176
Korean	17,962	17,453	16,680	11,803
Puerto Rican	f	f	f	6,649
Samoan	14,073	14,349	24,820[d]	11,173
Vietnamese	3,463	3,403	4,000	c
White	318,770	331,925	327,640	244,832
Other	42,537	21,444	20,560	10,723
Mixed, Part Hawaiian	g	g	g	166,087
Mixed, non-Hawaiian	g	g	g	87,840

Sources: Hawaii (State) DPED, Statistical Report No. 180, Table 1; 1983d, special tabulation; United States BOC 1982b, Table 58.

Note: See Table 4–2 for detailed Asian and Pacific Island resident population.

[a]The Bureau of the Census released three counts of racial statistics:
  (1) a full count, with only limited edit and review;
  (2) a one-in-six sample, with more extensive editing;
  (3) a five percent Public Use Microdata Sample (PUMS).

[b]The Hawaii Health Surveillance Program (HHSP) is an ongoing sample survey conducted by the Hawaii State Department of Health. It excludes persons in military barracks or aboard ships, inmates of institutions and most other group quarters, and residents of Ni'ihau and Kalawao. HHSP figures are commonly used by state planners for ethnic representation.

[c]Included with "Other."

[d]Includes Guamanian, Samoan, and other Asian and Pacific Islanders.

[e]Unmixed Hawaiian.

[f]Included with White.

[g]Tabulated with race by U.S. census.

Table 3–3.a. Black Ethnic Population by Age, Sex, and Percentage Distribution, Hawai'i, 1900–1980

Age	1900	1910	1920	1930	1940	1950	1960	1970	1980
Males									
0–4	NA	NA	NA	NA	NA	NA	319	493	1,000
5–9							222	436	640
10–14							95	303	434
15–19							410	540	1,241
20–24							1,007	1,693	4,320
25–29							507	495	1,822
30–34							247	468	919
35–39							202	203	505
40–44							99	179	317
45–49				a			57	117	194
50–54							44	70	124
55–59							31	47	123
60–64							20	44	85
65–69							4	7	37
70–74							4	13	26
75–79							4	0	9
80–84							0	0	4
85 +							0	14	4
Subtotal	158	415	218	322	172	2,033	3,272	5,122	11,804
Females									
0–4	NA	NA	NA	NA	NA	NA	355	469	988
5–9							219	371	612
10–14							94	243	412
15–19							61	167	430
20–24							153	306	1,119
25–29							228	350	839
30–34							131	232	461
35–39							72	112	227
40–44							33	39	128
45–49				a			9	27	97
50–54							23	20	82
55–59							4	0	55
60–64							18	46	40
65–69							8	0	27
70–74							9	13	19
75–79							0	0	16
80–84							0	0	4
85 +							5	0	4
Subtotal	75	280	130	241	83	618	1,422	2,395	5,560
Total	233	695	348	563	255	2,651	4,694	7,517	17,364

Sources: United States BOC 1913, Tables 8, 10, 25, 27; 1932, Table 4; Table 2; 1953, Tables 29, 30; 1961, Table 17; 1962, Table 96; 1963, Table 61; 1971b, Table 17; 1972a, Tables 96, 138, 139; 1982a, Tables 19 and 22.

Notes: Changes in U.S. census definition of race between 1960–1970 and again between 1970–1980 resulted in lack of comparability for ethnic data. U.S. census data on race are also not comparable to Hawaii

	Distribution (percent)								
Age	1900	1910	1920	1930	1940	1950	1960	1970	1980
Males									
0–4	NA	NA	NA	NA	NA	NA	9.74	9.62	8.47
5–9							6.79	8.51	5.42
10–14							2.91	5.91	3.68
15–19							12.53	10.54	10.51
20–24							30.78	33.05	36.60
25–29							15.50	9.66	15.44
30–34							7.55	9.13	7.79
35–39							6.17	3.96	4.28
40–44							3.03	3.49	2.69
45–49				a			1.74	2.28	1.64
50–54							1.34	1.38	1.05
55–59							0.95	0.93	1.04
60–64							0.61	0.86	0.72
65–69							0.12	0.15	0.31
70–74							0.12	0.25	0.22
75–79							0.12	0.00	0.08
80–84							0.00	0.00	0.03
85 +							0.00	0.28	0.03
Total							100.00	100.00	100.00
Females									
0–4	NA	NA	NA	NA	NA	NA	24.96	19.58	17.77
5–9							15.40	15.49	11.01
10–14							6.61	10.15	7.41
15–19							4.29	6.97	7.73
20–24							10.76	12.77	20.13
25–29							16.03	14.61	15.09
30–34							9.21	9.69	8.29
35–39							5.06	4.68	4.08
40–44							2.32	1.63	2.30
45–49				a			0.64	1.13	1.75
50–54							1.62	0.84	1.47
55–59							0.28	0.00	0.99
60–64							1.27	1.92	0.72
65–69							0.56	0.00	0.49
70–74							0.64	0.54	0.34
75–79							0.00	0.00	0.29
80–84							0.00	0.00	0.07
85 +							0.35	0.00	0.07
								0.00	0.00
Total							100.00	100.00	100.0

Health Surveillance Program (HHSP) data owing to different procedures.
See Table 4–3 for total resident population by age, sex and percentage distribution.

NA Not available.

aBetween 1900 and 1950, Blacks were included in the category "Other."

Table 3–3.b. Chinese Ethnic Population by Age, Sex and Percentage Distribution, Hawai'i, 1900–1980

Age	1900[a]	1910	1920[a]	1930[a]	1940[a]	1950	1960	1970	1980
Age and Sex									
Males									
0–4	722	859	1,450	1,753	1,116	2,042	2,169	2,181	1,613
5–9	839	999	1,281	1,808	1,388	1,586	2,263	2,708	1,625
10–14	438	856	1,052	1,547	1,840	1,184	2,126	2,865	1,964
15–19	1,240	650	1,002	1,354	1,809	1,315	1,500	2,566	2,507
20–24	2,337	405	828	1,078	1,520	1,377	858	2,015	2,542
25–29	3,968	790	667	1,076	1,267	1,531	1,023	1,594	2,443
30–34	3,362	1,828	426	1,139	975	1,471	1,430	1,321	2,373
35–39	2,912	2,714	719	792	1,081	1,323	1,612	1,568	1,673
40–44	2,467	2,299	1,592	437	1,056	1,017	1,478	1,792	1,333
45–49	1,442	2,040	2,110	567	739	1,017	1,239	1,890	1,532
50–54	989	1,399	1,693	1,172	351	936	929	1,622	1,783
55–59	644	870	1,417	1,331	403	585	997	1,353	1,823
60–64	645	872	945	962	734	296	834	881	1,548
65–69	134	368	470	704	880	249	487	893	1,182
70–74	55	152	402	438	467	398	207	731	808
75–79	11	30	90	252	299	402	154	290	1,122[b]
80–84	3	7	26	86	121	193	168	117	b
85+	1	5	17	57	78	121	135	85	b
Unknown	87	5	10	8	7	0	0	0	0
Subtotal	22,296	17,148	16,197	16,561	16,131	17,043	19,609	26,472	27,871
Females									
0–4	626	759	1,429	1,619	1,052	1,930	2,029	1,964	1,531
5–9	740	898	1,239	1,759	1,397	1,485	2,104	2,385	1,450
10–14	302	765	924	1,563	1,734	1,170	2,069	2,761	1,872
15–19	352	450	898	1,218	1,741	1,350	1,436	2,464	2,345
20–24	366	294	745	938	528	1,563	911	2,143	2,583
25–29	352	329	503	877	1,150	1,638	1,139	1,461	2,544
30–34	288	269	346	741	906	1,485	1,571	1,445	2,463
35–39	182	282	363	527	893	1,114	1,590	1,520	1,739
40–44	118	184	284	352	669	861	1,466	1,870	1,437
45–49	54	117	234	322	480	838	1,076	2,003	1,599
50–54	39	86	140	237	312	668	879	1,661	1,894
55–59	23	42	87	219	268	418	840	1,217	1,863
60–64	12	22	63	114	185	275	611	919	1,624
65–69	6	15	29	59	183	219	375	872	1,222
70–74	3	8	16	40	77	125	205	638	832
75–79	2	3	5	16	34	107	150	296	1,416[b]
80–84	1	2	3	11	21	64	72	175	b
85+	0	1	1	4	8	23	65	109	b
Unknown	5	0	1	2	5	0	0	0	0
Subtotal	3,471	4,526	7,310	10,618	12,643	15,333	18,588	25,903	28,414
Total	25,767	21,674	23,507	27,179	28,774	32,376	38,197	52,375	56,285

Sources: See Table 3.3.a.

Note: See Note, Table 3–3.a. After 1960, the U.S. census counted some Part Hawaiians with Chinese. NA Not available.

				Distribution (percent)					
Age	1900	1910	1920	1930	1940	1950	1960	1970	1980
Males									
0–4	3.24	5.01	8.95	10.59	6.92	11.98	11.06	8.24	5.79
5–9	3.76	5.83	7.91	10.92	8.60	9.31	11.54	10.23	5.83
10–14	1.96	4.99	6.50	9.34	11.41	6.95	10.84	10.83	7.05
15–19	5.56	3.79	6.19	8.18	11.21	7.72	7.65	9.69	9.00
20–24	10.48	2.36	5.11	6.51	9.42	8.08	4.38	7.61	9.12
25–29	17.80	4.61	4.12	6.50	7.85	8.98	5.22	6.02	8.77
30–34	15.08	10.66	2.63	6.87	6.04	8.63	7.29	4.99	8.51
35–39	13.06	15.83	4.44	4.78	6.70	7.76	8.22	5.92	6.00
40–44	11.07	13.41	9.83	2.64	6.55	5.96	7.54	6.77	4.78
45–49	6.47	11.90	13.03	3.42	4.58	5.97	6.32	7.14	5.50
50–54	4.43	8.16	10.45	7.08	2.18	5.49	4.74	6.13	6.40
55–59	2.89	5.07	8.75	8.04	2.50	3.49	5.08	5.11	6.54
60–64	2.89	5.08	5.83	5.81	4.55	1.74	4.25	3.33	5.55
65–69	0.60	2.14	2.90	4.25	5.46	1.46	2.48	3.37	4.24
70–74	0.25	0.89	2.48	2.65	2.90	2.34	1.05	2.76	2.90
75–79	0.05	0.17	0.56	1.52	1.86	2.36	0.79	1.10	4.02[b]
80–84	0.02	0.04	0.16	0.51	0.75	1.13	0.86	0.44	b
85 +	0.00	0.03	0.10	0.34	0.48	0.71	0.69	0.32	b
Unknown	0.39	0.03	0.06	0.05	0.04	0.00	0.00	0.00	0.00
Total	100.00	100.00	100.00	100.00	100.00	100.00	100.00	100.00	100.00
Females									
0–4	18.03	16.77	19.55	15.25	8.32	12.59	10.91	7.58	5.39
5–9	21.32	19.84	16.95	16.57	11.05	9.68	11.32	9.21	5.10
10–14	8.70	16.90	12.64	14.72	13.71	7.63	11.13	10.66	6.59
15–19	10.14	9.94	12.28	11.47	13.77	8.80	7.72	9.51	8.25
20–24	10.54	6.50	10.19	8.83	12.08	10.19	4.90	8.27	9.09
25–29	10.13	7.27	6.88	8.26	9.10	10.68	6.13	5.64	8.95
30–34	8.30	5.94	4.74	6.98	7.17	9.68	8.45	5.58	8.67
35–39	5.24	6.23	4.96	4.96	7.06	7.26	8.55	5.87	6.12
40–44	3.40	4.06	3.89	3.32	5.29	5.62	7.89	7.22	5.06
45–49	1.56	2.59	3.20	3.03	3.80	5.47	5.79	7.73	5.63
50–54	1.14	1.90	1.92	2.23	2.47	4.36	4.73	6.41	6.66
55–59	0.66	0.93	1.19	2.07	2.12	2.73	4.52	4.70	6.56
60–64	0.35	0.49	0.86	1.07	1.46	1.79	3.29	3.55	5.72
65–69	0.17	0.33	0.40	0.56	1.45	1.43	2.02	3.37	4.30
70–74	0.09	0.18	0.22	0.37	0.61	0.82	1.10	2.46	2.93
75–79	0.06	0.07	0.07	0.15	0.27	0.70	0.81	1.14	4.98[b]
80–84	0.03	0.04	0.04	0.10	0.17	0.42	0.39	0.68	b
85 +	0.00	0.02	0.01	0.04	0.06	0.15	0.35	0.42	b
Unknown	0.14	0.00	0.01	0.02	0.04	0.00	0.00	0.00	0.00
Total	100.00	100.00	100.00	100.00	100.00	100.00	100.00	100.00	100.00

[a]Age adjustments: 1900, ages 0–9, above age 25; 1920, above age 35; 1930, above age 35; 1940, above age 75.

[b]Includes age 75 + .

Table 3–3.c. Filipino Ethnic Population by Age, Sex, and Percentage Distribution, Hawai'i, 1910–1980

Age	1910[a]	1920[b]	1930[b]	1940[b]	1950	1960	1970	1980
Males								
0–4	NA	956	2,854	2,431	3,394	4,620	5,840	6,562
5–9		614	1,825	2,424	2,899	4,056	5,868	6,599
10–14		320	956	1,996	2,616	3,369	6,027	6,519
15–19		660	3,308	1,229	2,321	2,791	4,630	6,495
20–24		5,441	13,696	1,131	2,369	1,783	2,957	5,572
25–29		4,347	12,057	7,662	2,689	1,724	3,136	5,621
30–34		2,033	7,911	8,324	2,119	2,242	2,859	4,812
35–39		1,117	5,226	6,442	6,307	2,208	2,251	4,197
40–44		509	2,380	4,131	6,318	1,737	2,592	3,273
45–49		445	1,290	2,777	5,373	4,983	2,584	2,679
50–54		191	555	1,212	3,258	5,361	1,730	2,956
55–59		109	289	607	2,147	4,429	4,286	3,001
60–64		42	113	232	1,027	2,471	4,093	1,952
65–69		36	61	116	488	1,500	2,426	3,428
70–74		14	24	29	127	659	1,260	3,284
75–79		3	9	15	62	263	837	2,888[c]
80–84		2	3	7	24	74	230	c
85 +		0	1	1	9	69	183	c
Unknown		12	8	25	0	0	0	0
Subtotal	2,135	16,851	52,566	40,791	43,547	44,339	53,789	69,838
Females								
0–4	NA	989	2,858	2,238	3,256	4,465	5,302	6,090
5–9		552	1,794	2,296	2,705	3,756	5,649	6,128
10–14		241	930	2,046	2,381	3,241	5,540	6,039
15–19		258	566	1,206	2,228	2,529	4,119	6,493
20–24		721	792	713	1,878	1,779	3,272	6,076
25–29		643	1,388	563	1,259	1,985	3,419	6,052
30–34		313	852	667	741	1,907	3,213	5,331
35–39		237	654	871	665	1,358	2,565	4,430
40–44		113	312	494	601	834	2,425	3,672
45–49		61	175	353	805	686	2,070	3,256
50–54		29	83	159	456	666	1,068	3,167
55–59		10	38	92	262	694	848	2,545
60–64		5	18	43	135	404	617	1,696
65–69		3	11	20	81	246	816	1,230
70–74		2	5	8	34	101	320	864
75–79		2	5	4	10	49	142	1,033[c]
80–84		0	2	2	8	14	82	c
85 +		0	2	2	10	17	98	c
Unknown		1	1	1	0	0	0	0
Subtotal	226	4,180	10,486	11,778	17,515	24,731	41,565	64,102
Total	2,361	21,031	63,052	52,569	61,062	69,070	95,354	133,940

Sources: See Table 3–3.a.

Note: See Note, Table 3–3.a.

NA Not available.

				Distribution (percent)				
Age	1910	1920	1930	1940	1950	1960	1970	1980
Males								
0–4	NA	5.67	5.43	5.96	7.79	10.42	10.86	9.40
5–9		3.64	3.47	5.94	6.66	9.14	10.91	9.45
10–14		1.90	1.82	4.89	6.01	7.60	11.20	9.33
15–19		3.92	6.29	3.01	5.33	6.29	8.61	9.31
20–24		32.29	26.06	2.77	5.44	4.02	5.49	7.96
25–29		25.80	22.94	18.79	6.17	3.89	5.83	8.05
30–34		12.06	15.05	20.41	4.87	5.06	5.32	6.80
35–39		6.63	9.94	15.79	14.48	4.98	4.18	6.01
40–44		3.02	4.53	10.13	14.51	3.92	4.82	4.60
45–49		2.64	2.45	6.81	12.34	11.24	4.80	3.84
50–54		1.13	1.06	2.97	7.48	12.09	3.22	4.23
55–59		0.65	0.55	1.49	4.93	9.99	7.97	4.29
60–64		0.25	0.21	0.57	2.36	5.57	7.61	2.80
65–69		0.22	0.11	0.28	1.12	3.38	4.51	4.90
70–74		0.08	0.05	0.07	0.29	1.49	2.34	4.70
75–79		0.02	0.01	0.04	0.14	0.59	1.56	4.13[c]
80–84		0.01	0.01	0.02	0.06	0.17	0.43	c
85 +		0.00	0.00	0.00	0.02	0.16	0.34	c
Unknown		0.07	0.02	0.06	0.00	0.00	0.00	0.00
Total		100.00	100.00	100.00	100.00	100.00	100.00	100.00
Females								
0–4	NA	23.66	27.26	19.00	18.59	18.05	12.76	9.50
5–9		13.21	17.11	19.49	15.44	15.19	13.59	9.56
10–14		5.77	8.86	17.37	13.59	13.11	13.33	9.42
15–19		6.17	5.40	10.24	12.72	10.23	9.91	10.12
20–24		17.25	7.55	6.05	10.72	7.19	7.87	9.48
25–29		15.38	13.24	4.78	7.19	8.03	8.23	9.44
30–34		7.49	8.13	5.66	4.23	7.71	7.73	8.32
35–39		5.67	6.24	7.40	3.80	5.49	6.17	6.91
40–44		2.70	2.97	4.19	3.43	3.37	5.83	5.73
45–49		1.46	1.67	3.00	4.60	2.77	4.98	5.08
50–54		0.69	0.79	1.35	2.60	2.69	2.57	4.94
55–59		0.24	0.36	0.78	1.50	2.81	2.04	3.97
60–64		0.12	0.17	0.37	0.77	1.63	1.48	2.65
65–69		0.07	0.10	0.17	0.46	0.99	1.96	1.92
70–74		0.05	0.05	0.07	0.19	0.41	0.77	1.35
75–79		0.05	0.05	0.03	0.06	0.20	0.34	1.61[c]
80–84		0.00	0.02	0.02	0.05	0.06	0.20	c
85 +		0.00	0.02	0.02	0.06	0.07	0.24	c
Unknown		0.02	0.01	0.01	0.00	0.00	0.00	0.00
Total		100.00	100.00	100.00	100.00	100.00	100.00	100.00

[a]In 1900 and 1910, Filipinos were included in the category of "Other."

[b]Age adjustments: 1920, above age 35; 1930, above age 35; 1940, above age 75.

[c]Includes age 75 + .

Table 3–3.d. Hawaiian Ethnic Population by Age, Sex, and Percentage Distribution, Hawai'i, 1900–1980

Age	Age and Sex								
	1900[a]	1910	1920[a]	1930[a]	1940[a]	1950	1960	1970[b]	1980[b]
Males									
0–4	1,720	1,368	1,266	1,247	556	397	425	NA	NA
5–9	1,575	1,253	1,219	1,230	631	536	456		
10–14	1,528	1,307	1,122	1,161	705	591	470		
15–19	1,619	1,343	1,091	1,127	647	537	487		
20–24	1,160	1,129	1,038	952	688	486	409		
25–29	1,265	1,123	961	760	636	461	384		
30–34	943	837	770	728	543	527	434		
35–39	1,204	1,043	913	788	477	527	439		
40–44	847	734	630	669	502	455	421		
45–49	852	841	801	738	505	437	462		
50–54	647	638	567	446	438	375	399		
55–59	634	611	541	487	330	354	329		
60–64	422	407	394	350	237	256	306		
65–69	375	270	304	258	230	203	215		
70–74	281	202	193	161	143	81	109		
75–79	207	149	85	102	75	68	75		
80–84	113	81	42	46	31	41	26		
85 +	136	98	49	49	31	19	22		
Unknown	114	5	4	12	8	0	0		
Subtotal	15,642	13,439	11,990	11,311	7,413	6,351	5,868		
Females									
0–4	1,612	1,345	1,298	1,228	522	415	446	NA	NA
5–9	1,506	1,256	1,209	1,201	614	479	398		
10–14	1,390	1,221	1,207	1,222	728	559	485		
15–19	1,477	1,314	1,100	1,071	631	486	480		
20–24	1,369	1,138	1,102	1,031	586	442	326		
25–29	1,211	1,090	1,059	915	587	375	351		
30–34	1,053	947	819	794	529	479	385		
35–39	1,037	1,006	838	856	547	475	399		
40–44	756	734	709	662	457	419	391		
45–49	645	734	723	635	477	434	408		
50–54	531	604	481	512	360	432	337		
55–59	466	438	391	455	335	315	351		
60–64	260	244	306	240	176	213	237		
65–69	256	186	211	195	179	157	196		
70–74	190	138	117	125	114	107	116		
75–79	121	88	75	85	64	66	72		
80–84	80	58	45	45	30	18	28		
85 +	69	50	37	36	24	23	20		
Unknown	128	11	6	17	2	0	0		
Subtotal	14,157	12,602	11,733	11,325	6,962	5,894	5,426		
Total	29,799	26,041	23,723	22,636	14,375	12,245	11,294		

Sources: See Table 3–3.a.

Note: See Note, Table 3–3.a.

NA Not available.

	Distribution (percent)								
Age	1900	1910	1920	1930	1940	1950	1960	1970	1980
Males									
0–4	11.00	10.18	10.55	11.02	7.50	6.25	7.24	NA	NA
5–9	10.07	9.32	10.16	10.87	8.51	8.44	7.77		
10–14	9.77	9.73	9.36	10.27	9.51	9.31	8.01		
15–19	10.35	9.99	9.10	9.96	8.73	8.46	8.30		
20–24	7.41	8.40	8.66	8.42	9.28	7.65	6.97		
25–29	8.09	8.35	8.02	6.72	8.58	7.26	6.54		
30–34	6.03	6.23	6.42	6.44	7.32	8.30	7.40		
35–39	7.70	7.76	7.62	6.97	6.44	8.30	7.48		
40–44	5.41	5.46	5.25	5.92	6.77	7.16	7.17		
45–49	5.44	6.26	6.68	6.52	6.81	6.88	7.88		
50–54	4.14	4.75	4.73	3.94	5.91	5.90	6.80		
55–59	4.05	4.55	4.51	4.31	4.45	5.57	5.61		
60–64	2.70	3.03	3.29	3.09	3.20	4.03	5.21		
65–69	2.40	2.01	2.54	2.28	3.10	3.20	3.66		
70–74	1.80	1.50	1.61	1.42	1.93	1.27	1.86		
75–79	1.32	1.11	0.71	0.90	1.01	1.07	1.28		
80–84	0.72	0.60	0.35	0.41	0.42	0.65	0.44		
85 +	0.87	0.73	0.41	0.43	0.42	0.30	0.38		
Unknown	0.73	0.04	0.03	0.11	0.11	0.00	0.00		
Total	100.00	100.00	10.00	100.00	100.00	100.00	100.00	100.00	100.00
Females									
0–4	11.38	10.67	11.06	10.84	7.50	7.04	8.22	NA	NA
5–9	10.64	9.97	10.30	10.60	8.82	8.13	7.33		
10–14	9.82	9.69	10.29	10.79	10.46	9.48	8.94		
15–19	10.43	10.43	9.38	9.46	9.06	8.25	8.85		
20–24	9.67	9.03	9.39	9.10	8.42	7.50	6.01		
25–29	8.55	8.65	9.03	8.08	8.43	6.36	6.47		
30–34	7.44	7.50	6.98	7.01	7.60	8.13	7.09		
35–39	7.33	7.98	7.14	7.56	7.86	8.06	7.35		
40–44	5.34	5.82	6.04	5.85	6.56	7.11	7.21		
45–49	4.56	5.82	6.16	5.61	6.85	7.36	7.52		
50–54	3.75	4.79	4.10	4.52	5.17	7.33	6.21		
55–59	3.29	3.48	3.33	4.02	4.81	5.34	6.47		
60–64	1.84	1.94	2.61	2.12	2.53	3.61	4.37		
65–69	1.81	1.48	1.80	1.72	2.57	2.66	3.61		
70–74	1.34	1.10	1.00	1.10	1.64	1.82	2.14		
75–79	0.85	0.70	0.64	0.75	0.92	1.12	1.33		
80–84	0.57	0.46	0.38	0.40	0.43	0.31	0.52		
85 +	0.49	0.40	0.32	0.32	0.34	0.39	0.36		
Unknown	0.90	0.09	0.05	0.15	0.03	0.00	0.00		
Total	100.00	100.00	100.00	100.00	100.00	100.00	100.00	100.00	100.00

[a]Age adjustments: 1900, ages 0–9, above age 25; 1920, above age 35; 1930, above age 75; 1940, above age 55.

[b]Full Hawaiians are included with "Part Hawaiians." See Table 3-3.e.

Table 3-3.e. Part Hawaiian Ethnic Population by Age, Sex, and Percentage Distribution, Hawai'i, 1900–1980

Age					Age and Sex				
	1900[a]	1910	1920[a]	1930[a]	1940[a]	1950	1960	1970[b]	1980[b]
Males									
0–4	894	1,388	2,067	3,246	4,686	7,589	8,799	4,398	6,697
5–9	711	1,104	1,754	2,689	4,209	6,618	7,672	4,756	6,241
10–14	569	926	1,274	2,113	3,832	4,765	6,469	4,770	6,590
15–19	494	789	922	1,617	3,071	3,839	5,268	3,730	6,931
20–24	322	534	686	1,075	2,229	2,880	2,873	2,265	5,366
25–29	283	415	571	814	1,778	2,579	2,801	2,753	4,832
30–34	194	285	391	617	1,278	2,168	2,600	2,117	4,046
35–39	191	261	386	564	1,034	1,768	2,339	1,990	3,478
40–44	110	151	252	375	713	1,234	1,944	1,790	2,733
45–49	78	160	253	331	671	979	1,480	1,532	2,506
50–54	50	102	140	202	422	735	1,106	1,537	2,280
55–59	42	79	142	160	319	547	761	1,097	1,887
60–64	9	16	94	81	161	325	534	805	1,382
65–69	11	24	65	75	101	210	362	579	994
70–74	3	6	13	55	74	110	171	421	630
75–79	4	8	29	19	43	50	83	235	612[c]
80–84	0	1	5	4	12	15	35	81	c
85+	0	1	4	3	8	19	17	70	c
Unknown	6	0	4	2	9	0	0	0	0
Subtotal	3,971	6,250	9,052	14,042	24,650	36,430	45,314	34,926	57,205
Females									
0–4	869	1,343	2,059	3,088	4,696	7,392	8,414	4,012	6,311
5–9	682	1,053	1,566	2,654	4,147	6,133	7,344	4,514	5,938
10–14	547	829	1,238	2,096	3,698	4,796	6,235	4,494	6,305
15–19	506	816	986	1,599	3,083	4,086	5,039	4,082	6,861
20–24	353	667	754	1,202	3,514	3,355	3,301	2,973	5,747
25–29	308	490	636	917	1,833	2,536	3,117	2,766	4,909
30–34	176	279	502	663	1,385	2,382	2,866	2,466	4,071
35–39	177	282	411	620	1,111	1,852	2,456	2,087	3,602
40–44	96	152	249	412	779	1,479	2,072	1,984	2,867
45–49	57	127	206	327	701	1,072	1,546	1,737	2,609
50–54	50	113	123	216	480	851	1,178	1,454	2,493
55–59	26	46	94	150	332	571	815	1,495	2,014
60–64	13	22	77	106	234	385	566	838	1,591
65–69	6	14	37	61	126	259	397	691	1,223
70–74	6	15	17	40	83	130	234	361	828
75–79	2	6	9	17	50	79	134	195	926[c]
80–84	1	0	4	7	20	28	53	100	c
85+	0	1	2	6	10	29	28	99	c
Unknown	11	1	5	1	3	0	0	0	0
Subtotal	3,886	6,256	8,975	14,182	25,285	37,415	45,795	36,348	58,295
Total	7,857	12,506	18,027	28,224	49,935	73,845	91,109	71,274	115,500

Sources: See Table 3-3.a.

Note: See Note, Table 3-3.a. The Hawaii Health Surveillance Program in 1980 counted 176,713 Part Hawaiians (87,483 males and 89,230 females).

[a]Age adjustments: 1900, ages 0–9, above age 25; 1920, above age 35; 1930, above age 75; 1940, above age 55.

				Distribution (percent)					
Age	1900	1910	1920	1930	1940	1950	1960	1970	1980
Males									
0–4	22.51	22.21	22.83	23.12	19.01	20.83	19.42	12.59	11.70
5–9	17.91	17.66	19.38	19.15	17.08	18.17	16.93	13.62	10.90
10–14	14.32	14.82	14.07	15.04	15.55	13.08	14.27	13.66	11.52
15–19	12.44	12.62	10.19	11.52	12.46	10.53	11.62	10.68	12.12
20–24	8.11	8.54	7.58	7.65	9.04	7.91	6.34	6.49	9.38
25–29	7.12	6.64	6.31	5.80	7.21	7.08	6.18	7.88	8.45
30–34	4.84	4.56	4.32	4.39	5.18	5.95	5.74	6.06	7.07
35–39	4.81	4.18	4.26	4.02	4.19	4.85	5.16	5.70	6.08
40–44	2.79	2.41	2.79	2.67	2.89	3.39	4.29	5.12	4.78
45–49	1.96	2.56	2.79	2.36	2.72	2.69	3.27	4.39	4.38
50–54	1.26	1.63	1.55	1.44	1.71	2.02	2.44	4.40	3.99
55–59	1.06	1.26	1.57	1.14	1.29	1.50	1.68	3.14	3.30
60–64	0.22	0.26	1.04	0.58	0.66	0.89	1.18	2.30	2.42
65–69	0.28	0.38	0.72	0.53	0.41	0.58	0.80	1.66	1.74
70–74	0.08	0.10	0.14	0.39	0.30	0.30	0.38	1.21	1.10
75–79	0.09	0.13	0.32	0.14	0.17	0.14	0.18	0.67	1.07[c]
80–84	0.00	0.02	0.06	0.03	0.06	0.04	0.08	0.23	c
85 +	0.00	0.02	0.04	0.02	0.03	0.05	0.04	0.20	c
Unknown	0.15	0.00	0.04	0.01	0.04	0.00	0.00	0.00	0.00
Total	100.00	100.00	100.00	100.00	100.00	100.00	100.00	100.00	100.00
Females									
0–4	22.36	21.46	22.94	21.77	18.57	19.76	18.37	11.04	10.83
5–9	17.55	16.83	17.45	18.71	16.40	16.39	16.04	12.42	10.19
10–14	14.08	13.25	13.79	14.78	14.63	12.82	13.61	12.37	10.82
15–19	13.02	13.04	10.99	11.27	12.19	10.92	11.00	11.23	11.77
20–24	9.08	10.66	8.40	8.48	9.94	8.97	7.21	8.18	9.86
25–29	7.93	7.83	7.09	6.47	7.25	6.78	6.81	7.61	8.42
30–34	4.53	4.46	5.59	4.67	5.48	6.37	6.26	6.78	6.98
35–39	4.55	4.51	4.58	4.37	4.37	4.39	4.95	5.36	5.74	6.18
40–44	2.48	2.43	2.77	2.91	3.08	3.95	4.52	5.45	4.92
45–49	1.47	2.03	2.30	2.31	2.77	2.86	3.38	4.78	4.47
50–54	1.28	1.81	1.36	1.52	1.90	2.27	2.57	4.00	4.28
55–59	0.67	0.74	1.05	1.06	1.31	1.53	1.78	4.11	3.45
60–64	0.33	0.35	0.86	0.75	0.93	1.03	1.24	2.31	2.72
65–69	0.15	0.22	0.41	0.43	0.50	0.69	0.87	1.90	2.10
70–74	0.15	0.24	0.19	0.28	0.33	0.35	0.51	0.99	1.42
75–79	0.06	0.10	0.10	0.12	0.20	0.21	0.29	0.54	1.59[c]
80–84	0.03	0.00	0.05	0.05	0.08	0.07	0.12	0.28	c
85 +	0.00	0.02	0.02	0.04	0.04	0.08	0.06	0.27	c
Unknown	0.28	0.02	0.00	0.01	0.01	0.00	0.00	0.00	0.00
Total	100.00	100.00	100.00	100.00	100.00	100.00	100.00	100.00	100.00

[b]In 1970 and 1980, the U.S. census classified by self-identification of race or by race of father in 1970 or by race of mother in 1980. Many persons who would have been tabulated as Part Hawaiian under the definitions of earlier years were counted in 1970 and 1980 as White, Chinese, or some other race. Therefore, figures for 1970 and 1980 are not directly comparable with those for other years. See Table 3-3.d. for pure Hawaiian population.

[c]Includes age 75 + .

193

Table 3–3.f. Japanese Ethnic Population by Age, Sex, and Percentage Distribution, Hawai'i, 1900–1980

Age				Age and Sex					
Age	1900[a]	1910	1920[a]	1930[a]	1940[a]	1950	1960	1970	1980
Males									
0–4	1,720	4,945	9,552	11,149	7,327	11,315	10,897	7,240	5,998
5–9	1,228	3,532	6,842	11,795	9,067	9,443	11,403	9,222	6,449
10–14	219	1,655	4,499	9,483	11,329	7,561	10,866	10,561	7,643
15–19	1,901	1,743	4,416	6,722	11,364	8,704	8,393	10,347	9,395
20–24	9,791	7,707	3,320	4,335	9,192	8,988	4,606	7,481	10,075
25–29	10,128	7,457	2,391	4,193	6,474	9,657	5,788	6,958	10,469
30–34	12,176	8,965	6,730	3,168	4,353	8,315	8,064	5,418	9,624
35–39	5,137	7,749	5,786	2,161	4,084	6,235	9,064	6,124	7,471
40–44	3,752	5,659	6,728	5,617	2,978	4,301	8,023	8,252	5,778
45–49	849	3,093	5,294	4,353	1,975	4,015	5,841	8,592	6,444
50–54	414	1,508	3,732	4,784	4,618	2,740	4,153	7,860	8,249
55–59	73	424	2,006	3,463	3,223	1,712	3,644	5,303	8,770
60–64	47	274	966	2,269	3,157	3,949	2,416	3,719	7,281
65–69	9	53	214	954	2,045	2,442	1,432	2,769	4,913
70–74	1	7	131	447	1,048	2,047	2,810	2,074	3,115
75–79	0	3	11	57	341	1,163	1,441	844	4,289[b]
80–84	63	1	3	19	129	479	847	1,494	b
85+	0	2	7	24	94	180	447	818	b
Unknown	0	7	16	15	22	0	0	0	0
Subtotal	47,508	54,784	62,644	75,008	82,820	93,246	100,135	105,076	115,963
Females									
0–4	1,628	4,855	9,237	10,636	7,089	10,789	10,361	6,960	5,811
5–9	1,138	3,393	6,682	11,474	8,837	9,049	10,969	9,187	6,228
10–14	153	1,443	4,125	9,111	10,838	3,347	10,474	10,563	7,367
15–19	599	941	3,439	6,445	10,956	8,826	8,355	10,488	9,079
20–24	2,872	2,457	4,270	3,984	8,927	10,477	5,465	8,803	9,999
25–29	2,757	3,299	4,785	4,109	6,017	10,474	7,227	6,716	10,153
30–34	2,955	3,536	3,941	4,235	3,715	8,518	9,935	6,101	9,519
35–39	895	2,600	3,200	4,042	3,831	5,892	10,040	8,183	7,609
40–44	498	1,448	3,292	3,214	3,730	3,651	8,099	10,069	6,546
45–49	70	632	1,932	2,433	3,400	3,657	5,641	9,495	8,492
50–54	23	204	1,057	2,359	2,567	3,443	3,549	7,861	10,507
55–59	6	56	455	1,413	1,898	3,030	3,449	5,078	9,902
60–64	2	21	156	750	1,671	2,267	3,136	3,470	7,768
65–69	2	1	32	276	934	1,638	2,579	3,196	5,231
70–74	0	1	14	106	462	1,253	1,804	2,675	3,107
75–79	0	1	4	15	120	666	1,167	1,981	6,467[b]
80–84	0	1	3	10	66	285	734	997	b
85+	0	0	0	2	13	90	336	770	b
Unknown	5	2	6	9	14	0	0	0	0
Subtotal	13,603	24,891	46,630	64,623	75,085	91,352	103,320	112,593	123,785
Total	61,111	79,675	109,274	139,631	157,905	184,598	203,455	217,669	239,748

Sources: See Table 3–3.a.

Note: See Note, Table 3–3.a.

				Distribution (percent)				
Age	1900	1910	1920	1930	1940	1950	1960	1970	1980
Males									
0–4	3.62	9.03	15.25	14.86	8.85	12.13	10.88	6.89	5.17
5–9	2.58	6.45	10.92	15.72	10.95	10.12	11.39	8.77	5.56
10–14	0.47	3.02	7.18	12.64	13.68	8.11	10.85	10.05	6.59
15–19	4.00	3.18	7.05	8.96	13.72	9.33	8.38	9.85	8.10
20–24	20.61	14.07	5.30	5.80	11.09	9.64	4.60	7.12	8.69
25–29	21.32	13.61	3.82	5.59	7.82	10.36	5.78	6.62	9.03
30–34	25.63	16.37	10.74	4.22	5.25	8.92	8.05	5.16	8.30
35–39	10.81	14.14	9.24	2.88	4.93	6.68	9.05	5.83	6.44
40–44	7.90	10.33	10.74	7.49	3.60	4.61	8.01	7.85	4.98
45–49	1.79	5.65	18.45	5.80	2.38	4.30	5.83	8.18	5.55
50–54	0.87	2.75	5.96	6.38	5.58	2.94	4.15	7.48	7.11
55–59	0.15	0.77	3.20	4.62	3.89	1.84	3.64	5.05	7.56
60–64	0.10	0.50	1.54	3.02	3.81	4.24	2.41	3.54	6.29
65–69	0.01	0.10	0.34	1.27	2.47	2.62	1.43	2.64	4.24
70–74	0.01	0.01	0.21	0.60	1.27	2.20	2.81	1.97	2.69
75–79	0.00	0.01	0.01	0.08	0.41	1.25	1.44	0.80	3.70[b]
80–84	0.13	0.00	0.01	0.03	0.16	0.51	0.85	1.42	[b]
85 +	0.00	0.00	0.01	0.02	0.11	0.19	0.45	0.78	[b]
Unknown	0.00	0.01	0.03	0.02	0.03	0.00	0.00	0.00	0.00
Total	100.00	100.00	100.00	100.00	100.00	100.00	100.00	100.00	100.00
Females									
0–4	11.97	19.51	19.81	16.46	9.44	11.81	10.02	6.18	4.09
5–9	8.36	13.63	14.33	17.76	11.77	9.91	10.61	8.16	5.03
10–14	1.13	5.80	8.85	14.10	14.43	8.04	10.13	9.38	5.95
15–19	4.40	3.78	7.36	9.96	14.59	9.66	8.08	9.32	7.33
20–24	21.11	9.87	9.16	6.17	11.89	11.47	5.29	7.82	8.08
25–29	20.27	13.25	10.27	6.36	8.01	11.47	7.00	5.96	8.20
30–34	21.72	14.21	8.45	6.55	4.94	9.32	9.62	5.42	7.69
35–39	6.58	10.45	6.86	6.25	5.10	6.45	9.72	7.27	6.15
40–44	3.66	5.82	7.06	4.97	4.97	4.00	7.84	8.94	5.29
45–49	0.51	2.54	4.14	3.76	4.53	4.00	5.46	8.43	6.86
50–54	0.17	0.82	2.27	3.65	3.42	3.77	3.43	6.98	8.49
55–59	0.04	0.22	0.98	2.19	2.53	3.32	3.34	4.51	8.00
60–64	0.02	0.08	0.33	1.16	2.23	2.48	3.04	3.08	6.28
65–69	0.01	0.01	0.07	0.43	1.24	1.79	2.50	2.84	4.23
70–74	0.01	0.00	0.03	0.16	0.62	1.37	1.75	2.38	2.51
75–79	0.00	0.00	0.01	0.02	0.16	0.73	1.13	1.76	5.22[b]
80–84	0.00	0.00	0.01	0.02	0.09	0.31	0.71	0.89	[b]
85 +	0.00	0.00	0.00	0.00	0.02	0.10	0.33	0.68	[b]
Unknown	0.04	0.01	0.01	0.01	0.02	0.00	0.00	0.00	0.00
Total	100.00	100.00	100.00	100.00	100.00	100.00	100.00	100.00	100.00

[a]Age adjustments: 1900, ages 0–9, above age 25; 1920, above age 35; 1930, above age 35; 1940, above age 75.

[b]Includes age 75 + .

Table 3–3.g. Korean Ethnic Population by Age, Sex, and Percentage Distribution, Hawai'i, 1910–1980

Age	Age and Sex							
	1910	1920	1930	1940	1950	1960	1970	1980
Males								
0–4	140	398	464	NA	NA	NA	400	557
5–9	91	209	530				471	647
10–14	65	123	401				628	720
15–19	81	78	222				433	762
20–24	255	52	120				306	632
25–29	889	68	76				286	580
30–34	994	301	55				143	609
35–39	636	624	61				269	550
40–44	394	700	266		b		315	434
45–49	210	432	526				456	408
50–54	78	269	589				259	424
55–59	40	141	346				126	451
60–64	44	53	214				123	325
65–69	9	18	81				72	171
70–74	2	18	30				68	114
75–79	0	4	8				17	111[c]
80–84	0	0	5				36	c
85+	1	0	4				106	c
Unknown	2	10	1					0
Subtotal	3,931	3,498	3,999	3,965	3,849	NA	4,514	7,495
Females								
0–4	123	375	456	NA	NA	NA	375	615
5–9	99	183	509				507	655
10–14	45	123	407				579	664
15–19	32	84	176				383	783
20–24	42	237	121				478	977
25–29	60	99	152				339	1,168
30–34	56	77	235				315	1,267
35–39	43	71	91				311	918
40–44	37	66	70		b		523	718
45–49	23	46	71				367	634
50–54	20	38	65				297	559
55–59	6	20	40				148	482
60–64	6	18	33				115	375
65–69	6	7	17				162	222
70–74	3	6	14				119	165
75–79	1	2	5				36	265[c]
80–84	0	0	0				30	c
85+	0	0	0				27	c
Unknown	0	0	0					0
Subtotal	602	1,452	2,462	2,886	3,181	NA	5,111	10,467
Total	4,533	4,950	6,461	6,851	7,030	NA	9,625	17,962

Sources: See Table 3–3.a.

Note: See Note, Table 3–3.a.

NA Not available.

	Distribution (percent)					
Age	1910	1920	1930	1940–60	1970	1980
Males						
0–4	3.56	11.38	11.60	NA	8.86	7.43
5–9	2.31	5.97	13.25		10.43	8.63
10–14	1.65	3.52	10.03		13.91	9.61
15–19	2.06	2.23	5.55		9.59	10.18
20–24	6.49	1.49	3.00		6.78	8.42
25–29	22.62	1.94	1.90		6.34	7.74
30–34	25.29	8.61	1.38		3.17	8.13
35–39	16.18	17.83	1.53		5.96	7.34
40–44	10.02	20.02	6.65	b	6.98	5.79
45–49	5.34	12.35	13.15		10.10	5.44
50–54	1.98	7.69	14.73		5.74	5.66
55–59	1.02	4.03	8.65		2.79	6.01
60–64	1.12	1.52	5.35		2.72	4.34
65–69	0.23	0.51	2.03		1.59	2.28
70–74	0.05	0.51	0.75		1.51	1.52
75–79	0.00	0.11	0.45		0.38	1.48[c]
80–84	0.00	0.00	0.00		0.80	c
85 +	0.03	0.00	0.00		2.35	c
Unknown	0.05	0.29	0.02		0.00	0.00
Total	100.00	100.00	100.00	NA	100.00	100.00
Females						
0–4	20.43	25.83	18.52	NA	7.34	5.88
5–9	16.45	12.60	20.67		9.93	6.26
10–14	7.47	8.47	16.53		11.34	6.34
15–19	5.32	5.78	7.15		7.49	7.48
20–24	6.98	16.32	4.91		9.35	9.34
25–29	9.96	6.82	6.17		6.63	11.16
30–34	9.30	5.30	9.55		6.16	12.10
35–39	7.14	4.89	3.70		6.08	8.77
40–44	6.15	4.55	2.84	b	10.23	6.86
45–49	3.82	3.17	2.89		7.18	6.06
50–54	3.32	2.61	2.64		5.81	5.34
55–59	1.00	1.38	1.63		2.90	4.60
60–64	1.00	1.24	1.34		2.25	3.58
65–69	1.00	0.49	0.69		3.17	2.12
70–74	0.50	0.41	0.57		2.32	1.58
75–79	0.16	0.14	0.20		0.70	2.53[c]
80–84	0.00	0.00	0.00		0.59	c
85 +	0.00	0.00	0.00		0.53	c
Unknown	0.00	0.00	0.00		0.00	0.00
Total	100.00	100.00	100.00	NA	100.00	100.00

[a]Age adjustments: 1920, above age 35; 1930, above age 35.

[b]Between 1940 and 1960 the Korean population was not tabulated separately by the U.S. census, and Koreans were included in the category "Other."

[c]Includes age 75 + .

Table 3–3.h. Samoan Ethnic Population by Age, Sex, and Percentage Distribution, Hawai'i, 1980

Age	1980[a] Age and Sex	Distribution (percent)
Males		
0–4	1,096	15.76
5–9	1,016	14.61
10–14	929	13.36
15–19	892	12.83
20–24	593	8.53
25–29	569	8.18
30–34	456	6.56
35–39	356	5.12
40–44	272	3.91
45–49	216	3.11
50–54	162	2.33
55–59	152	2.19
60–64	101	1.45
65–69	73	1.05
70–74	34	.49
75 +	36	.52
Subtotal	6,953	100.00
Females		
0–4	1,061	14.91
5–9	938	13.14
10–14	1,011	14.21
15–19	862	12.12
20–24	664	9.33
25–29	598	8.40
30–34	461	6.47
35–39	354	4.97
40–44	309	4.34
45–49	244	3.43
50–54	193	2.71
55–59	145	2.04
60–64	108	1.52
65–69	85	1.19
70–74	35	.49
75 +	52	.73
Subtotal	7,120	100.00
Total	14,073	

Source: See Table 3–3.a.

Note: See Note, Table 3–3.a.

[a]Between 1920 and 1970, Samoans were included in the category "Other."

Table 3–3.i. Vietnamese Ethnic Population by Age, Sex, and Percentage Distribution, Hawai'i, 1980

Age	1980[a] Age and Sex	Distribution (percent)
Males		
0–4	147	9.68
5–9	207	13.64
10–14	222	14.62
15–19	250	16.47
20–24	179	11.79
25–29	165	10.87
30–34	81	5.34
35–39	79	5.20
40–44	44	2.90
45–49	35	2.31
50–54	36	2.37
55–59	23	1.52
60–64	17	1.12
65–69	14	.92
70–74	15	.99
75 +	4	.26
Subtotal	1,518	100.00
Females		
0–4	123	6.32
5–9	204	10.49
10–14	185	9.51
15–19	211	10.85
20–24	192	9.87
25–29	281	14.46
30–34	278	14.30
35–39	169	8.69
40–44	83	4.27
45–49	56	2.88
50–54	38	1.95
55–59	36	1.85
60–64	31	1.59
65–69	24	1.23
70–74	25	1.28
75 +	9	.46
Subtotal	1,945	100.00
Total	3,463	

Sources: See Table 3–3.a; Hawaii (State) DPED 1985, Statistical Report No. 180, p. 2.

Note: See Note, Table 3–3.a.

[a]Vietnamese refugees arrived in Hawai'i during the 1970s.

Table 3-3j. White Ethnic population by Age, Sex, and Percentage Distribution, Hawaii'i, 1900-1980[a]

				Age and Sex					
Age	1900[b]	1910	1920[b]	1930[b]	1940[b]	1950	1960	1970	1980
Males									
0-4	2,082	3,360	3,757	3,765	3,504	6,629	13,065	14,559	12,785
5-9	1,900	2,584	3,512	3,957	3,281	4,412	10,322	16,325	11,346
10-14	1,705	2,213	2,851	3,517	3,288	2,903	8,580	15,592	10,988
15-19	1,357	2,276	3,346	4,948	7,177	5,622	11,324	14,670	14,552
20-24	1,433	2,836	3,434	10,492	16,400	9,804	18,224	28,444	26,086
25-29	1,508	2,506	2,596	6,328	8,711	7,781	9,713	15,020	19,635
30-34	1,223	2,031	2,244	3,627	5,640	7,551	8,641	10,643	18,075
35-39	1,373	1,754	2,095	3,132	4,567	5,772	8,723	10,213	13,037
40-44	1,011	1,291	1,634	2,388	3,343	4,095	7,353	8,589	8,666
45-49	910	1,126	1,542	1,979	2,744	3,207	5,210	7,989	6,881
50-54	701	867	971	1,472	2,019	2,427	3,717	7,076	6,675
55-59	422	598	738	970	1,372	1,890	2,812	4,738	6,748
60-64	466	660	692	783	965	1,377	1,919	3,378	5,783
65-69	188	330	500	600	667	892	1,422	2,481	4,298
70-74	108	190	285	370	376	534	982	1,341	2,787
75-79	57	101	188	230	235	295	539	874	1,550
80-84	13	23	51	73	87	126	238	369	743
85+	13	23	46	60	66	88	131	357	429
Unknown	61	13	23	15	31	0	0	0	0
Subtotal	16,531	24,782	30,505	48,706	64,473	65,405	112,915	162,658	171,064
Females									
0-4	2,043	3,346	3,617	3,704	3,272	6,099	12,689	14,226	11,998
5-9	1,896	2,620	3,250	3,770	3,227	4,251	10,041	15,248	10,749
10-14	1,549	2,047	2,891	3,434	3,258	2,824	8,112	14,401	10,312
15-19	1,262	2,109	2,303	3,053	3,345	2,575	5,790	11,852	11,312
20-24	1,026	1,798	2,102	2,894	3,969	4,145	7,831	15,942	16,490
25-29	976	1,668	2,120	2,967	4,504	6,127	7,697	13,684	17,457
30-34	782	1,335	1,743	2,667	4,210	5,406	7,477	9,826	15,564
35-39	759	1,163	1,677	2,483	3,316	4,385	7,651	8,535	10,989
40-44	555	849	1,203	1,757	2,697	3,480	5,648	7,332	7,126
45-49	479	683	940	1,515	2,192	2,708	4,356	7,078	5,981
50-54	385	549	670	1,072	1,663	2,230	3,418	5,818	6,328
55-59	206	360	478	739	1,231	1,691	2,538	4,292	6,359
60-64	164	288	473	590	898	1,242	2,060	3,680	5,306
65-69	84	202	311	363	614	979	1,542	2,464	4,200
70-74	50	120	209	267	422	572	1,149	1,837	3,165
75-79	34	80	144	220	260	345	719	1,294	2,020
80-84	11	25	53	96	132	204	381	719	1,333
85+	8	19	38	65	84	125	216	543	1,017
Unknown	19	5	15	11	24	0	0	0	0
Subtotal	12,288	19,266	24,237	31,667	39,318	49,388	89,315	138,771	147,706
Total	28,819	44,048	54,742	80,373	103,791	114,793	202,230	301,429	318,770

Sources: See Table 3-3.a.

Note: See Note, Table 3-3.a. After 1960, the U.S. census counted some Part Hawaiians with Whites.

				Sex Distribution (percent)					
Age	1900	1910	1920	1930	1940	1950	1960	1970	1980
Males									
0–4	13.62	13.56	12.32	7.73	5.43	10.14	11.57	8.95	7.47
5–9	10.47	10.43	11.51	8.13	5.08	6.75	9.14	10.04	6.63
10–14	10.31	8.93	9.35	7.22	5.10	4.44	7.60	9.58	6.42
15–19	8.21	9.18	10.97	10.16	11.13	8.60	10.03	9.02	8.51
20–24	8.67	11.44	11.26	21.54	25.44	14.99	16.14	17.49	15.25
25–29	9.12	10.11	8.51	12.99	13.51	11.90	8.60	9.23	11.48
30–34	7.40	8.20	7.36	7.45	8.75	11.54	7.65	6.54	10.57
35–39	8.30	7.08	6.86	6.43	7.09	8.83	7.73	6.28	7.62
40–44	6.12	5.21	5.36	4.90	5.19	6.26	6.51	5.28	5.07
45–49	5.51	4.54	4.68	4.06	4.26	4.90	4.61	4.91	4.02
50–54	4.24	3.50	3.56	3.02	3.13	3.71	3.29	4.35	3.90
55–59	2.55	2.41	2.73	1.99	2.14	2.89	2.49	2.91	3.94
60–64	2.82	2.66	1.96	1.61	1.49	2.11	1.70	2.08	3.38
65–69	1.14	1.34	1.61	1.23	0.94	1.36	1.26	1.53	2.51
70–74	0.65	0.77	0.96	0.76	0.68	0.81	0.87	0.82	1.63
75–79	0.34	0.41	0.61	0.47	0.36	0.45	0.48	0.54	0.91
80–84	0.08	0.09	0.17	0.16	0.13	0.19	0.21	0.23	0.43
85 +	0.08	0.09	0.15	0.12	0.10	0.13	0.12	0.22	0.25
Unknown	0.37	0.05	0.07	0.03	0.05	0.00	0.00	0.00	0.00
Total	100.00	100.00	100.00	100.00	100.00	100.00	100.00	100.00	100.00
Females									
0–4	17.98	17.37	14.92	11.70	8.32	12.35	14.21	10.25	8.12
5–9	14.08	13.60	13.41	11.91	8.21	8.61	11.24	10.99	7.28
10–14	12.61	10.62	11.93	10.84	8.29	5.72	9.08	10.38	6.98
15–19	10.27	10.95	9.50	9.64	8.51	5.21	6.48	8.54	7.66
20–24	8.35	9.33	8.67	9.14	10.09	8.39	8.77	11.49	11.16
25–29	7.95	8.65	8.75	9.37	11.46	12.41	8.65	9.86	11.82
30–34	6.36	6.93	7.19	8.42	10.71	10.95	8.37	7.09	10.54
35–39	6.17	6.04	6.76	7.84	8.43	8.88	8.57	6.15	7.44
40–44	4.52	4.41	5.12	5.55	6.86	7.05	6.32	5.28	4.82
45–49	3.90	3.55	3.78	4.78	5.58	5.48	4.87	5.10	4.05
50–54	3.13	2.85	2.86	3.38	4.23	4.52	3.83	4.19	4.28
55–59	1.68	1.87	2.21	2.33	3.26	3.42	2.84	3.09	4.31
60–64	1.33	1.48	1.72	1.86	2.15	2.51	2.31	2.65	3.59
65–69	0.67	1.05	1.30	1.15	1.52	1.98	1.73	1.78	2.84
70–74	0.41	0.62	0.85	0.84	1.11	1.16	1.29	1.32	2.14
75–79	0.28	0.42	0.59	0.69	0.66	0.70	0.80	0.93	1.37
80–84	0.09	0.13	0.22	0.30	0.34	0.41	0.43	0.52	0.90
85 +	0.07	0.10	0.16	0.21	0.21	0.25	0.24	0.39	0.70
Unknown	0.15	0.03	0.06	0.05	0.06	0.00	0.00	0.00	0.00
Total	100.00	100.00	100.00	100.00	100.00	100.00	100.00	100.00	100.00

[a]Includes Portuguese, Puerto Ricans, Spaniards, and other Whites.

[b]Age adjustments: 1900, age 0–9, above age 25; 1920, above age 35; 1930, above age 75; 1940, above age 55.

Table 3–3.k. Other Ethnic Populations by Age, Sex, and Percentage Distribution, Hawai'i, 1900–1980

Age	1900[a]	1910[a]	1920[a,b]	1930[a,b]	1940[a,b,c]	1950[a,c]	1960[a]	1970[a]	1980[a]
Males									
0–4	NA	110	50	52	791	1,441	972	1,173	3,549
5–9		79	46	60	951	1,130	781	1,032	2,785
10–14		87	22	57	1,120	779	704	871	2,450
15–19		983	31	26	1,062	1,128	449	581	2,648
20–24		742	21	30	884	1,633	643	885	3,705
25–29		271	38	29	586	1,267	471	545	2,728
30–34		131	32	18	458	989	519	510	1,995
35–39		100	26	40	284	711	580	350	1,338
40–44		65	31	30	240	500	388	232	915
45–49		59	37	17	237	325	295	248	694
50–54		43	11	24	362	234	167	129	609
55–59		26	18	12	593	206	100	94	524
60–64		23	20	18	578	262	72	47	397
65–69		19	10	14	393	496	105	50	274
70–74		8	10	15	198	367	79	19	178
75–79		4	0	1	60	224	175	0	183[f]
80–84		6	4	1	31	81	158	14	f
85+		4	2	2	28	76	63	6	f
Unknown		5	0	1	1	0	0	0	0
Subtotal	421	2,765	409	447	8,857	11,849	6,721	6,786	24,972
	(263)	(215)	(191)	(125)	(4,720)	(5,967)			
					[313]	[960]			

			Distribution (percent)					
Age	1910	1920	1930	1940	1950	1960	1970	1980[a]
Males								
0–4	3.98	12.22	11.63	8.93	12.16	14.46	17.20	14.21
5–9	2.86	11.26	13.42	10.74	9.54	11.62	15.21	11.51
10–14	3.15	5.38	12.75	12.64	6.57	10.48	12.83	9.81
15–19	35.55	7.58	5.82	11.98	9.52	6.68	8.55	10.61
20–24	26.83	5.13	6.71	9.98	13.79	9.57	13.04	14.84
25–29	9.80	9.29	6.49	6.61	10.69	7.01	8.03	10.92
30–34	4.74	7.82	4.03	5.17	8.35	7.72	7.52	7.99
35–39	3.62	6.36	8.95	3.21	6.00	8.63	5.16	5.36
40–44	2.35	7.58	6.71	2.71	4.22	5.77	3.42	3.66
45–49	2.13	9.05	3.80	2.68	2.74	4.39	3.65	2.78
50–54	1.56	2.69	5.37	4.09	1.97	2.48	1.90	2.44
55–59	0.94	4.40	2.69	6.70	1.74	1.49	1.39	2.10
60–64	0.83	4.89	4.03	6.52	2.21	1.07	0.69	1.59
65–69	0.69	2.44	3.13	4.44	4.19	1.56	0.74	1.10
70–74	0.29	2.44	3.36	2.24	3.10	1.18	0.28	0.71
75–79	0.14	0.00	0.22	0.68	1.89	2.60	0.00	0.73[f]
80–84	0.22	0.98	0.22	0.35	0.68	2.35	0.21	f
85+	0.14	0.49	0.45	0.32	0.64	0.94	0.09	f
Unknown	0.18	0.00	0.22	0.01	0.00	0.00	0.00	0.00
Total	100.00	100.00	100.00	100.00	100.00	100.00	100.00	100.00

continued

Table 3-3.k. *(continued)*

Age				Age and Sex					
Age	1900[a]	1910[a]	1920[a,b]	1930[a,b]	1940[a,b,c]	1950[a,c]	1960[a]	1970[d]	1980[e]
Females									
0–4	NA	124	50	61	805	1,292	937	1,107	3,316
5–9		94	37	64	962	1,069	772	1,057	2,600
10–14		78	48	44	1,082	874	629	739	2,244
15–19		123	31	38	1,017	890	509	709	2,397
20–24		72	12	27	796	954	437	772	2,765
25–29		59	11	13	561	938	398	543	2,422
30–34		31	17	24	404	757	487	494	1,909
35–39		33	9	18	350	540	512	363	1,227
40–44		12	9	11	322	408	372	219	817
45–49		11	12	6	236	326	196	173	683
50–54		14	2	4	153	309	139	104	645
55–59		8	5	11	141	193	218	88	480
60–64		3	0	4	103	146	167	60	384
65–69		5	4	3	70	117	89	23	305
70–74		0	1	2	53	85	49	21	191
75–79		0	0	0	46	31	65	37	229[f]
80–84		0	1	2	15	38	17	11	f
85+		0	0	1	5	34	9	10	f
Unknown		0	0	0	3	0	0	0	0
Subtotal	227	667	249	333	7,124	9,001	6,002	6,530	22,614
	(152)	(161)	(119)	(92)	(4,155)	(5,202)			
					[266]	[650]			
Total	648	3,432	658	780	15,981	20,850	12,723	13,316	47,586
	(415)	(376)	(310)	(217)	(8,875)	(11,169)			
					[579]	[1,618]			

Sources: See Table 3-3.a.

Note: See Note, Table 3-3.a.

NA Not available.

[a]Refers to races such as Indian, Samoan, Micronesian and "Other." Blacks included in 1900–1950. Filipinos included in 1910, Koreans included in 1940, 1950, 1960. Subtotals and total in parentheses refer to "Other" excluding Filipinos in 1910; excluding Blacks in 1900, 1910, 1920, 1930, 1940, 1950, and excluding Koreans in 1940, 1950; includes 8,296 Puerto Ricans in 1940 and 9,551 in 1950. Puerto Ricans were counted as White since 1950.

	Distribution (percent)							
Age	1910	1920	1930	1940	1950	1960	1970	1980
Females								
0–4	18.59	20.08	18.32	11.30	14.35	15.61	16.95	14.67
5–9	14.09	14.86	19.22	13.50	11.88	12.86	16.19	11.50
10–14	11.69	19.28	13.21	15.19	9.71	10.48	11.32	9.92
15–19	18.44	12.45	11.41	14.28	9.89	8.48	10.86	10.60
20–24	10.79	4.82	8.11	11.18	10.61	7.28	11.82	12.23
25–29	8.85	4.42	3.91	7.87	10.42	6.63	8.32	10.71
30–34	4.05	6.83	7.21	5.67	8.41	8.12	7.56	8.44
35–39	4.95	3.61	5.41	4.91	6.00	8.53	5.56	5.43
40–44	1.80	3.61	3.30	4.52	4.53	6.20	3.35	3.61
45–49	1.65	4.82	1.80	3.31	3.62	3.27	2.65	3.02
50–54	2.10	0.80	1.20	2.15	3.43	2.32	1.59	2.85
55–59	1.20	2.01	3.30	1.98	2.15	3.63	1.35	2.12
60–64	0.45	0.00	1.20	1.45	1.62	2.78	0.92	1.70
65–69	0.75	1.61	0.90	0.98	1.30	1.48	0.35	1.35
70–74	0.00	0.40	0.60	0.74	0.94	0.82	0.32	0.84
75–79	0.00	0.00	0.00	0.65	0.34	1.08	0.57	1.01[f]
80–84	0.00	0.40	0.60	0.21	0.42	0.28	0.17	f
85 +	0.00	0.00	0.30	0.07	0.38	0.15	0.15	f
Unknown	0.00	0.00	0.00	0.04	0.00	0.00	0.00	0.00
Total	100.00	100.00	100.00	100.00	100.00	100.00	100.00	100.00

[b]Age adjustments: 1920, above age 35; 1930, above age 35; 1940, above age 75.

[c]Puerto Ricans were included with "Other" in 1940 and 1950. Figures in brackets exclude Puerto Ricans.

[d]Figures are overstated by census tabulation. See U.S. Bureau of Census, *Census of Population: 1970, Detailed Characteristics*. Final Report PC(1)–D13 *Hawaii*. Appendix B, p. 5.

[e]In 1980, "Other" included American Indian (2,655), Eskimo (68), Aleut (45), Asian Indian (604), Guamanian (1,677), and Other (42,537). See Table 4-2 for sample count of other ethnic groups.

[f]Includes age 75 + .

Table 3-4. Population and Percentage Distribution by Ethnicity and Counties, Hawai'i, 1970 and 1980

	State Total 1970[a]	State Total 1980[b]	Hawaii County 1970[a]	Hawaii County 1980[b]	Honolulu County 1970[a]	Honolulu County 1980[b]	Kauai County 1970[a]	Kauai County 1980[b]	Maui County 1970[a]	Maui County 1980[b]
All Races	768,561[c]	964,691	63,468	92,053	629,176[c]	762,565	29,761	39,082	46,156	70,991
Percent	100.0	100.0	100.0	100.0	100.0	100.0	100.0	100.0	100.0	100.0
Black	7,573	17,364	114	286	7,388	16,843	41	66	30	169
Percent	1.0	1.8	0.2	0.3	1.2	2.2	0.1	0.2	0.1	0.2
Chinese	52,039	56,285	1,841	1,672	48,288	52,814	538	520	1,372	1,279
Percent	6.8	5.8	2.9	1.8	7.7	6.9	1.8	1.3	3.0	1.8
Filipino	93,915	133,940	10,454	12,709	65,553	97,565	8,135	10,237	9,773	13,429
Percent	12.2	13.9	16.5	13.8	10.4	12.8	27.3	26.2	21.2	18.9
Hawaiian	71,375	115,500	7,809	17,274	53,709	80,172	3,011	5,704	6,846	12,350
Percent	9.3	12.0	12.3	18.8	8.5	10.5	10.1	14.6	14.8	17.4
Japanese	217,307	239,748	23,817	24,476	169,078	189,828	9,780	9,775	14,632	15,669
Percent	28.3	24.9	37.5	26.6	26.9	24.9	32.9	25.0	31.7	22.1
Korean	8,656	17,962	330	580	8,058	16,880	83	136	185	366
Percent	1.1	1.9	0.5	0.6	1.3	2.2	0.3	0.4	0.4	0.5
Samoan	NA	14,073	NA	132	NA	13,811	NA	33	NA	97
Percent	NA	1.5	NA	0.2	NA	1.8	NA	0.1	NA	0.1
Vietnamese	NA	3,463	NA	127	NA	3,293	NA	5	NA	38
Percent	NA	0.4	NA	0.2	NA	0.4	NA	0.0	NA	0.1
White	298,160	318,770	18,298	31,316	259,519	252,455	7,733	11,147	12,610	23,852
Percent	38.8	33.0	28.8	34.0	41.2	33.1	26.0	28.5	27.3	33.6

Other										
Aleutian	NA	45	NA	12	NA	27	NA	2	NA	4
Percent	NA	0.0	NA	0.0	NA	0.0	NA	0.0	NA	0.0
American Indian	1,126	2,655	72	315	996	2,088	30	75	28	177
Percent	0.1	0.3	0.1	0.3	0.2	0.3	0.1	0.2	0.1	0.2
Asian Indian	NA	604	NA	25	NA	543	NA	12	NA	24
Percent	NA	0.1	NA	0.0	NA	0.1	NA	0.0	NA	0.0
Eskimo	NA	68	NA	6	NA	57	NA	1	NA	4
Percent	NA	0.0	NA	0.0	NA	0.0	NA	0.0	NA	0.0
Guamanian	NA	1,677	NA	68	NA	1,559	NA	20	NA	30
Percent	NA	0.2	NA	0.1	NA	0.2	NA	0.1	NA	0.0
Other	18,410	42,537	733	3,055	16,587	34,630	410	1,349	680	3,503
Percent	2.4	4.4	1.2	3.3	2.6	4.5	1.4	3.5	1.5	4.9

Sources: Hawaii (State) DPED, Statistical Report No. 152, Tables 1, 2, 6, 7; United States BOC, 1973b, 1981a.

Notes: This table uses U.S. census definition of race and is not comparable to Hawaii Health Surveillance Program tabulations of ethnic distribution in Hawai'i. Percentages may not add to 100 because of rounding.

NA Not available.

[a]By self-identification or race of father.

[b]By self-identification or race of mother.

[c]Revised totals for the state in 1970, not tabulated by race, are 769,913 state total and 630,528 for the city and county of Honolulu. Difference between this table and Tables 3-1 and 3-3 reflects differences in the underlying census tables.

Table 3-5. Births and Deaths by Ethnic Population, Hawai'i, 1900-1985[a,b,c,d]

	Total		Black[e]		Chinese		Filipino		Hawaiian	
	Births	Deaths	Births	Deaths	Births	Deaths	Births	Deaths	Births	Deaths
1900	1,026	2,376	NA	NA	160	228	NA	NA	303	991
1901	2,035	3,029			428	292			406	1,209
1902	2,350	2,578			414	238			527	967
1903	2,526	2,657			420	228			533	1,033
1904	2,510	2,783			379	239			541	1,000
1905	2,609	2,685			360	217			504	985
1906	2,830	2,854			376	227			532	1,035
1907	3,574	3,063			370	231			519	1,105
1908[f]	4,609	1,376			164	103			246	482
1909	4,946	2,851			409	224			676	1,003
1910	4,302	2,840			456	235			639	1,005
1911	4,487	3,295			423	253			582	1,010
1912	5,147	3,071			444	225		59	649	932
1913	5,568	3,232			489	230	92	178	574	941
1914	5,756	3,707			548	247	154	223	586	966
1915	7,278	3,556			607	276	219	209	533	888
1916	7,899	3,940			655	274	251	223	617	942
1917	8,707	3,498			680	271	346	229	597	844
1918	9,404	4,010			666	331	456	364	635	883
1919	9,164	4,051			717	322	470	408	659	891
1920	10,165	4,563			661	364	584	440	676	1,010
1921	10,246	3,789			717	298	577	340	620	713
1922	11,249	4,113			762	335	748	497	611	780
1923	11,335	4,654			790	332	863	629	564	834
1924	12,128	4,218			800	309	1,375	636	594	791
1925	13,109	4,071			837	292	1,806	834	588	714
1926	12,417	4,056			832	323	1,796	718	544	635
1927	12,296	3,929			777	282	1,653	637	527	648
1928	11,543	3,992			773	343	1,448	675	420	631
1929	11,498	4,481			694	331	1,411	817	445	686
1930[c]	10,873	3,976			694	321	1,404	686	422	626
1931	10,463	3,731			649	311	1,478	544	367	567
1932	10,493	3,670			584	304	1,476	536	415	541
1933	10,014	3,646			574	279	1,377	483	376	585
1934	9,431	3,679			492	295	1,306	478	370	598
1935	9,252	3,236			NA	248	NA	425	NA	482
1936	8,960	3,335			499	285	1,132	379	354	465
1937	8,763	3,684			468	282	1,143	466	328	522
1938	8,986	3,219			491	222	1,123	384	326	460
1939	9,038	3,216			460	290	1,108	402	332	409
1940	9,524	3,025			474	271	1,032	298	317	430
1941[g]	9,603	3,047			490	286	1,040	286	287	388
1942[g]	10,376	3,272			530	272	1,059	287	268	381
1943[g]	10,977	3,373			614	252	1,092	313	232	346
1944[g]	12,211	3,613			797	278	1,202	342	238	347
1945	12,597	2,840			781	264	1,221	315	228	315
1946	11,945	3,068			800	274	1,176	353	202	349
1947	14,050	3,129			832	291	1,435	332	233	359
1948	14,522	2,976	NA	NA	859	259	1,434	343	188	298

Part Hawaiian		Japanese		Korean		Samoan[e]		White		Other	
Births	Deaths	Births	Deaths	Births	Deaths	Births	Deaths	Births	Deaths	Births	Deaths
24	59	221	735	NA	NA	NA	NA	306	318	12	45
58	78	486	830					657	569	21	51
70	68	590	839					718	424	31	42
69	74	643	905					836	381	25	36
74	75	604	1,000					885	412	27	57
81	76	669	902					950	413	45	92
127	82	705	881					1,030	533	60	96
108	103	1,487	953					1,049	594	41	77
63	49	1,220	462					422	238	23	42
148	94	2,347	983					1,297	488	69	59
195	145	1,784	945					1,165	510	63	101
467	172	1,726	1,030					1,200	673	89	157
625	200	2,021	942					1,305	651	103	62
627	178	2,230	1,012					1,486	621	70	72
708	202	3,039	1,296					1,652	708	69	65
786	188	3,377	1,301					1,640	612	0	82
833	275	3,662	1,385					1,760	766	121	75
917	239	4,260	1,246	144	47			1,739	602	24	20
992	275	4,579	1,363	183	73			1,862	693	31	28
1,001	260	4,391	1,469	175	73			1,725	603	26	25
1,190	353	4,963	1,596	192	77			1,882	698	17	25
1,229	282	4,910	1,315	219	87			1,961	638	13	26
1,321	300	5,590	1,398	218	75			1,979	700	20	28
1,376	356	5,689	1,645	232	73			1,796	771	25	14
1,346	284	5,820	1,388	258	93			1,910	697	25	20
1,496	264	6,186	1,168	243	81			1,939	641	17	23
1,594	340	5,594	1,244	234	85			1,803	685	20	26
1,569	390	5,751	1,174	233	61			1,753	675	33	36
1,713	374	5,148	1,169	210	76			1,799	687	32	37
1,775	474	5,184	1,339	172	83			1,782	714	35	37
1,757	446	4,655	1,157	190	81			1,715	631	36	28
1,767	395	4,365	1,096	152	75			1,640	719	45	24
1,909	442	4,265	1,050	151	66			1,659	710	34	21
1,910	443	3,922	1,074	129	82			1,667	678	59	22
1,931	449	3,693	1,060	101	71			1,500	651	38	27
NA	411	NA	919	NA	74			NA	666	NA	11
2,044	415	3,251	1,015	84	73			1,578	695	18	8
2,084	535	3,118	1,032	102	85			1,492	742	28	20
2,135	425	3,163	916	91	86			1,623	713	34	13
2,210	405	3,130	945	95	92			1,678	660	25	13
2,395	346	3,337	890	99	73			1,828	698	42	19
2,357	379	3,247	853	111	76			2,043	767	28	12
2,583	385	3,589	923	118	84			2,196	921	33	19
3,008	395	3,990	870	171	86			1,806	1,086	64	25
3,102	337	4,491	875	193	79			2,128	1,254	60	101
3,212	323	4,504	855	226	97			2,358	654	67	17
3,093	343	4,420	972	192	90			2,032	673	50	14
3,314	393	4,817	952	228	85			3,128	704	63	13
3,372	342	4,890	934	179	81	NA	NA	3,496	707	104	12

continued

Table 3–5. *(continued)*

	Total		Black[e]		Chinese		Filipino		Hawaiian	
	Births	Deaths	Births	Deaths	Births	Deaths	Births	Deaths	Births	Deaths
1949	14,223	2,965	NA	NA	860	273	1,564	299	166	270
1950	14,059	2,883			840	260	1,567	303	166	244
1951	14,471	2,859			853	256	1,602	331	158	247[h]
1952	15,618	2,831			901	230	1,684	307	150	248[h]
1953	16,130	2,349			894	253	1,706	301	166	233
1954	16,222	2,934			897	255	1,720	345	132	207
1955	16,339	3,087			820	255	1,798	330	121	255
1956	17,142	3,038			825	240	1,803	360	141	230
1957	17,023	3,285			826	233	1,806	398	115	253
1958	16,726	3,096			812	222	1,864	357	108	241
1959	17,033	3,246			777	227	1,965	423	114	228
1960	17,177	3,456			721	264	1,891	428	90	232
1961	17,543	3,293			767	213	1,927	401	77	234
1962	17,932	3,409			734	221	2,030	445	105	203
1963	17,714	3,556	285	17	721	219	2,034	446	80	216
1964	17,262	3,539	281	10	660	241	1,996	472	80	196
1965	16,228	3,571	273	15	610	233	1,905	449	61	186
1966	14,920	3,632	155	11	595	241	1,964	496	74	206
1967	14,735	3,732	175	16	543	236	1,954	524	68	195
1968	14,470	4,004	168	17	532	229	2,059	615	40	202
1969	15,550	3,962	150	14	587	235	2,233	545	46	210
1970	16,361	3,942	217	21	515	224	2,507	576	46	200
1971	15,845	4,107	210	19	583	261	2,498	606	44	187
1972	15,413	4,219	210	18	482	252	2,696	623	45	208
1973	15,358	4,286	281	27	507	277	2,591	615	36	191
1974	15,472	4,286	299	22	572	245	2,682	536	46	200
1975	15,689	4,272	333	23	563	262	2,739	589	48	191
1976	16,292	4,349	366	20	614	305	2,792	598	55	199
1977	16,874	4,348	409	36	625	258	2,850	559	38	184
1978	16,717	4,508	458	29	566	260	2,803	595	53	179
1979	17,513	4,791	535	32	697	292	2,741	622	53	200
1980	18,129	4,903	603	33	681	328	2,885	618	51	20
1981	18,174	4,927	652	30	725	295	2,856	684	46	198
1982	18,675	5,123	707	39	708	337	2,864	763	60	202
1983	19,090	5,409	826	30	719	332	2,833	753	39	225
1984	18,667	5,571	870	48	696	362	2,743	797	49	190
1985	18,267	5,751	897	49	695	376	2,783	797	60	243

Sources: Hawaii (Territory) Board of Health, Annual Reports 1910–1958; Hawaii (State) DOH, Annual Reports 1959–1985; United States, BOC 1931, Table 3; United States Department of Health, Education, and Welfare 1931, Table 2; 1932, Table 2.

Note: Variations with Table 4–6 reflect differences of underlying sources.

NA Not available.

[a]Births are recorded by race of child and by place of residence, by fiscal year to 1948, and by calendar year thereafter.

[b]Persons of unmixed race are classified by race of parents. Persons of mixed background, other than Part Hawaiian, are tabulated by race of non-White parent if part-White or by race of father if non-White.

[c]Hawaii was admitted to the United States vital statistics registration area for deaths in 1918 and for births in 1929. Registration of vital events in years prior to 1930 may be incomplete.

Part Hawaiian		Japanese		Korean		Samoan[e]		White		Other	
Births	Deaths	Births	Deaths	Births	Deaths	Births	Deaths	Births	Deaths	Births	Deaths
3,426	318	4,712	1,004	230	78	NA	NA	3,140	707	125	16
3,595	307	4,568	979	192	87			3,001	691	130	12
3,639	309[h]	4,641	944	NA	NA			2,893	628	685	144
3,935	311[h]	4,831	901	NA	NA			3,398	684	719	150
3,975	330	4,817	941	NA	NA			4,195	691	168	15
4,229	379	4,747	932	206	86			4,107	714	184	16
4,175	356	4,606	1,015	208	71			4,394	778	217	27
4,290	357	4,668	1,003	190	75			4,963	759	262	14
4,398	387	4,270	1,054	191	98			5,072	836	345	26
4,362	370	4,054	1,022	155	84			4,988	831	383	23
4,529	406	4,063	1,047	172	64			5,002	825	411	26
4,691	449	3,849	1,090	159	83			5,343	881	433	29
4,879	437	3,801	1,065	156	64			5,423	840	513	39
4,977	461	3,687	1,074	172	79			5,572	889	655	37
4,993	482	3,514	1,079	171	71	289	27	5,507	991	120	8
4,824	482	3,397	1,051	171	70	276	24	5,451	986	126	7
4,665	421	3,280	1,173	154	63	285	27	4,876	995	119	9
4,512	463	2,930	1,089	165	81	310	26	4,086	1,006	129	11
4,364	494	2,776	1,152	178	64	278	18	4,281	1,025	118	8
4,129	548	2,701	1,204	143	64	124	22	4,310	1,100	264	3
4,543	495	2,792	1,180	140	60	146	32	4,637	1,183	276	8
4,741	520	2,860	1,162	144	69	288	37	4,879	1,123	164	10
4,486	481	2,685	1,241	150	51	203	22	4,598	1,222	203	17
4,332	509	2,474	1,229	170	54	245	32	4,397	1,281	245	13
4,442	520	2,376	1,272	176	59	277	28	4,318	1,279	277	18
4,359	586	2,369	1,252	198	63	290	40	4,346	1,324	290	18
4,470	527	2,236	1,269	215	56	339	39	4,338	1,299	339	17
4,695	597	2,422	1,203	193	59	388	38	4,302	1,318	465	12
5,022	569	2,420	1,306	235	58	448	44	4,388	1,309	439	25
5,001	599	2,336	1,322	242	70	485	38	4,321	1,397	453	19
5,227	651	2,488	1,419	309	61	509	53	4,420	1,456	534	32
5,473	653	2,622	1,337	314	72	487	61	4,380	1,551	633	38
5,690	643	2,526	1,359	343	98	512	60	4,136	1,588	688	38
5,678	625	2,589	1,428	309	72	512	50	4,599	1,642	649	44
5,709	671	2,518	1,468	312	98	515	56	4,957	1,727	736	39
5,699	713	2,488	1,574	323	82	510	56	4,779	1,735	599	58
5,485	734	2,328	1,617	316	88	487	55	4,696	1,749	520	43

[d]Resident deaths only.

[e]Black and Samoan births and deaths are included with "Other" until 1963.

[f]Birth figures are for six months only.

[g]The 2,500 casualties in the 1941 Pearl Harbor attack are not included in this tabulation. The increased number of White deaths may be partially attributed to the large influx of transitory wartime White population.

[h]Adjusted from Hawaiian and Part Hawaiian totals of 556 in 1951 and 559 in 1952.

Table 3-6. Fertility in Total, Military, and Ethnic Populations, Hawai'i, 1900–1980

	1900	1910	1920[a]	1930[a]	1940[a]	1950[a]	1960	1970[b]	1980[b]
Crude Birth Rate[c] (per 1,000 persons)									
Total Population	6.7	22.4	38.2	29.4	22.6	28.2	26.8	21.3	18.8
By Military Status									
Civilian				NA	——	——	22.9	19.1	16.6
Military				NA	——	——	48.8	35.1	33.7
By Ethnic Population									
Black				NA			41.8		
Chinese	6.2	21.0	28.1	26.4	17.9	25.9	18.7		
Filipino	NA	NA	27.8	23.2	20.4	25.7	27.4		
Hawaiian	10.2	24.5	28.5	18.8	19.8		8.0		
Part Hawaiian	3.1	15.6	66.0	63.0	31.2	43.7	51.5		
Japanese	3.6	22.4	43.5	33.0	20.6	24.8	19.3		
Korean	NA	NA	38.8	29.4	NA	NA	19.1		
Samoan				NA	NA	NA			
White	10.6	26.4	34.4	20.1	18.7	23.5	26.3		
General Fertility Rate[c] (per 1,000 women)									
Total Population	39.1	124.6	245.7	185.0	112.1	125.2	128.0	96.4	78.8
By Military Status									
Civilian				NA	——	——	106.2	84.8	68.5
Military				NA	——	——	250.5	169.5	157.2

212

	1	2	3	4	5	6	7	8
By Ethnic Population								
Black	96.5	NA	NA	NA	74.8	104.9	289.1	
Chinese	252.2	NA	210.6	154.1	237.3	212.6	88.3	
Filipino	NA	102.6	255.6	320.6	85.4	38.6	182.1	
Hawaiian	43.9	73.1	120.1	79.8	145.7	204.8	b	
Part-Hawaiian	14.9	124.9	336.3	328.7	87.4	95.8	249.1	
Japanese	20.9	NA	207.1	176.9	NA	NA	80.0	
Korean	NA	NA	302.8	224.9	NA	NA	NA	
Samoan	NA	NA	NA	NA	NA	NA	NA	
White	57.1	130.6	168.8	101.8	87.8	103.5	125.4	
Total Fertility Rate[c] (per 1,000 women)								
Total Population	NA	7,070.5	5,542.5	3,205.0	3,321.0	3,886.5	2,728.5	2,091.5
By Military Status								
Civilian			NA			3,360.5	2,461.5	1,903.5
Military			NA			6,480.5	4,275.0	3,789.5
By Ethnic Population								
Black	NA	NA	NA	4,820.0	2,298.0	NA	2,946.5	
Chinese	NA	NA	NA	8,427.0	7,252.0	NA	3,787.0	
Filipino	NA	NA	NA	2,347.5	2,509.5	4,399.0	b	
Hawaiian	NA	NA	NA	9,703.5	3,957.0	5,666.0	5,268.0	
Part Hawaiian	NA	NA	NA	5,618.4	2,784.5	2,490.0	2,711.0	
Japanese	NA	NA	NA	6,051.0	NA	NA	NA	
Korean	NA	NA	NA	NA	NA	NA	NA	
Samoan	NA	NA	NA	NA	NA	NA	NA	
White	NA	NA	NA	2,887.5	2,428.5	2,838.5	3,571.0	

continued

Table 3-6. *(continued)*

	1900	1910	1920ᵃ	1930ᵃ	1940ᵃ	1950ᵃ	1960	1970ᵇ	1980ᵇ
Gross Reproduction Rate[c]									
Total Population	NA	NA	3,432.3	2,668.8	1,551.5	1,635.5	1,883.2	1,318.7	1,010.5
By Military Status									
Civilian				NA			1,633.7	1,191.0	915.5
Military				NA			3,140.0	2,065.5	1,830.0
Net Reproduction Rate[c]									
Total Population	NA	NA	2,383.7	2,188.1	1,413.6	1,568.1	1,821.5	1,281.4	990.7
By Military Status									
Civilian				NA			1,573.6	1,154.8	898.8
Military				NA			3,037.8	2,006.1	1,799.9
Child-Woman Ratio[d] (per 1,000 women in age group 15–44)									
Total Population	575.2	697.0	780.6	767.3	454.9	569.1	602.8	414.3	338.6
By Military Status									
Civilian				NA			562.1	400.0	278.5
Military				NA			832.2	508.9	603.8
By Ethnic Population									
Black	NA		NA	NA			994.1		
Chinese	813.0	894.9	917.2	724.7	314.8	495.8	517.4		
Filipino	NA	NA	851.2	1,251.5	1,034.3	902.1	874.2		
Hawaiian	482.7	435.5	455.7	464.4	323.0	303.4	373.5		
Part Hawaiian	1,091.0	1,024.4	1,166.2	1,170.1	876.4	954.8	913.1		
Japanese	316.6	686.2	819.5	837.0	387.8	462.1	432.8		
Korean	NA	NA	1,219.2	1,088.8	387.0	462.1	NA		
Samoan	NA		NA	NA			NA		
White	769.6	751.6	661.5	472.1	307.4	487.3	611.8		

Median Age of Mothers									
Total Population	NA	NA	28.9	28.9	27.4	26.9	25.7	26.1	26.3
By Military Status									
Civilian			NA	——	——		26.3	26.2	27.0
Military			NA	——	——		24.2	25.2	23.5

Sources: United States, BOC 1913, Tables 8, 10, 13, 24, 25, 27; 1931, Table 6; 1932, Table 4; 1953, Tables 11, 29, 30; 1961, Tables 16, 17; 1962, Tables 96, 139; 1963, Table 61; 1971b, Tables 17, 20, 28; 1971c, Table 53; 1972a, Tables 96, 138, 139; 1982a, Table 19, 22. United States, Department of Health, Education, and Welfare 1940, part 1, Tables 2, 3, 5; 1950, vol. 1, Table 10.09; 1960, vol. 1, Tables 1–A–C, 2–4, 2–14. Hawaii (Territory) Board of Health 1920 p. 11; Annual Report 1950, Table 2. Hawaii (State) DOH, Annual Report, Statistical Supplement 1960, Tables 3, 10, 12; 1970, Table 13; 1980, Tables 18, 26. Gardner, Nordyke, and Schmitt 1987, Tables 19, 22.

Note: All rates are per 1,000 designated population. See Glossary for explanation of rates. Births to women under age 15 are assigned to those age 15–19; births to women over age 44 are included with those age 40–44.

NA Not available.

[a] Corrected for under-registration.

[b] Figures for 1970 and 1980 are not directly comparable with earlier years because of changed definitions of ethnic groups. See Note, Table 3–3.a. and findings in Table 3–7.

[c] Population data is based on U.S. census tabulations, and birth data is based on Hawaii Health Department figures.

[d] From U.S. census count.

Table 3-7. Fertility in Total and Ethnic Populations According to Both U.S. Census and Hawaii Health Surveillance Program Definitions, Hawaii, 1970 and 1980

	1970		1980	
	U.S. Census	Health Survey[a,b]	U.S. Census	Health Survey[a,b]
Crude birth rate (per 1,000 persons)				
Total population	21.3	22.3	18.8	18.8
By ethnic population (by race of mother)				
Black	23.9	37.1	23.4	21.9
Chinese	10.5	17.7	12.5	11.7
Filipino	26.2	42.6	22.7	22.2
Hawaiian (part)	50.9	26.8	34.7	22.7
Japanese	13.5	14.8	11.1	11.0
Korean	16.5	25.0	22.5	24.3
Samoan	NA	NA	34.8	37.9
White	20.0	26.1	18.4	20.7
General Fertility Rate (per 1,000 women)				
Total population	96.4	95.8	78.8	80.7
By ethnic population				
Black	149.3	147.4	126.7	105.1
Chinese	50.4	82.7	53.7	46.2
Filipino	131.4	197.2	94.9	97.8
Hawaiian (part)	221.7	129.5	142.7	91.9
Japanese	58.3	63.1	50.2	52.2
Korean	67.7	85.2	69.3	71.5
Samoan	NA	NA	150.9	162.5
White	90.1	101.9	74.2	88.2
Total Fertility Rate (per 1,000 women)				
Total population	2,728.5	2,738.5	2,091.5	2,166.0
By ethnic population				
Black	3,505.5	4,814.0	2,620.5	2,384.0
Chinese	1,636.0	2,551.0	1,463.0	1,321.0
Filipino	3,787.0	5,900.0	2,625.5	2,885.0
Hawaiian (part)	6,121.5	3,658.0	3,766.5	2,543.5
Japanese	1,978.5	2,147.0	1,383.5	1,552.0
Korean	2,074.0	3,415.0	1,857.5	1,886.0
Samoan	NA	NA	4,123.5	5,200.0
White	2,276.5	2,595.5	1,897.5	2,271.0

Table 3-7. *(continued)*

	1970		1980	
	U.S. Census	Health Survey[a,b]	U.S. Census	Health Survey[a,b]
Child Woman Ratio (per 1,000 women in age group 15–44)				
Total population	414.3	427.7	338.6	324.7
By ethnic population				
Black	797.7	445.5	620.5	781.5
Chinese	380.2	201.5	239.8	166.7
Filipino	586.0	416.1	394.7	394.5
Hawaiian (part)	514.1	727.9c	463.6	496.2
Japanese	282.0	230.3	223.2	184.3
Korean	329.9	244.3	201.0	212.9
Samoan	NA	NA	664.1	660.1
White	428.5	360.8	314.0	280.6

Sources: Hawaii, DOH 1981, Health Surveillance Program, special tables; R and S Report, No. 1; Annual Report, Statistical Supplement 1970, Table 13; 1980, Tables 18, 26; United States, BOC 1971c, Table 20; 1972, Table 139; 1982, Tables 19, 22.

Note: The ratios in this table use vital statistics from the State Department of Health in the numerators, and population count from the U.S. census and Hawaii Health Surveillance Program in the denominators. The interpretation of such fertility rates is problematic because of the lack of comparability of data. (See Chapter 4, Ethnicity.)

NA Not available.

[a]The population estimates by age, sex, and race prepared for the Hawaii Health Surveillance Program are taken from interviews in randomly selected households per year throughout the state. Persons from Ni'ihau, Kalawao County, and inmates of institutions and military barracks were excluded in the sample but added to the survey total from census calculations.

[b]Race was determined by questions following the 1960 decennial census criteria in which the racial grouping of each individual is determined by his parents' racial background. Any indication of Hawaiian blood resulted in a classification of Part Hawaiian.

[c]The U.S. census count of 8,410 children aged 1–4 years in 1970 contrasts with the Health Survey count of 20,410 children of the same age at that time; this disparity accounts for the higher child-woman ratio in the Health Survey tabulations.

Table 3–8. Age-specific Fertility Rates by Total, Ethnic, and Civilian and Military Populations, Hawai'i, 1930–1980

	1930	1940	1950	1960	1970[a]	1980[a]
Total Population						
Ages 15–19	66.7	52.1	58.6	75.5	62.6	51.2
20–24	243.6	176.4	200.7	284.3	173.8	125.6
25–29	260.9	179.8	195.6	221.0	169.8	122.3
30–34	215.8	109.3	125.9	125.1	91.7	83.0
35–39	148.9	73.5	64.4	54.8	38.5	30.4
40–44	82.0	32.2	17.3	15.8	8.8	5.5
45–49	12.9	3.2	1.0	0.9	0.6	0.3
Black						
Ages 15–19	NA	NA	NA	NA	155.7	104.7
20–24	NA	NA	NA	NA	219.0	196.6
25–29	NA	NA	NA	NA	182.9	120.4
30–34	NA	NA	NA	NA	73.3	71.6
35–39	NA	NA	NA	NA	44.6	30.8
40–44	NA	NA	NA	NA	25.6	0.0
45–49	NA	NA	NA	NA	0.0	0.0
Chinese						
Ages 15–19	38.4	16.1	NA	23.0	18.3	9.8
20–24	170.6	95.5	NA	169.0	70.9	44.9
25–29	232.6	141.7	NA	203.7	132.1	103.4
30–34	236.2	104.9	NA	130.5	67.8	96.6
35–39	154.0	69.4	NA	52.2	29.6	31.6
40–44	116.1	29.9	NA	10.9	8.0	6.3
45–49	16.1	2.1	NA	0.0	0.5	0.0
Filipino						
Ages 15–19	253.1	184.8	NA	101.7	83.1	57.5
20–24	434.3	440.4	NA	356.4	235.0	158.5
25–29	397.7	342.8	NA	273.0	212.1	156.0
30–34	309.9	220.4	NA	155.2	127.0	101.3
35–39	201.5	166.5	NA	100.1	75.6	42.2
40–44	57.9	87.0	NA	38.4	23.1	9.3
45–49	31.0	8.5	NA	5.8	1.5	0.3
Hawaiian						
Ages 15–19	37.3	50.2	NA	62.5	b	b
20–24	116.4	141.6	NA	288.3	b	b
25–29	114.8	122.7	NA	267.8	b	b
30–34	100.8	94.5	NA	145.5	b	b
35–39	71.3	60.3	NA	92.7	b	b
40–44	24.2	28.4	NA	23.0	b	b
45–49	4.7	4.2	NA	0.0	b	b
Part Hawaiian						
Ages 15–19	148.1	92.3	NA	117.3	187.8	125.2
20–24	503.0	232.7	NA	413.5	480.0	264.1
25–29	500.5	206.8	NA	277.2	323.9	203.5
30–34	402.7	137.2	NA	150.4	141.5	117.4
35–39	251.6	77.4	NA	72.5	69.0	37.8
40–44	116.5	43.6	NA	20.8	18.6	4.9
45–49	18.3	1.4	NA	1.9	3.5	0.4

Table 3-8. *(continued)*

	1930	1940	1950	1960	1970[a]	1980[a]
Japanese						
Ages 15–19	39.1	13.6	12.0	20.7	19.6	13.8
20–24	223.1	123.9	116.2	152.4	92.9	51.8
25–29	287.4	186.6	174.0	187.1	159.2	96.2
30–34	255.3	111.7	121.4	118.7	87.2	85.9
35–39	196.7	78.6	59.4	49.4	30.6	25.4
40–44	114.8	38.1	14.2	13.2	6.0	3.5
45–49	7.3	4.4	0.8	0.7	0.2	0.1
Korean						
Ages 15–19	39.8	NA	NA	NA	41.8	21.7
20–24	223.1	NA	NA	NA	131.8	95.2
25–29	282.9	NA	NA	NA	123.9	126.7
30–34	400.0	NA	NA	NA	73.0	84.5
35–39	164.8	NA	NA	NA	38.6	39.2
40–44	71.4	NA	NA	NA	5.7	4.2
45–49	28.2	NA	NA	NA	0.0	0.0
Samoan						
Ages 15–19						57.5
20–24						283.
25–29						269.2
30–34			NA			147.5
35–39						48.0
40–44						19.4
45–49						0.0
White						
Ages 15–19	70.7	70.2	60.6	111.0	59.1	47.4
20–24	181.8	173.3	192.3	298.3	160.8	123.5
25–29	139.5	127.8	159.3	202.0	133.1	109.2
30–34	89.2	70.1	98.0	109.8	69.3	67.5
35–39	64.4	37.4	47.4	45.5	27.4	26.2
40–44	27.9	6.0	10.1	14.2	5.5	5.5
45–49	4.0	0.9	0.0	0.0	0.1	0.2

	Civilian			Military		
	1960	1970	1980	1960	1970	1980
Ages 15–19	55.8	56.3	40.8	257.9	135.1	184.3
20–24	229.1	151.9	103.0	464.7	281.6	279.3
25–29	204.3	158.0	116.5	297.6	227.2	172.0
30–34	116.1	81.3	82.5	164.6	135.3	87.3
35–39	52.0	36.6	30.6	74.1	49.0	28.4
40–44	14.8	8.2	5.7	37.2	26.8	6.6

Sources: See Table 3-6.

NA Not available.

[a]Figures for 1970 and 1980 are not directly comparable with earlier years because of changed definitions of racial groups. The population denominator for this table is based on U.S. census tabulations of race. See Note, Table 3-3.a. and Chapter 4, Ethnicity.

[b]Hawaiian and Part Hawaiian are combined as Part Hawaiian in 1970 and 1980.

Table 3–9. Elective Abortions by Ethnicity of Mother, Hawai'i, 1971–1985

	Total	Black	Chinese	Filipino	Hawaiian[a]	Japanese	Korean	Samoan	White	Other
1971 Abortions	4,135	47	203	398	540	1,969	127	48	1,733	70
Births[b]	15,845	169	550	2,584	3,320	2,745	189	338	5,746	204
Ratio[c]	26	28	37	15	16	35	67	14	30	34
1972 Abortions	4,547	45	236	517	591	1,085	150	51	1,781	91
Births	15,413	167	511	2,759	3,210	2,451	215	343	5,526	231
Ratio	30	27	46	19	18	44	70	15	32	39
1973 Abortions	4,534	62	229	563	666	1,049	196	77	1,566	126
Births	15,358	206	533	2,616	3,300	2,371	229	330	5,499	274
Ratio	30	30	43	22	20	44	86	23	28	46
1974 Abortions	4,158	94	179	586	618	842	205	57	1,464	113
Births	15,472	221	552	2,667	3,262	2,414	241	336	5,457	322
Ratio	27	43	32	22	19	35	85	17	27	35
1975 Abortions	4,545	117	193	629	657	888	233	82	1,547	199
Births	15,689	243	566	2,827	3,302	2,239	83	411	5,245	573
Ratio	29	48	34	22	20	40	82	20	29	35
1976 Abortions	5,163	120	226	687	700	880	260	94	1,712	484
Births	16,292	268	636	2,860	3,465	2,398	289	395	5,536	445
Ratio	32	45	36	24	20	37	90	24	31	109
1977 Abortions	5,249	128	199	651	727	789	264	78	1,719	694
Births	16,874	273	608	2,933	3,667	2,482	298	451	5,722	440
Ratio	31	47	33	22	20	32	89	17	30	158
1978 Abortions	6,014	143	221	735	761	958	274	99	2,027	796
Births	16,717	326	609	2,997	3,630	2,365	289	467	5,588	446
Ratio	36	44	36	25	21	41	95	21	36	179

1979 Abortions	6,125	84	199	723	843	1,016	220	104	1,924	994
Births	17,513	369	664	2,877	3,859	2,532	373	487	5,434	918
Ratio	35	23	30	25	22	40	59	21	36	108
1980 Abortions	6,462	86	253	883	945	1,152	232	116	2,125	670
Births	18,129	406	704	3,042	4,004	2,655	404	490	5,488	936
Ratio	36	21	36	29	24	43	57	24	39	72
1981 Abortions	6,692	126	280	959	1,071	1,111	287	120	2,184	554
Births	18,174	478	700	3,105	4,243	2,654	411	492	5,103	1,078
Ratio	37	26	40	31	25	42	70	24	43	51
1982 Abortions	6,224	102	250	950	1,044	1,022	246	116	2,089	405
Births	18,675	497	748	3,053	4,211	2,638	390	521	5,976	641
Ratio	33	21	33	31	25	39	63	22	35	63
1983 Abortions	6,041	164	229	916	972	1,031	287	121	1,959	362
Births	19,090	608	731	3,048	4,227	2,542	412	518	6,383	621
Ratio	32	27	31	30	23	41	70	23	31	58
1984 Abortions	5,334	131	198	758	953	897	220	104	1,669	404
Births	18,667	652	700	2,998	4,184	2,555	401	516	6,105	556
Ratio	29	20	28	25	23	35	55	20	27	72
1985 Abortions	5,670	120	230	847	940	869	211	92	1,827	534
Births	18,267	657	706	2,944	4,025	2,460	401	472	6,101	501
Ratio	31	18	33	29	24	35	53	20	30	107

Source: Hawaii (State) DOH, Annual Report, Statistical Supplement, 1971–1985.

[a]Includes Hawaiian and Part Hawaiian.

[b]Births by ethnicity of mother.

[c]Number of elective abortions per 100 live births.

Table 3–10. Interracial Marriages as Percentage of All Marriages by Sex and Ethnic Group, Hawai'i, 1912–1985

		1912–1916	1920–1929	1930–1939	1940–1949	1950–1959	1960–1969	1970–1979	1980–1985	Resident Population 1985[a]
Black	Grooms	NA	NA	NA	NA	NA	45.9	60.2	52.7	51.1
	Brides	NA	NA	NA	NA	NA	13.2	16.1	17.2	19.3
Chinese	Grooms	41.7	24.8	28.0	31.2	43.6	58.2	60.2	60.1	61.8
	Brides	5.7	15.7	28.5	38.0	45.2	61.5	65.2	63.9	66.4
Filipino	Grooms	21.8	25.6	37.5	42.0	44.5	50.6	47.0	44.3	42.2
	Brides	2.8	1.0	4.0	21.0	35.8	47.9	50.9	54.6	55.5
Hawaiian	Grooms	19.4	33.3	55.2	66.3	78.9	85.8	87.1	89.2	84.2
	Brides	39.9	52.1	62.7	77.2	81.5	90.1	85.9	84.5	78.8
Part Hawaiian	Grooms	52.1	38.8	41.0	36.9	41.3	61.3	57.2	55.8	56.1
	Brides	66.2	57.7	57.9	64.2	58.4	56.7	57.9	59.1	57.3
Japanese	Grooms	0.5	2.7	4.3	4.3	8.7	19.6	33.1	40.5	41.0
	Brides	0.2	3.1	6.3	16.9	19.1	28.1	40.3	47.4	50.0
Korean	Grooms	26.4	17.6	23.5	49.0	70.3	75.1	62.0	47.3	44.1
	Brides	0.0	4.9	39.0	66.7	74.5	82.1	82.4	77.2	77.7
Puerto Rican	Grooms	24.4	18.6	29.8	39.5	51.3	69.6	79.1	82.0	83.8
	Brides	26.4	39.7	42.8	50.3	60.5	70.3	77.5	73.3	69.7
Samoan	Grooms	NA	NA	NA	NA	NA	39.2	41.0	44.0	54.7
	Brides	NA	NA	NA	NA	NA	50.7	40.3	39.9	47.1
Vietnamese	Grooms	NA	NA	NA	NA	NA	NA	14.4	23.8	34.8
	Brides	NA	NA	NA	NA	NA	NA	77.7	62.7	64.3
White	Grooms	17.3	24.3	22.4	33.8	37.4	28.2	26.1	21.9	38.3
	Brides	11.7	13.8	10.7	10.2	16.4	19.8	20.8	15.8	28.2
Total		11.5	19.2	22.8	28.6	32.8	36.0	38.4	35.5	45.0

Sources: Lind 1980, p. 114; Hawaii (State) DOH, Annual Report, Statistical Supplement, 1971–1985.
NA Not available.

[a]These figures are derived from 9,893 marriages among residents of Hawai'i in 1985, in contrast to the 1980–1985 column based on 15,421 annual marriages that took place among residents as well as visitors to Hawai'i.

Table 3-11. Arrivals of Chinese in Hawai'i, 1852–1899

Year	Number of Arrivals	Year	Number of Arrivals
1852	293	1876	1,283
1853	64	1877	557
1854	12	1878	2,464
1855	61	1879	3,812
1856	23	1880	2,505
1857	14	1881	3,924
1858	13	1882	1,362
1859	171	1883	4,243
1860	21	1884	2,708
1861	2	1885	3,108
1862	13	1886	1,766
1863	8	1887	1,546
1864	9	1888	1,526
1865	615	1889	439
1866	117	1890	654
1867	210	1891	1,386
1868	51	1892	1,802
1869	78	1893	981
1870	305	1894	1,459
1871	223	1895	2,734
1872	61	1896	5,280
1873	48	1897	4,481
1874	62	1898	3,100
1875	151	1899	975
		Total	56,720

Source: Glick, 1980, p. 12.

Note: Several thousand duplications are included in the number of arrivals owing to the reentry of migrants who had temporarily left the islands.

Table 3–12. Arrivals of Filipinos through HSPA to Hawai'i, 1909–1946

Year	Men	Women	Ratio (M/W)	Children	Total
1909	554	57	8:1	28	639
1910	2,633	169	16:1	93	2,915
1911	1,363	173	8:1	74	1,610
1912	4,319	553	8:1	362	5,234
1913	3,258	573	6:1	351	4,182
1914	1,848	360	5:1	228	2,436
1915	1,363	238	6:1	185	1,786
1916	1,674	141	12:1	134	1,949
1917	2,536	182	14:1	210	2,928
1918	2,196	298	7:1	395	2,889
1919	2,642	312	9:1	278	3,232
1920	3,030	232	13:1	181	3,443
1921	3,982	434	9:1	240	4,656
1922	8,513	704	12:1	457	9,674
1923	4,830	1,482	3:1	787	7,099
1924	4,915	1,414	3:1	648	6,977
1925	9,934	459	22:1	252	10,645
1926	3,960	121	33:1	96	4,177
1927	8,976	95	95:1	88	9,158
1928	10,508	193	55:1	156	10,857
1929	6,971	152	46:1	186	7,309
1930	6,904	177	39:1	291	7,372
1931	5,597	217	26:1	200	6,014
1932	953	151	6:1	122	1,226
1933	9	22	1:2	10	41
1934	25	43	1:2	39	107
1946	6,000	446	14:1	915	7,361
Total	109,513	9,398	12:1	7,006	125,917

Source: Dorita 1954, p. 131.

Table 4-1. Resident and De Facto Population, Land Area, and Density, Islands and Counties, Hawai'i, 1985

Place	Population, 1985[a]		Land Area		Density Resident Population		Density De Facto Population	
	Resident	De Facto[b]	Square Miles	Square Kilometers	Per Square Mile	Per Square Kilometer	Per Square Mile	Per Square Kilometer
Hawaii State	1,053,885	1,152,025	6,425	16,641	164	63	179	69
Counties								
Hawaii	109,159	115,758	4,034	10,449	27	11	29	11
Honolulu	814,642	865,114	596	1,544	1,367	528	1,451	560
Kauai	44,781	55,635	620	1,605	72	28	90	35
Maui[c]	85,303	115,518	1,175	3,043	73	28	98	38
Islands								
Hawai'i	109,200	115,800	4,034	10,449	27	11	29	11
Kaho'olawe	0	0	45	117	0	0	0	0
Kaua'i	44,600	55,400	549	1,423	81	31	101	40
Lāna'i	2,200	2,200	140	364	16	6	16	6
Maui	76,600	105,600	729	1,887	105	41	145	56
Moloka'i[c]	6,500	7,800	261	676	25	10	30	12
Ni'ihau	180	180	70	181	3	1	3	1
O'ahu[d]	814,611	865,083	593	1,538	1,374	530	1,451	560
City of Honolulu[d]	381,676	NA	87	225	4,387	1,696	NA	NA
Outside Central City	432,935	NA	509	1,315	851	329	NA	NA
Northwestern Hawaiian Islands[e]	31	31	3	8	10	4	10	4

Sources: Hawaii (State) DPED, 1986 Data Book, Tables 7, 151; Statistical Report No. 190, Tables 1, 3, 5, 6, 7; 195, Table 1.

Note: Totals may not equal sums because of rounding.

NA Not available.

[a]These population estimates as of July 1, 1985, were prepared jointly by the U.S. Bureau of the Census, the Hawaii State Department of Health, and the Research and Economic Analysis Division of the DPED as part of the Federal-State Cooperative Program for Local Population Estimates.

[b]The de facto population is the number of persons physically present in an area; it includes visitors present and excludes residents absent from the state.

[c]Includes Kalawao County (Kalaupapa Settlement) of 13.3 square miles (34.4 square kilometers) and 150 residents.

[d]Northwestern Hawaiian Islands are included with the count of the city and county of Honolulu.

[e]As of April 1, 1980.

Table 4-2. Resident Population by Detailed Asian and Pacific Island Group, Based on a Sample, Hawai'i, 1980

	Number	Percent		Number	Percent
Total	964,691	100.0			
White	331,925	34.4	Pacific Islander	137,696	14.3
Black	17,687	1.8	Polynesian		
			Hawaiian	118,251	12.3
Asian	452,951	46.9	Samoan	14,349	1.5
			Tahitian	269	0.0
Chinese	55,916	5.8	Tongan	1,482	0.2
Filipino	132,075	13.7	Other	336	0.0
Japanese	239,734	24.9			
Indian (Asian)	708	0.1			
Korean	17,453	1.8	Micronesian		
Vietnamese	3,403	0.4	Guamanian	1,630	0.2
Bangladeshi	—	—	Other Mariana Islanders	56	0.0
Burmese	16	0.0	Marshallese	78	0.0
Cambodian	58	0.0	Palauan	305	0.0
Hmong	52	0.0	Other	579	0.1
Indonesian	153	0.0			
Laotian	1,369	0.1	Melanesian		
Malayan	59	0.0	Fijian	260	0.0
Okinawan	935	0.1	Other Melanesian	95	0.0
Pakistani	59	0.0			
Sri Lankan	26		Other Pacific Islanders[b]	6	0.0
Thai	765	0.1			
Other[a]	170	0.0	Other	24,432	2.5

Source: United States BOC 1983, Tables 1, 2, 4, 5.

Note: Difference between the 100 percent count and sample figures for Asian and Pacific Islander groups is a result of additional edit and review procedures performed during the processing of sample questionnaires as well as sampling variability and non-sampling errors. Percentages may not add to total percentage because of rounding. See Tables 3-1, 3-2, and 3-3 for other ethnic population figures.

[a]Includes census entries such as Asian American, Asian, and Asiatic.

[b]Includes census entry only as "Pacific Islander."

Table 4–3. Total Resident Population by Age, Sex, and Percentage Distribution, Hawai'i, 1900–1980

	Age and Sex								
Age	1900	1910	1920	1930	1940	1950	1960	1970	1980
Males									
0–4	7,734	12,170	19,496	24,530	20,411	32,817	41,266	36,256	40,004
5–9	5,701	9,642	15,477	23,894	21,951	26,626	37,175	40,990	37,555
10–14	4,484	7,109	11,263	19,235	24,110	20,402	32,679	40,791	38,459
15–19	6,633	7,865	11,546	19,324	26,359	23,467	30,622	37,275	45,673
20–24	15,067	13,608	14,820	31,778	32,044	27,539	30,403	46,807	59,070
25–29	20,008	13,451	11,639	25,333	27,114	25,967	22,411	30,358	48,864
30–34	15,107	15,071	12,927	17,263	21,571	23,143	24,177	23,846	42,990
35–39	11,302	14,257	11,827	12,844	17,969	22,644	25,167	23,084	32,684
40–44	7,793	10,593	11,915	12,082	12,963	17,915	21,443	23,749	23,765
45–49	4,364	7,529	10,972	10,077	9,648	15,353	19,567	23,347	21,589
50–54	2,626	4,635	7,516	8,968	9,422	10,704	15,876	19,620	23,298
55–59	1,529	2,648	4,541	6,882	6,853	7,445	13,103	17,037	23,502
60–64	1,907	2,296	3,777	4,966	6,058	7,491	8,572	13,791	18,871
65–69	851	1,073	1,887	2,849	4,472	4,979	5,527	9,671	15,384
70–74	434	567	796	1,438	2,295	3,665	5,021	5,781	10,991
75+	459	548	668	1,115	1,792	3,738	5,164	6,802	11,984[c]
Unknown	370	37	79	62	103	0	0	0	0
Subtotal	106,369	123,099	151,146	222,640	245,135	273,895	338,173	399,205	494,683
Females									
0–4	7,350	11,895	19,054	23,650	19,674	31,174	39,696	34,555	37,844
5–9	5,448	9,413	14,718	23,225	21,840	25,168	35,603	38,846	35,502
10–14	3,954	6,428	10,797	18,807	23,384	19,950	31,339	39,021	36,411
15–19	4,211	5,785	9,099	14,166	21,979	20,441	24,199	34,568	40,773
20–24	6,003	6,468	9,943	10,989	19,033	22,817	20,203	34,748	46,612
25–29	6,533	6,995	9,856	11,338	15,215	23,717	22,142	29,101	46,423
30–34	4,371	6,453	7.758	10.211	11,816	19,747	24,759	23,787	41,324
35–39	3,102	5,409	7,085	9,407	10,919	14,883	24,078	23,601	31,264
40–44	2,004	3,416	5,646	6,674	9,148	10,831	18,915	25,095	23,703
45–49	1,447	2,327	4,144	5,560	7,839	9,7901	13,918	22,852	23,651
50–54	900	1,590	2,550	4,472	5,694	8,202	10,189	18,433	25,906
55–59	617	956	1,540	3,061	4,275	6,480	8,909	13,306	23,881
60–64	566	606	1,098	1,859	3,332	4,662	7,199	9,581	18,923
65–69	332	431	651	1,009	2,193	3,449	5,432	7,987	13,769
70–74	263	284	365	575	1,152	2,306	3,667	6,050	9,231
75+	338	335	428	652	1,010	2,282	4,351	7,825	14,791[c]
Unknown	193	19	34	41	52	0	0	0	0
Subtotal	47,632	68,810	104,766	145,696	178,195	225,899	294,599	369,356	470,008
Total	154,001	191,909[a]	255,912[a]	368,336[a]	423,330[a]	499,794	632,772	768,561[b]	964,691

Sources: United States, BOC 1953, Table 11; 1961, Table 16; 1971b, Table 20; 1982a, Tables 19 and 22.
Note: See Tables 3–3.a. to 3–3.k. for U.S. census count of ethnic populations by age and percentage distribution, Hawai'i, 1900–1980.

228

				Distribution (percent)					
Age	1900	1910	1920	1930	1940	1950	1960	1970	1980
Males									
1–4	7.26	9.88	12.90	11.01	8.33	11.99	12.22	9.08	8.09
5–9	5.36	7.82	10.24	10.73	8.95	9.72	10.99	10.27	7.59
10–14	4.22	5.78	7.45	8.64	9.84	7.45	9.66	10.22	7.77
15–19	6.24	6.39	7.64	8.68	10.75	8.57	9.06	9.34	9.23
20–24	14.16	11.05	9.80	14.27	13.08	10.05	8.99	11.73	11.94
25–29	18.81	10.93	7.70	11.38	11.05	9.48	6.63	7.60	9.89
30–34	14.20	12.24	8.56	7.75	8.80	8.45	7.15	5.97	8.69
35–39	10.63	11.58	7.83	5.77	7.33	8.27	7.44	5.78	6.61
40–44	7.33	8.61	7.89	5.43	5.29	6.54	6.34	5.95	4.80
45–49	4.10	6.12	7.26	4.53	3.94	5.61	5.79	5.85	4.36
50–54	2.47	3.77	4.97	4.03	3.84	3.91	4.69	4.91	4.71
55–59	1.44	2.15	3.01	3.09	2.80	2.72	3.87	4.27	4.75
60–64	1.79	1.87	2.50	2.23	2.47	2.73	2.53	3.45	3.82
65–69	0.80	0.87	1.25	1.28	1.82	1.82	1.63	2.42	3.11
70–74	0.41	0.46	0.53	0.65	0.94	1.34	1.48	1.45	2.22
75+	0.43	0.45	0.44	0.50	0.73	1.36	1.53	1.71	2.42[c]
Unknown	0.35	0.03	0.05	0.03	0.04	0.00	0.00	0.00	0.00
Total	100.00	100.00	100.00	100.00	100.00	100.00	100.00	100.00	100.00
Females									
1–4	15.44	17.29	18.18	16.23	11.04	13.80	13.49	9.38	8.05
5–9	11.44	13.68	14.05	15.94	12.05	11.14	12.09	10.52	7.55
10–14	8.30	9.34	10.31	12.91	13.12	8.83	10.64	10.56	7.75
15–19	8.84	8.41	8.69	9.72	12.33	9.05	8.21	9.36	8.68
20–24	12.60	9.40	9.49	7.53	10.68	10.10	6.86	9.41	9.92
25–29	13.72	10.17	9.41	7.78	8.54	10.50	7.52	7.88	9.88
30–34	9.18	9.38	7.41	7.01	6.63	8.74	8.40	6.44	8.79
35–39	6.51	7.86	6.76	6.46	6.13	6.59	8.17	6.39	6.65
40–44	4.21	4.96	5.39	4.58	5.13	4.79	6.42	6.79	5.04
45–49	3.04	3.38	3.96	3.82	4.40	4.33	4.72	6.19	5.03
50–54	1.89	2.31	2.43	3.07	3.20	3.63	3.46	4.99	5.51
55–59	1.30	1.39	1.47	2.10	2.40	2.87	3.02	3.60	5.08
60–64	1.19	0.88	1.05	1.28	1.87	2.06	2.44	2.59	4.03
65–69	0.70	0.63	0.62	0.69	1.23	1.53	1.84	2.14	2.93
70–74	0.55	0.41	0.35	0.39	0.65	1.02	1.24	1.64	1.96
75+	0.71	0.49	0.41	0.45	0.57	1.01	1.48	2.12	3.15[c]
Unknown	0.41	0.03	0.03	0.03	0.03	0.00	0.00	0.00	0.00
Total	100.00	100.00	100.00	100.00	100.00	100.00	100.00	100.00	100.00

[a]Includes population of outlying islands; see footnote b, Table 2–1.

[b]Census unrevised totals; the revised 1970 state total was 769,913.

[c]Includes age 75+; see Table 4–11 for ages 75–79, 80–84, and 85+.

Table 4-4. Population by Military Status, Age, and Sex, Hawai'i, 1970 and 1980

	1970					1980			
Age	Total	Military	Military Dependents	Civilians	Age	Total	Military	Military Dependents	Civilians
Males					Males				
0–4	36,284	0	6,029	30,255	0–4	39,538	0	7,088	32,450
5–9	40,818	0	6,150	34,668	5–9	37,859	0	5,529	32,330
10–14	41,617	33	5,229	36,355	10–14	38,633	0	3,772	34,861
15–19	37,497	3,781	2,363	31,353	15–19	45,740	5,598	2,184	37,958
20–24	46,046	22,122	288	23,636	20–24	59,293	21,970	636	36,687
25–29	30,787	7,326	77	23,384	25–29	48,617	9,960	408	38,249
30–34	23,479	5,327	30	18,122	30–34	43,449	7,345	144	35,960
35–39	22,968	5,111	15	17,842	35–39	33,336	4,939	82	28,315
40–44	23,741	2,655	6	21,080	40–44	23,428	2,534	18	20,876
45–49	23,408	1,616	0	21,792	45–49	20,760	1,001	34	19,725
50–54	20,283	826	4	19,453	50–54	23,115	428	93	22,594
55–59	17,044	140	23	16,881	55–59	24,116	185	57	23,874
60–64	13,090	18	37	13,035	60–64	18,914	63	33	18,818
65–69	9,277	21	16	9,240	65–69	15,238	0	80	15,158
70–74	5,927	0	17	5,910	70–74	10,952	0	24	10,928
75+	7,077	34	50	6,993	75+	11,984	9	10	11,965
Subtotal	399,343	49,010	20,334	329,999	Subtotal	494,972	54,032	20,192	420,748

Females

Age				
0–4	34,415	0	5,700	28,715
5–9	38,918	0	6,042	32,876
10–14	39,320	0	4,917	34,403
15–19	34,264	32	2,973	31,259
20–24	34,689	440	5,511	28,738
25–29	29,278	131	4,446	24,701
30–34	24,092	95	4,065	19,932
35–39	23,676	66	3,427	20,183
40–44	24,461	57	1,807	22,597
45–49	22,950	36	1,166	21,748
50–54	18,283	40	482	17,761
55–59	13,166	27	149	12,990
60–64	9,745	4	84	9,657
65–69	8,224	8	56	8,160
70–74	5,984	7	53	5,924
75 +	7,751	0	49	7,702
Subtotal	369,216	943	40,927	327,346
Total	768,559	49,953	61,261	657,345

Females

Age				
0–4	37,446	0	6,910	30,536
5–9	35,452	0	5,161	30,291
10–14	36,114	0	3,617	32,497
15–19	40,314	411	2,841	37,062
20–24	46,694	1,937	5,738	39,019
25–29	46,836	1,237	5,923	39,676
30–34	41,332	447	5,104	35,781
35–39	31,973	113	3,210	28,650
40–44	23,312	83	1,537	21,692
45–49	22,726	88	812	21,826
50–54	26,496	65	422	26,009
55–59	24,039	18	169	23,852
60–64	19,194	12	99	19,083
65–69	13,415	0	121	13,924
70–74	9,572	0	76	9,496
75 +	14,804	0	42	14,762
Subtotal	469,719	4,411	41,782	423,526
Total	964,691	58,443	61,974	844,274

Sources: Hawaii (State) DPED 1970, Statistical Report No. 105; Data Book, 1986, Table 17.

Note: Civilians other than military dependents are calculated as a residual. Figures for 1980 are based on a 15.7 percent sample; therefore the age and sex samples do not exactly match those in other tables.

Table 4-5. Military Population by Race, Hawai'i, 1980

Ethnic Group	Total Population[a]	Armed Forces	Military Dependents	Other Civilians
Total	964,691	58,443	61,974	844,274
White	331,854	43,130	41,708	247,372
Percent	34.4	73.8	67.3	29.3
Black	17,364	7,773	4,648	5,066
Percent	1.8	13.3	7.5	0.6
American Indian, Eskimo, Aleut	2,894	526	248	2,533
Percent	0.3	0.9	0.4	0.3
Asian & Pacific Islander	591,356	4,734	12,891	572,418
Percent	61.3	8.1	20.8	67.8
Other	21,223	2,279	2,479	16,885
Percent	2.2	3.9	4.0	2.0

Source: Hawaii (State) DPED 1986, Data Book, Table 34.

[a]Differences between these figures and Table 3-1 relate to differences in underlying census tables.

Table 4-6. Vital Events and Vital Rates, Resident Population, Hawai'i, 1900–1985

Year	Resident Population[a]	Births[b] Number	Births[b] Rate[d]	Deaths[b] Number	Deaths[b] Rate[d]	Marriages[b] Number	Marriages[b] Rate[d]	Marriages[b] Percent Interracial	Divorces[b,c] Number	Divorces[b,c] Rate[d]
1900	154,193	1,026	6.7	2,376	15.4	NA	NA	NA	48	0.3
1901	155,547	2,058	13.2	3,029	19.5	NA	NA	NA	85	0.5
1902	157,436	2,350	14.9	2,578	16.4	1,155	7.3	NA	56	0.4
1903	162,634	2,526	15.5	2,657	16.3	1,184	7.3	NA	62	0.4
1904	167,976	2,510	14.9	2,783	16.6	1,125	6.7	NA	89	0.5
1905	166,728	2,609	15.6	2,686	16.1	1,223	7.3	NA	109	0.7
1906	166,895	2,830	17.0	2,854	17.1	1,264	7.6	NA	87	0.5
1907	174,740	3,574	20.5	3,065	17.5	2,143	12.3	NA	271	1.6
1908	182,662	4,609	25.2	2,811	15.4	1,875	10.3	NA	131	0.7
1909	188,316	4,536	24.1	2,801	14.9	1,799	9.6	NA	223	1.2
1910	193,225	4,472	23.1	3,194	16.5	2,065	10.7	NA	197	1.0
1911	196,735	4,776	24.3	3,102	15.8	2,673	13.6	NA	284	1.4
1912	207,276	5,420	26.1	3,128	15.1	3,223	15.5	NA	352	1.7
1913	218,417	6,128	28.1	3,543	16.2	3,184	14.6		337	1.5
1914	226,868	6,971	30.7	3,682	16.2	2,769	12.2		324	1.4
1915	231,515	7,719	33.3	3,447	14.9	2,705	11.7	11.5	389	1.7
1916	237,538	7,989	33.6	3,879	16.3	2,778	11.7		379	1.6
1917	250,138	9,095	36.4	3,769	15.1	2,635	10.5	NA	383	1.5
1918	254,465	9,220	36.2	3,959	15.6	2,398	9.4	NA	557	2.2
1919	260,408	9,633	37.0	3,881	14.9	2,013	7.7	NA	525	2.0
1920	260,726	9,950	38.2	4,601	17.6	2,127	8.2	NA	570	2.2
1921	271,790	10,649	39.2	3,921	14.4	2,338	8.6		562	2.1
1922	284,290	11,171	39.3	4,354	15.3	2,493	8.8	18.0	555	2.0
1923	299,507	11,724	39.1	4,644	15.3	2,795	9.3		560	1.9
1924	308,912	12,911	41.8	4,020	13.0	3,354	10.9		557	1.8

1925	325,960	12,602	38.7	4,111	12.6	2,736	8.4		627	1.9
1926	331,126	12,282	37.1	3,886	11.7	2,617	7.9	21.9	618	1.9
1927	337,294	11,821	35.0	4,037	12.0	2,626	7.8		676	2.0
1928	351,382	11,662	33.2	4,124	11.7	2,737	7.8		595	1.7
1929	360,406	11,235	31.2	4,383	12.2	2,565	7.1	21.3	563	1.6
1930	367,880	10,803	29.4	3,864	10.5	2,443	6.6		529	1.4
1931	377,530	10,469	27.7	3,730	9.9	2,629	7.0		598	1.6
1932	385,013	10,500	27.3	3,670	9.5	2,726	7.1	21.6	527	1.4
1933	383,973	9,635	25.1	3,648	9.5	2,621	6.8		541	1.4
1934	384,331	9,313	24.2	3,455	9.0	2,838	7.4		595	1.6
1935	389,562	9,199	23.6	3,306	8.5	2,985	7.7	20.0	690	1.8
1936	396,072	8,594	21.7	3,434	8.7	3,292	8.3	22.1	730	1.8
1937	400,816	8,984	22.4	3,547	8.8	3,556	8.9	24.6	815	2.0
1938	409,960	9,066	22.1	3,229	7.9	3,868	9.4	24.2	862	2.1
1939	415,705	9,271	22.3	3,128	7.5	3,963	9.5	22.6	686	1.7
1940	427,884	9,650	22.6	3,086	7.2	5,355	12.5	25.0	946	2.2
1941	459,335	10,124	22.0	5,351	11.6	6,066	13.2	23.9	1,147	2.5
1942	582,026	10,406	17.9	3,397	5.8	7,093	12.2	25.7	1,517	2.6
1943	649,650	11,638	17.9	3,343	5.1	4,984	7.7	29.1	1,610	2.5
1944	858,945	12,697	14.8	3,728	4.3	4,882	5.7	31.9	1,574	1.8
1945	814,601	12,299	15.1	3,396	4.2	4,978	6.1	32.2	1,530	1.9
1946	545,439	12,684	23.3	3,229	5.9	5,945	10.9	27.1	1,453	2.7
1947	526,238	14,589	27.7	3,219	6.1	5,846	11.1	28.8	1,178	2.2
1948	517,013	14,481	28.0	3,104	6.0	5,671	11.0	29.5	1,388	2.7
1949	511,039	14,249	27.9	3,020	5.9	5,316	10.4	29.9	1,052	2.1
1950	497,980	14,054	28.2	2,919	5.9	5,575	11.2	29.7	1,173	2.4
1951	514,256	14,446	28.1	2,877	5.6	5,860	11.4	30.6	1,185	2.3
1952	517,378	15,596	30.1	2,887	5.6	5,743	11.1	31.5	1,300	2.5
1953	509,947	16,103	31.6	2,905	5.7	5,633	11.0	30.5	1,287	2.5
1954	505,461	16,191	32.0	3,000	5.9	5,362	10.6	31.2	1,270	2.5
1955	539,292	16,305	30.2	3,223	6.0	5,431	10.1	31.3	1,343	2.5

continued

Table 4-6. *(continued)*

Year	Resident Population[a]	Births[b] Number	Births[b] Rate[d]	Deaths[b] Number	Deaths[b] Rate[d]	Marriages[b] Number	Marriages[b] Rate[d]	Marriages[b] Percent Interracial	Divorces[b,c] Number	Divorces[b,c] Rate[d]
1956	558,575	17,122	30.7	3,143	5.6	5,158	9.2	35.1	1,305	2.3
1957	584,466	17,040	29.2	3,422	5.9	4,897	8.4	34.4	1,182	2.0
1958	605,356	16,710	27.6	3,185	5.3	4,727	7.8	37.6	1,228	2.0
1959	622,087	17,050	27.4	3,374	5.4	4,958	8.0	37.3	1,378	2.2
1960	641,520	17,193	26.8	3,593	5.6	5,237	8.2	37.3	1,270	2.0
1961	658,684	17,558	26.7	3,428	5.2	5,298	8.0	36.1	1,556	2.4
1962	683,513	17,932	26.2	3,575	5.2	5,484	8.0	37.7	1,471	2.2
1963	682,241	17,744	26.0	3,709	5.4	5,750	8.4	38.6	1,515	2.2
1964	699,858	17,284	24.7	3,696	5.3	5,790	8.3	38.3	1,690	2.4
1965	703,804	16,259	23.1	3,764	5.3	6,071	8.6	38.1	1,111	1.6
1966	710,325	14,943	21.0	3,839	5.4	5,792	8.2	37.7	897	1.3
1967	722,528	14,765	20.4	3,973	5.5	7,345e	10.2	33.5	1,451	2.0
1968	734,456	14,595	19.9	4,250	5.8	9,021e	12.3	33.8	1,865	2.5
1969	750,228	15,690	20.9	4,214	5.6	9,891e	13.2	33.7	2,314	3.1
1970	771,600	16,361	21.2	3,971	5.1	10,599e	10.1	33.7	2,589	3.4
1971	801,600	15,780	19.7	4,130	5.2	9,734e	10.1	38.7	3,691	4.6
1972	828,300	15,364	18.5	4,245	5.1	9,750	10.2	38.6	3,891	4.7
1973	851,600	15,328	18.0	4,356	5.1	9,776	10.2	40.6	4,170	4.9
1974	868,000	15,472	17.8	4,286	4.9	9,649	9.8	40.1	4,111	4.7
1975	886,200	15,689	17.7	4,272	4.8	9,673	9.5	39.6	4,265	4.8
1976	904,200	16,292	18.0	4,350	4.8	9,769	9.2	38.8	4,712	5.2
1977	918,300	16,874	18.4	4,349	4.7	10,266	9.2	37.5	4,601	5.0
1978	931,600	16,717	17.9	4,508	4.8	10,736	9.3	37.9	4,837	5.2
1979	953,300	17,513	18.4	4,791	5.0	11,678	9.9	38.2	5,055	5.3
1980	968,900	18,129	18.7	4,903	5.1	11,856	9.7	37.6	4,438	4.6

Year									
1981	980,200	18,174	18.5	4,927	5.0	12,218	9.6	36.1	4,253	4.3
1982	997,600	18,675	18.7	5,123	5.1	13,483	10.1	35.7	4,233	4.2
1983	1,018,600	19,090	18.7	5,409	5.3	14,062	10.0	35.5	4,583	4.5
1984	1,036,000	18,667	18.0	5,571	5.4	14,982	9.7	33.4	4,769	4.6
1985	1,051,500	18,267	17.3	5,751	5.5	15,421	9.4	33.6	4,887	4.6

Sources: Hawaii (State) DOH 1974, R & S Report, No. 5, Tables 1, 2, 3; 1981, R & S Report No. 33, Tables 1, 6; Annual Report, Statistical Supplement, 1952–1985; Hawaii (State) DPED Data Book, 1986, Tables 3, 56, 94; Schmitt 1977, Tables 1.4, 2.11.

Note: Variations with Table 3–5 reflect differences of underlying sources.

NA Not available.

[a]As of July 1, estimated.

[b]Includes military dependents. Non-resident births and deaths and resident births and deaths occurring out of state are excluded. See Table 3–10 for interracial marriages.

[c]Final decrees; an interlocutory decree for six months was abolished July 1, 1971.

[d]Per 1,000 resident population.

[e]Figure inflated by non-resident military personnel on "rest and recuperation" in Hawai'i.

Table 4–7. Births to Unmarried Mothers, Infant Deaths, Abortions, and Maternal Deaths, Hawai'i, 1910–1985

	Births to Un-married Mothers		Infant Deaths[a]		Abortions[b,c]		Maternal Deaths
	Number	Rate Per 1,000 Live Births	Number	Rate Per 1,000 Live Births	Number	Rate Per 1,000 Live Births	Number
1910	NA	NA	1,013	226.5	NA	NA	47
1920	NA	NA	1,083	108.8	NA	NA	87
1930	317	29	889	82.3	NA	NA	67
1940	563	58	442	43.7	NA	NA	23
1950	698	50	335	23.8	NA	NA	12
1960	882	51	399	23.2	NA	NA	5
1961	1,011	58	381	21.7	NA	NA	4
1962	1,081	60	369	20.6	NA	NA	5
1963	1,137	64	399	22.5	NA	NA	3
1964	1,151	67	342	19.8	NA	NA	2
1965	1,177	72	349	21.5	NA	NA	2
1966	1,253	84	282	18.9	NA	NA	3
1967	1,292	88	250	16.9	NA	NA	1
1968	1,383	95	277	19.0	NA	NA	3
1969	1,516	97	302	19.2	NA	NA	1
1970	1,577	96	315	19.1	NA	NA	3
1971	1,400	88	254	16.0	4,135	262.0	3
1972	1,433	93	270	17.5	4,547	296.0	2
1973	1,597	104	210	13.7	4,534	295.8	2
1974	1,684	109	241	16.0	4,158	268.7	0
1975	1,936	123	201	13.7	4,545	289.7	1
1976	2,036	125	172	11.2	5,163	316.9	0
1977	2,419	143	196	12.3	5,249	311.1	0
1978	2,677	160	185	12.0	6,014	359.7	1
1979	2,687	164	179	10.9	6,125	349.7	0
1980	3,188	176	183	10.8	6,462	356.4	1
1981	3,303	182	178	10.5	6,692	364.1	3
1982	3,472	186	158	8.5	6,224	330.7	1
1983	3,766	197	175	10.0	6,041	313.9	0
1984	3,585	192	186	9.2	5,277	282.7	2
1985	3,650	200	159	8.7	5,670	310.4	2

Sources: Hawaii (State) DOH 1974, R & S Report No. 5, Table 1; 1981, R & S Report No. 33, Tables 1, 3, 7, 9; Annual Report, Statistical Supplement, 1952–1985.

NA Not available.

[a]Resident population.

[b]Legal restrictions for elective abortions were removed by State Law of Hawaii, Act 1, March 11, 1970.

[c]See Table 3–9 for abortions by ethnicity.

Table 4–8. Life Expectancy at Birth in Selected Areas of the World

	Year	Males	Females
Hawai'i	1980	75.0[a]	81.5[a]
Africa			
Ethiopia	1980–1985	39.3	42.5
Morocco	1980–1985	56.6	60.0
Sierra Leone	1980–1985	32.5	35.5
South Africa	1980–1985	51.8	55.2
Sudan	1980–1985	46.6	49.0
America, North			
Canada	1980–1982	71.9	78.9
Haiti	1980–1985	51.2	54.4
Mexico	1979	62.1	66.0
Nicaragua	1980–1985	58.7	61.0
United States	1984	71.2	78.2
America, South			
Argentina	1980–1981	65.5	72.7
Bolivia	1980–1985	48.6	53.0
Chile	1975–1980	61.3	67.6
Asia			
Afghanistan	1980–1985	36.6	37.3
Bangladesh	1981	55.3	54.4
China	1980–1985	66.7	68.9
Hong Kong	1985	73.8	79.2
India	1980–1985	55.6	55.2
Indonesia	1980–1985	52.2	54.9
Japan	1985	74.8	80.5
Korea, North	1980–1985	64.6	71.0
Korea, Republic of	1978–1979	62.7	69.1
Malaysia	1984	67.6	72.7
Nepal	1981	50.9	48.1
Pakistan	1976–1978	59.0	59.2
Philippines	1980–1985	60.2	63.7
Europe			
Czechoslovakia	1984	67.1	74.3
Denmark	1984–1985	71.6	77.5
France	1983–1985	71.0	75.0
Germany, Federal Republic of	1985	71.2	78.1
Hungary	1985	65.6	73.6
Norway	1984–1985	72.8	79.5
Sweden	1985	73.8	79.7
Switzerland	1984–1985	73.5	80.0
United Kingdom	1982–1984	71.4	77.2
Oceania			
American Samoa	1976	61.0	64.3
Australia	1985	72.3	78.8
Fiji	1980–1985	67.0	71.0
New Zealand	1985	71.0	76.8
Papua New Guinea	1980–1985	51.2	52.7
USSR	1984–1985	62.9	72.3

Source: Gardner 1984, p. 9; Han, Tuan, and Liu 1987; United Nations, Department of International Economic and Social Affairs 1985, Table 22; 1988, Table 4.

[a]This figure is given as 74.0 years for males and 80.3 years for females in the tabulations of the U.S. DHHS, Public Health Service 1987, which used a 3-year denominator in contrast with Gardner's two-year base.

239

Table 4-9. Life Expectancy by Age and Sex, Hawaiʻi, 1920–1980

Age	1920 Males	1920 Females	1930 Males	1930 Females	1940 Males	1940 Females	1950 Males	1950 Females	1960 Males	1960 Females	1970 Males	1970 Females	1980 Males	1980 Females
0–1	47.8	47.3	53.1	56.3	59.5	62.6	67.8	71.3	69.8	74.0	71.0	76.8	75.0	81.5
1	52.6	51.3	58.3	59.9	61.8	64.3	68.8	71.8	70.6	74.5	71.5	77.0	74.9	81.2
5	51.0	49.7	56.6	57.8	58.6	61.1	65.2	68.2	66.9	70.7	67.7	73.1	71.1	77.3
10	47.2	45.8	52.3	53.5	54.0	56.5	60.4	63.4	62.0	65.9	62.8	68.2	66.2	73.4
15	43.1	41.8	47.6	48.9	49.4	51.7	55.5	58.5	57.1	60.9	57.9	63.3	61.3	67.4
20	39.5	38.6	43.5	44.6	44.9	46.9	50.9	53.7	52.4	56.1	53.2	58.5	56.6	61.4
25	36.3	35.8	39.3	40.7	40.3	42.5	46.2	48.9	47.8	51.3	48.5	53.6	52.0	57.5
30	33.1	33.3	35.1	36.8	35.9	38.1	41.5	44.2	42.9	46.5	43.8	48.8	47.3	52.7
35	29.8	30.8	31.1	33.0	31.6	33.8	36.9	39.5	38.3	41.6	39.2	44.1	42.6	48.0
40	26.5	27.9	27.2	29.1	27.4	29.4	32.4	34.9	33.7	36.9	34.6	39.4	38.0	43.8
45	23.2	24.7	23.5	25.5	23.4	25.3	28.0	30.5	29.2	32.3	30.1	34.7	33.4	38.5
50	20.0	21.4	19.9	21.9	19.6	21.1	23.9	26.3	24.8	28.0	25.9	30.2	29.2	32.3
55	17.0	18.1	16.9	18.3	15.9	17.3	20.0	22.1	20.9	23.9	21.9	25.9	25.1	29.5
60	14.1	14.9	13.9	15.1	12.5	13.6	16.8	18.4	17.3	20.0	18.2	21.8	21.3	25.3
65	11.3	12.3	11.1	11.8	9.1	9.9	13.7	15.1	14.0	16.3	14.8	17.9	17.5	21.1
70	8.8	10.1	8.7	9.3	5.9	6.3	10.9	12.1	11.3	12.9	11.8	14.3	14.2	17.3
75	6.6	8.9	7.1	7.1	3.0	3.0	8.8	9.5	8.6	9.9	9.2	11.1	11.0	13.4
80	4.6	6.7	NA	NA	NA	NA	6.9	7.2	6.4	7.2	7.1	8.3	8.7	10.6
85	2.6	4.7	NA	NA	NA	NA	5.4	5.7	4.7	4.8	5.1	6.1	6.5	7.7

Sources: Gardner and Nordyke 1974, Tables 28, 29, 30, 31, 32; Gardner 1984, Table 1; United States Department of Health, Education, and Welfare 1976, Tables 2, 3.

NA Not available.

Table 4-10. Life Expectancy by Ethnicity and Sex, Hawai'i and the United States, 1920-1980

Population	Total					Males					Females				
	1920	1940	1960	1980	1985a	1920	1940	1960	1980	1985a	1920	1940	1960	1980	1985a
Hawai'i Total	46.9	62.8	72.3	78.0	—	47.0	60.9	70.4	75.0	—	46.8	66.1	74.8	81.5	—
Chinese	54.7	65.1	73.8	80.2	NA	53.9	64.1	71.8	78.4	NA	57.2	67.8	76.4	81.7	NA
Filipino	33.0	62.9	71.6	78.8	NA	32.8	62.3	71.2	77.3	NA	29.1	63.0	72.1	81.0	NA
Hawaiian	35.0	52.4	64.9	74.0	—	35.9	51.0	63.0	70.9	—	34.2	53.8	67.1	76.0	—
Japanese	51.2	67.5	75.6	79.7	—	51.3	65.5	73.6	77.7	—	52.0	70.8	77.6	81.5	—
White	57.0	64.9	72.8	76.4		55.0	61.5	70.0	74.2		60.1	70.5	76.2	79.1	
U.S. Total	54.1	62.9	69.7	73.7	74.7	53.6	60.8	66.6	70.0	71.1	54.6	65.2	73.1	77.5	78.3
Black & Other	45.3	53.1	63.6	69.5	71.2	45.5	51.5	61.1	65.3	67.2	45.2	54.9	66.3	73.6	75.2
White	54.9	64.2	70.6	74.4	75.3	54.4	62.1	67.4	70.7	71.8	55.6	66.6	74.1	78.1	78.7

Sources: Gardner 1984, p.7 (revised); Park, Gardner and Nordyke 1979 (revised); United States, BOC 1987, Table 105.

NA Not available.

[a]Preliminary, 1985.

241

Table 4-11. Numbers, Median Age, and Growth Rates of Total and Elderly Populations, Hawai'i, 1900–2000

Population	1900			1910			1920			1930		
	Males	Females	Total	Males	Females	Total	Males	Females	Total	Males	Females	Total
All Ages	106,369	47,632	154,001	123,099	68,810	191,909	151,146	104,766	255,912	222,640	145,696	368,336
Ages 65+	1,744	933	2,677	2,188	1,050	3,238	3,351	1,444	4,795	5,402	2,236	7,638
65–69	851	332	1,183	1,073	431	1,504	1,887	651	2,538	2,849	1,009	3,858
70–74	434	263	697	567	284	851	796	365	1,161	1,438	575	2,013
75+	459	338	797	548	335	883	668	428	1,096	1,115	652	1,767
Median Age (years)												
Total Population	28.3	22.3	26.9	29.1	20.7	26.4	26.3	19.3	23.3	23.8	17.5	21.7
Ages 65+	70.2	72.5	71.1	70.2	71.7	70.7	69.4	71.0	69.7	69.7	70.2	69.9
Growth Rate[a]												
Total Population	5.94	4.21	5.37	1.46	3.68	2.20	2.05	4.20	2.95	3.87	3.30	3.64
Ages 65+	NA	NA	NA	2.27	1.18	1.90	4.26	3.19	3.93	4.78	4.37	4.66
Percentage of Ages 65+ in Total Population	1.6	2.0	1.7	1.8	1.5	1.7	2.2	1.4	1.9	2.4	1.5	2.1
Percentage of Elderly Population												
Ages 65+	100.0	100.0	100.0	99.9	100.0	100.0	100.0	100.0	100.0	99.9	100.0	100.0
65–69	48.8	35.6	44.2	49.0	41.1	46.4	56.3	45.1	52.9	52.7	45.1	50.5
70–74	24.9	28.2	26.0	25.9	27.0	26.3	23.8	25.3	24.2	26.6	25.7	26.4
75+	26.3	36.2	29.8	25.0	31.9	27.3	19.9	29.6	22.9	20.6	29.2	23.1

Table 4-11. (continued)

Population	1940			1950			1960			1970		
	Males	Females	Total	Males	Females	Total	Males	Females	Total	Males	Females	Total
All Ages	245,135	178,195	423,330	273,895	225,899	499,794	338,173	294,599	632,772	399,205	369,356	768,561
Ages 65+	8,559	4,355	12,914	12,382	8,037	20,419	15,712	13,450	29,162	22,254	21,862	44,116
65–69	4,472	2,193	6,665	4,979	3,449	8,428	5,527	5,432	10,959	9,671	7,987	17,658
70–74	2,295	1,152	3,447	3,665	2,306	5,971	5,021	3,667	8,688	5,781	6,050	11,831
75–79	1,792	1,010	2,802	3,738	2,282	3,570	5,164	4,351	5,090	6,802	7,825	7,021
80–84	b	b	b	b	b	1,604	b	b	2,845	b	b	4,593
85+	b	b	b	b	b	846	b	b	1,580	b	b	3,013
Median Age (years)												
Total Population	24.6	20.7	23.2	26.2	23.6	24.9	24.5	24.1	24.3	24.7	25.5	25.0
Ages 65+	69.8	70.0	69.8	71.6	71.2	71.5	72.3	71.8	72.1	71.3	72.4	71.9
Growth Rate[a]												
Total Population	0.96	2.01	1.39	1.10	2.37	1.66	2.11	2.66	2.36	1.66	2.26	1.94
Ages 65+	4.60	6.67	5.25	3.69	6.13	4.58	2.38	5.15	3.56	3.48	4.86	4.14
Percentage of Ages 65+ in Total Population	3.5	2.4	3.1	4.5	3.6	4.1	4.6	4.6	4.6	5.6	5.9	5.7
Percentage of Elderly Population												
Ages 65+	99.9	100.1	100.0	100.0	100.0	100.0	100.1	100.0	100.1	100.1	100.0	99.9
65–69	52.2	50.4	51.6	40.2	42.9	41.3	35.2	40.4	37.6	43.5	36.5	40.0
70–74	26.8	26.5	26.7	29.6	28.7	29.2	32.0	27.3	29.8	26.0	27.7	26.8
75–79	20.9	23.2	21.7	30.2	28.4	17.5	32.9	32.3	17.5	30.6	35.8	15.9
80–84	b	b	b	b	b	7.9	b	b	9.8	b	b	10.4
85+	b	b	b	b	b	4.1	b	b	5.4	b	b	6.8

continued

243

Table 4-11. (continued)

Population	1980			1990 (projected)[c]			2000 (projected)[c]		
	Males	Females	Total	Males	Females	Total	Males	Females	Total
All Ages	494,683	470,008	964,691	578,500	560,000	1,138,400	639,900	627,900	1,267,800
Ages 65+	38,359	37,791	76,150	58,300	66,000	124,100	70,300	89,100	159,500
65–69	15,384	13,769	29,153	19,100	20,900	40,000	20,900	24,200	45,200
70–74	10,991	9,231	20,222	15,500	16,700	32,200	17,400	20,900	38,300
75–79	6,796	6,877	13,673	11,100	12,100	23,100	13,400	17,000	30,400
80–84	3,177	4,364	7,541	6,900	8,000	14,800	9,200	12,400	21,600
85+	2,011	3,550	5,561	5,700	8,300	14,000	9,400	14,600	24,000
Median Age (years)									
Total Population	27.7	29.1	28.4	30.1	32.5	31.3	32.2	35.3	33.7
Ages 65+	71.7	72.8	72.1	73.2	73.6	73.4	74.1	74.9	74.5
Growth Rate[a]									
Total Population	2.14	2.41	2.27	1.53	1.72	1.62	1.01	1.14	1.08
Ages 65+	5.44	5.47	5.46	4.19	5.58	4.88	1.87	3.00	2.51
Percentage of Ages 65+ in Total Population	7.8	8.0	7.9	10.1	11.8	10.9	11.0	14.2	12.6
Percentage of Elderly Population									
Ages 65+	100.0	99.9	100.0	100.0	100.0	99.9	100.1	100.1	99.9
65–69	40.1	36.4	38.3	32.8	31.7	32.2	29.7	27.2	28.3
70–74	28.7	24.4	26.6	26.6	25.3	25.9	24.8	23.5	24.0
75–79	17.7	18.2	17.9	19.0	18.3	18.6	19.1	19.1	19.1
80–84	8.3	11.5	9.9	11.8	12.1	11.9	13.1	13.9	13.5
85+	5.2	9.4	7.3	9.8	12.6	11.3	13.4	16.4	15.0

Sources: Hawaii (State) DPED 1984a, Table 13; Nordyke 1977, Table 4A; Schmitt 1977, Tables 1.9 and 1.11; United States, BOC 1953, Table 10; 1961, Table 16; 1971, Table 20; 1982, Table 19.

Note: For projections, total may not exactly equal male plus female figures because of rounding. Percentages may not sum to 100.0 because of rounding. NA Not available.

[a]Average annual growth rate in preceding decade.

[b]Data for this age group included with ages 75+.

[c]According to Hawaii (State) DPED 1984 population and economic projections, Series M-F.

Table 4-12. Elderly Population by Age and Ethnicity, Hawai'i, 1980

Age Group	All Ethnicities	Blacks	Chinese	Filipinos	Hawaiians	Japanese	Koreans	Samoans	Whites	Others[a]
65–69	29,153	64	2,404	4,658	2,217	10,144	393	158	8,498	617
70–74	20,222	45	1,640	4,148	1,458	6,222	279	69	5,952	409
75–79[b]	13,673	25	2,538	3,921	1,538	10,756	376	88	3,570	425
80–84[b]	7,541	8	NA	NA	NA	NA	NA	NA	2,076	NA
85+[b]	5,561	8	NA	NA	NA	NA	NA	NA	1,446	NA
65+										
Number	76,150	150	6,582	12,727	5,213	27,122	1,048	315	21,542	1,451
Percentage	100.0	0.20	8.64	16.71	6.85	35.62	1.38	0.41	28.29	1.90
All Ages										
Number	964,691	17,364	56,285	133,940	115,500	239,748	17,962	14,073	318,770	51,049
Percentage	100.0	1.80	5.83	13.89	11.97	24.85	1.86	1.46	33.05	5.29
Percentage 65+ of the Total Population of Each Ethnicity	7.89	0.86	11.69	9.50	4.51	11.31	5.83	2.24	6.76	2.84

Source: United States, BOC 1982, Tables 19, 22.

Note: U.S. census data on race are not comparable to HHSP data on ethnicity (see Note, Table 3-3.a. and Chapter 4, Ethnicity).

NA Not available.

[a]Category includes American Indians, Eskimos, Aleuts, Asian Indians, Vietnamese, Guamanians, and Others.

[b]Age group 75+ for Chinese, Filipinos, Hawaiians, Japanese, Koreans, Samoans, and Others.

Table 4-13. Residence by County and Sex for Total and Elderly Populations, Hawai'i, 1980

	Population								
	State			Hawaii County			Honolulu County		
Item	Males	Females	Total	Males	Females	Total	Males	Females	Total
Population									
All Ages	494,683	470,008	964,691	46,665	45,388	92,053	391,903	370,662	762,565
Elderly									
65+	38,359	37,791	76,150	5,102	4,276	9,378	27,051	28,317	55,368
65–74	26,375	23,000	49,375	3,445	2,645	6,090	18,740	17,192	35,932
75–84	9,973	11,241	21,214	1,364	1,220	2,584	6,943	8,485	15,428
85+	2,011	3,550	5,561	293	411	704	1,368	2,640	4,008
Population as Percentage of State									
Total Population									
Total	100.0	100.0	100.0	9.4	9.7	9.5	79.2	78.9	79.1
Elderly	100.0	99.9	100.0	13.3	11.3	12.3	70.5	74.9	72.7
Elderly Population as Percentage of State or County Population	7.8	8.0	7.9	10.9	9.4	10.2	6.9	7.6	7.3

Table 4–13. *(continued)*

Item	Population					
	Kauai County			Maui County		
	Males	Females	Total	Males	Females	Total
Population						
All Ages	20,052	19,030	39,082	36,063	34,928	70,991
Elderly						
65+	2,480	1,859	4,339	3,726	3,339	7,065
65–74	1,672	1,138	2,810	2,518	2,025	4,543
75–84	664	573	1,237	1,002	963	1,965
85+	144	148	292	206	351	557
Population as Percentage of State						
Total Population						
Total	4.1	4.0	4.0	7.3	7.4	7.4
Elderly	6.5	4.9	5.7	9.7	8.8	9.3
Elderly Population as Percentage of State or County Population	12.4	9.8	11.1	10.3	9.6	10.0

Source: United States, BOC 1981a.

Note: Percentages may not sum to 100.0 because of rounding.

Table 4-14. Origins of Early Contract Labor Immigrants to Hawai'i, 1852-1905

Place of Origin	Number of Immigrants
Korea	6,925
China	45,064
Japan	140,457
South Sea Islands	2,450
Norway	615
Germany	1,279
Italy	84
Austria	372
Portugal	14,670
Spain	2,299
Puerto Rico	5,200
U.S. (Black)	200
U.S. (White)	100
Russia	110

Source: Ivers 1909.

Table 4-15. Migration to Hawai'i, 1901–1985

Year	Total[b]	From Other States[a] Total[c]	Military Personnel	Military Dependents	Other Civilians	From Abroad[a] Total[d,e]	Canada
1901	NA	NA	NA	NA	NA	1,826	NA
1902						9,914	
1903						14,581	
1904						9,108	
1905						11,978	
1906						9,445	
1907						24,588	
1908						10,516	
1909						1,932	
1910						4,186	
1911						3,885	
1912						6,654	
1913						5,837	
1914						5,622	
1915						2,934	
1916						3,194	
1917						3,607	
1918						3,100	
1919						2,619	
1920						2,578	
1921						2,632	
1922						2,800	
1923						2,565	
1924						3,186	
1925						471	
1926						227	
1927						226	
1928						132	
1929						191	
1930						209	
1931						174	
1932						132	
1933						83	
1934						65	
1935						82	
1936						71	
1937						100	
1938						91	
1939						133	
1940						98	
1941						126	
1942						59	
1943						0	
1944						6	
1945						2	
1946						65	
1947						276	
1948						736	
1949						1,542	
1950						179	

| From Abroad[a] | | | | | | | | Rate of Alien Immigration per 1,000 Population |
China and Taiwan	Japan	Korea	Philippines[d]	Portugal	Spain	Vietnam	Other[f]	
1,094	338	4	NA	85	2	NA	303	11.8
297	9,125	12		35	0		445	63.1
573	13,045	515		12	1		435	89.8
415	6,590	1,884		12	0		207	54.3
205	6,692	4,892		3	0		186	71.9
106	9,051	98		5	0		185	56.7
8	20,865	9		1,328	2,251		127	141.1
27	9,153	8		1,115	18		195	57.8
58	1,679	2	639	1	10		182	10.4
91	1,239	7	2,915	864	1		1,984	21.8
130	1,883	8	1,610	548	868		448	20.0
114	2,816	17	5,234	1,114	2,156		437	31.8
143	4,062	45	4,182	228	1,043		316	26.8
129	3,817	92	2,436	13	1,362		209	24.7
111	2,625	78	1,786	2	3		115	121.7
119	2,797	80	1,949	2	0		196	13.4
141	3,178	116	2,928	6	4		162	14.4
101	2,856	78	2,889	0	0		65	12.1
72	2,384	66	3,232	0	0		97	9.9
107	2,138	45	3,443	1	0		287	9.9
161	2,153	41	4,656	9	1		267	9.5
275	2,212	58	9,674	4	4		247	9.8
304	1,989	53	7,099	3	7		209	8.6
293	2,635	75	6,977	2	2		179	10.4
68	274	7	10,645	0	0		122	1.5
30	61	9	4,177	0	0		127	0.7
36	70	10	9,158	0	0		110	0.7
18	25	0	10,857	0	0		89	0.4
21	58	7	7,309	0	0		105	0.5
22	61	4	7,372	0	0		122	0.6
21	68	0	6,014	1	0		84	0.5
18	57	1	1,226	0	3		53	0.3
NA	NA	NA	41	NA	NA		NA	0.2
			107					0.2
			NA					0.2
								0.2
								0.3
								0.2
								0.3
								0.2
								0.3
								0.1
								0.0
								0.0
								0.0
								0.1
								0.5
								1.4
								3.0
								0.4

continued

251

Table 4–15. (continued)

Year	Total[b]	From Other States[a]				From Abroad[a]	
		Total[c]	Military Personnel	Military Dependents	Other Civilians	Total[d,e]	Canada
1951	NA	NA	NA	NA	NA	294	NA
1952	6,833	6,131				702	
1953	7,589	6,976				613	
1954	6,549	5,728				821	
1955	7,451	6,500				951	
1956	11,047	9,960				1,087	
1957	14,908	13,524				1,384	
1958	19,547	18,140				1,407	
1959	17,492	15,876				1,616	
1960	19,589	17,970				1,619	
1961	15,837	14,075	1,690	1,723	10,662	1,762	
1962	21,503	19,455	3,302	5,176	10,977	2,048	
1963	22,222	20,455	3,280	5,760	11,415	1,767	
1964[g]	29,069	27,446	5,782	6,899	14,765	1,623	
1965	30,694	28,973	9,697	5,732	13,544	1,721	
1966	35,101	32,031	9,655	5,640	16,736	3,070	
1967	47,942	44,117	14,496	8,702	20,919	3,825	
1968	46,929	42,236	12,655	7,619	21,962	4,693	
1969	46,361	41,162	12,198	8,336	20,628	5,199	
1970	49,086	40,073	8,561	7,129	24,383	9,013[h]	90
1971	47,617	41,562	9,355	8,649	23,558	6,055	81
1972	51,153	44,388	10,267	11,637	22,484	6,765	92
1973	43,767	36,886	9,200	6,180	21,506	6,881	64
1974	43,556	37,007	9,421	8,744	18,842	6,549	64
1975	46,245	39,233	10,006	10,887	18,340	7,012	87
1976	50,461	40,690	10,991	10,518	19,181	9,771[i]	155
1977	51,442	43,617	12,361	12,771	18,485	7,825	175
1978	48,529	39,476	12,294	11,783	15,399	9,053	223
1979	31,503	22,559	5,283	4,699	12,577	8,944	135
1980	NA	13,922	5,559	5,097	3,266	NA	NA
1981	NA	18,134	6,981	7,694	3,459	NA	NA
1982	29,625	21,068	8,018	9,741	3,309	8,557	84
1983	28,838	21,720	7,353	8,562	5,805	7,118	109
1984	36,031	27,050	10,410	12,150	4,490	8,981	97
1985	33,638	25,770	11,247	11,599	2,924	7,868	130

Sources: Clifford 1975, Table 1; Hawaii (State) DPED, 1981 Data Book, Table 28; 1985, Table 3. Statistical Report No. 101, Table 11, 13; No. 108, Tables 1, 12, 13; No. 112, Tables 12, 13; No. 174, Table 12; No. 189, Tables 1, 3, 12, 13. Schmitt, 1977, Tables 3.1, 3.10.

NA Not available.

[a]Reporting Hawai'i as state on intended future permanent residence; excludes Filipinos before July 4, 1946.

[b]Includes intended residents from other states and from abroad; not adjusted for double counting of aliens aboard civilian carriers arriving from other states. Excludes American citizens and nationals migrating directly to Hawai'i from points outside the United States, such as from American Samoa, Canada, and Guam.

[c]By calendar year.

China and Taiwan	Japan	Korea	Philippines[d]	Portugal	Spain	Vietnam	Other[f]	Rate of Alien Immigration per 1,000 Population
			From Abroad[a]					
NA	NA	NA	NA	NA	NA	NA	NA	0.6
								1.4
								1.2
								1.6
								1.8
123	329						635	1.9
112	522						750	2.4
91	484						832	2.3
153	435						1,028	2.6
101	360						1,158	2.5
123	349		530				760	2.7
109	348		776				815	3.0
121	314		569				763	2.6
96	281		455				791	2.3
92	261		447				921	2.4
322	344		1,352				1,052	4.3
327	382		2,147				969	5.3
238	186	91	3,033	1			1,144	6.4
389	317	284	3,181	14			1,014	6.9
423	363	596	6,426[h]	NA			1,115	11.7
271	409	568	3,704				1,022	7.7
392	603	868	3,764				1,046	8.4
455	544	1,305	3,179				1,334	8.3
429	464	1,127	3,418				1,047	7.7
555	587	1,476	2,913			196	1,198	10.4
784	556	1,793	4,081			341	1,961	10.8
527	495	1,488	3,568			137	1,435	8.5
409	394	965	4,398			1,136	1,528	9.7
586	365	1,192	5,016			286	1,364	9.4
NA	NA	NA	NA			NA	NA	NA
NA	NA	NA	NA			NA	NA	NA
650	j	1,007	4,748			597	1,471	8.6
676	269	883	4,070			139	972	7.0
825	223	948	4,662			795	1,431	8.7
799	286	988	4,231			280	1,154	7.5

[d]Filipinos were not included in the total count for immigrants from abroad until 1961; tabulations for Filipino nationals who arrived in 1909-1946 were made by the Hawaii Sugar Planter's Association.

[e]Years ended June 30 through 1976 and September 30 thereafter.

[f]Includes all nationalities not shown separately.

[g]For 1964 and thereafter, the figures have been adjusted for non-response to questions on passenger and military status.

[h]Tabulation procedures may have caused a double count in 1970 totals.

[i]There were 7,789 immigrants through June 30, with 1,882 arrivals included through September 30, 1976.

[j]Included with "Other."

253

Table 4-16. Components of Change in the Total, Military, and Civilian Resident Population, Hawai‘i, 1970–1985

	1970[a]		1980[a]		1985[a,b]	
	Number	Percent	Number	Percent	Number	Percent
Population						
Total[c]	769,913	100.0	964,691	100.0	1,053,885	100.0
Military[d]	117,000	15.2	121,079	12.6	120,664	11.5
Civilian	652,913	84.8	843,612	87.4	933,221	88.5

	1960–1970[e]		1970–1980[e]		1980–1985[e]	
	Number	Percent	Number	Percent	Number	Percent
Population Growth[f]						
Total	136,256	100.0	190,702	100.0	89,609	100.0
By Net Migration[g]	52,446	38.5	107,834	56.6	39,049	43.6
By Natural Increase	83,810	61.5	82,868	43.4	50,560	56.4
Net Migration						
Total	11,896	100.0	77,939	100.0	18,930	100.0
Military[h]	-40,550	-340.9	-29,895	-38.4	-20,119	-106.3
Civilian	52,446	440.9	107,834	138.4	39,049	206.3
Natural Increase						
Total	126,161	100.0	118,654	100.0	70,286	100.0
Military	42,351	33.6	35,786	30.2	19,726	28.1
Civilian	83,810	66.4	82,868	69.8	50,560	71.9

	Number	%	Number	%	Number	%
Births						
Total	163,762	100.0	161,831	100.0	97,932	100.0
Military	43,908	26.8	37,234	23.0	20,302	20.7
Civilian	119,854	73.2	124,597	77.0	77,630	79.3
Deaths						
Total	37,601	100.0	43,177	100.0	27,646	100.0
Military	1,557	4.1	1,448	3.4	576	2.1
Civilian	36,044	95.9	41,729	96.6	27,070	97.9

Sources: Hawaii (State) DPED, 1972 Data Book, Table 17; Statistical Report No. 173, Table 1; 182, Table 1; 184, Table 2; 189, Table 17; 190, Table 2.

[a]April 1 for 1970 and 1980; July 1 for 1985.

[b]Provisional estimates.

[c]Resident population.

[d]Includes dependents.

[e]April 1, 1960 to March 31, 1970; April 1, 1970 to March 31, 1980; April 1, 1980 to June 30, 1985.

[f]Civilian population.

[g]Includes military separations less inductions (4,120 persons in 1960–70, 1,815 persons in 1970-80, and 22 persons in 1980–85).

[h]The net outmigration of military and dependents correlates to the transfer of military families with their Hawaii-born infants.

255

Table 5-1. State Population and Economic Projections: Comparison of 1984 Series M-F "Most Likely Visitor Industry Growth Rate" and Series M-B "Slow Visitor Industry Growth Rate," Hawai'i, 1980-2005, and 1988 Revised Series M-K, Hawai'i, 1985-2010

	1980	1985	1990	1995	2000	2005	2010	25-year change 1980-2005	25-year change 1985-2010
Series M-B[a]									
Population—Resident (1,000)	969.0	1,025.0	1,047.2	1,072.0	1,096.0	1,120.0	NA	151.0	NA
Population—De Facto (1,000)	1,055.9	1,115.0	1,136.9	1,161.0	1,185.0	1,208.7		152.8	
Visitors—Average Daily (1,000)	96.5	105.0	105.0	105.0	105.0	105.0		8.5	
Visitors—Annual (1,000)	3,935.0	4,357.0	4,357.0	4,357.0	4,357.0	4,357.0		422.0	
Hotel Rooms (1,000)	54.2	58.0	58.0	58.0	58.0	58.0		3.8	
Jobs (1,000)	499.5	510.2	520.8	535.6	549.8	561.6	NA	62.1	
Net Annual Migration	2,000	-2,500	-500	-600	1,600	NA		0.0	
Gross State Product (millions of $ 1980)	11,336.2	11,635.9	12,726.0	14,022.8	15,398.4	16,924.6		5,588.4	
Personal Income (millions of $ 1980)	9,862.0	10,791.5	11,899.3	13,173.8	14,546.3	15,973.0		6,111.0	
Per Capita Personal Income ($ 1980)	10,188.0	10,528.0	11,363.0	12,289.0	13,272.0	14,262.0		4,074.0	
Resident Population Annual Growth Rate		1.1	0.4	0.5	0.4	0.4		0.6	
Series M-F[a,b]									
Population—Resident (1,000)	969.0	1,057.8	1,138.4	1,211.5	1,267.8	1,310.0	NA	341.0	NA
Population—De Facto (1,000)	1,055.9	1,166.4	1,277.5	1,373.0	1,447.2	1,501.0		445.1	
Visitors—Average Daily (1,000)	96.5	124.0	155.6	179.0	197.6	207.7		111.2	
Visitors—Annual (1,000)	3,935.0	5,000.0	6,083.3	7,052.2	7,786.2	8,183.4		4,248.4	
Hotel Rooms (1,000)	54.2	63.6	79.2	91.7	101.4	106.5		52.3	
Jobs (1,000)	499.5	529.0	572.3	613.4	644.5	663.9		164.4	
Net Annual Migration	8,500	7,200	6,600	4,200	2,500	NA		145,000	
Gross State Product (millions of $ 1980)	11,336.2	12,106.4	14,061.8	16,192.3	18,264.4	20,180.8		8,844.6	
Personal Income (millions of $ 1980)	9,862.0	11,127.8	12,896.3	14,774.3	16,611.9	18,336.8		8,474.8	
Per Capita Personal Income ($ 1980)	10,188.0	10,520.0	11,328.0	12,195.0	13,103.0	13,998.0		3,810.0	
Resident Population Annual Growth Rate		1.75	1.47	1.06	1.05	0.7		1.2	

Series M-Kᶜ	NA							NA	
Population—Resident (1,000)	NA	1,051.5	1,142.5	1,228.9	1,294.2	1,359.5	1,435.1	NA	466.1
Population—De Facto (1,000)		1,149.7	1,283.9	1,397.3	1,489.2	1,580.7	1,687.2		631.3
Visitors—Average Daily (1,000)		116.7	161.7	190.0	217.7	244.9	277.1		180.6
Visitors—Annual (1,000)		4,900.0	6,600.0	7,800.0	9,000.0	10,200.0	11,600.0		7,665.0
Hotel Rooms (1,000)		65.9	77.4	91.3	105.1	118.5	134.4		80.2
Jobs (1,000)		493.3	557.1	609.9	656.8	694.7	728.9		229.4
Net Annual Migration		10,000	9,800	6,400	6,800	9,200	NA		211,000
Gross State Product (millions of $ 1982)		15,100.0	18,400.0	21,900.0	25,000.0	27,900.0	31,000.0		19,664.0
Personal Income (millions of $ 1982)		13,100.0	15,800.0	18,500.0	20,700.0	22,700.0	25,000.0		14,812.0
Per Capita Personal Income ($ 1982)		12,400.0	13,900.0	15,000.0	16,000.0	16,700.0	17,400.0		7,538.0
Resident Population Annual Growth Rate		1.6	1.7	1.5	1.0	1.0	1.1		1.3

Sources: Hawaii (State) DPED 1984a, Tables 1, 3, 11, 14, 15, 19, pp. 24, 67–71; personal communication with DPED, May 1987. Hawaii (State) DBED 1988, Tables 1, 2, 3, 4, 5, 7, 8.

NA Not available.

ᵃSeries M-B and M-F use the same fertility and mortality levels, based on nationwide projections prepared by the U.S. Census in 1982. "M" designated "medium," with a total fertility rate of 1.941 and nationwide life expectancy at birth in 2005 of 73.3 years for males and 81.3 years for females. The variable between Series M-B and M-F is the rate in the growth of the visitor industry. For Series M-B, the number of visitors would be constant at 4,357,000 annual tourists. In Series M-F, visitor arrivals are expected to reach 8.2 million by the year 2005, growing at a declining rate: 1980–1985, 5 percent; 1985–1990, 4 percent; 1990–1995, 3 percent; 1995–2000, 2 percent; and 2000–2005, 1 percent. In Series M-K, annual visitor arrivals would reach 11.6 million, growing at 1985–1990, 4.4 percent; 1990–1995, 6.1 percent; 1995–2000, 3.5 percent; 2000–2005, 3.0 percent; and 2005–2010, 2.5 percent.

ᵇSeries M-F was recommended by the State DPED in 1984 to be used for planning purposes.

ᶜFigures are derived from a preliminary report. Some changes may be presented in the final version.

Table 5-2. Visitors, Visitor Expenditures, and Hotel Units, Hawai'i, 1927-1986

Year	Average Daily Visitor Census	Visitors Staying Overnight or Longer				Visitor Expenditures In Hawaii ($)	Hotel Units
		Both Directions	% Change from Previous Year	Westbound[a]	Eastbound[b]		
1927	NA	17,451	—	15,693	1,758	8,200,000	2,729
1928	NA	19,980	+ 14.5	18,275	1,705	9,200,000	
1929	NA	22,190	+ 11.1	20,041	2,149	10,300,000	
1930	NA	18,651	− 15.9	16,995	1,656	8,700,000	
1931	1,200	15,780	− 15.4	14,402	1,378	6,900,000	[c]
1932	NA	10,370	− 34.3	9,464	906	4,100,000	
1933	NA	10,111	− 2.5	9,345	766	3,800,000	
1934	NA	16,161	+ 59.8	14,841	1,320	6,300,000	
1935	NA	19,933	+ 23.3	18,030	1,903	7,900,000	
1936	NA	22,199	+ 11.4	20,039	2,160	8,900,000	
1937	NA	21,987	− 1.0	19,489	2,498	9,500,000	
1938	NA	23,043	+ 4.8	20,853	2,190	10,200,000	2,607
1939	NA	24,390	+ 5.8	21,737	2,653	11,000,000	
1940	1,648	25,373	+ 4.0	(NA)	(NA)	12,000,000	[c]
1941	2,069	31,846	+ 25.5	30,425	1,421	16,400,000	2,502
1942–1945	—	War years—visitor industry suspended					
1946	975	15,000	—	NA	NA	6,300,000	1,572
1947	1,625	25,000	+ 66.7	NA	NA	12,100,000	1,958
1948	2,366	36,397	+ 45.6	NA	NA	18,900,000	1,958
1949	2,235	34,386	− 5.5	NA	NA	17,700,000	1,980
1950	3,027	46,593	+ 35.5	NA	NA	24,200,000	2,003
1951	3,350	51,565	+ 10.7	47,634	3,931	28,980,000	2,197

Year							
1952	3,796	60,539	+ 17.4	54,618	5,921	32,800,000	2,412
1953	4,746	80,346	+ 32.7	72,152	8,194	42,600,000	2,925
1954	5,369	91,289	+ 13.6	81,388	9,901	48,900,000	3,101
1955	6,042	109,798	+ 20.3	98,105	11,693	55,000,000	4,115
1956	6,947	133,815	+ 21.9	114,813	19,002	65,000,000	4,327
1957	8,205	168,829	+ 26.2	141,518	27,311	77,600,000	4,754
1958	8,397	171,588	+ 1.6	139,984	31,604	82,700,000	5,494
1959	10,390	243,216	+ 41.7	207,645	35,571	109,000,000	6,802
1960	11,797	296,517	+ 21.9	250,795	45,722	131,000,000	9,522
1961	11,960	319,807	+ 7.9	248,540	71,267	137,000,000	10,193
1962	13,125	362,145	+ 13.2	279,625	82,520	154,000,000	10,915
1963	15,316	429,140	+ 18.5	332,680	96,460	186,000,000	11,403
			Revised Series (1964–1970)				
1964	16,354	563,925	—	460,290	103,635	205,000,000	11,453
1965	17,369	686,928	+ 21.8	567,218	119,710	225,000,000	12,903
1966	20,918	835,456	+ 21.6	686,886	148,570	280,000,000	14,827
1967	27,630	1,124,818	+ 34.6	893,103	231,715	380,000,000	17,217
1968	32,335	1,314,571	+ 16.9	1,015,844	298,727	440,000,000	18,657
1969	37,198	1,527,012	+ 16.2	1,181,029	345,983	550,000,000	22,801
1970	36,943	1,746,970	+ 14.4	1,326,135	420,835	595,000,000	26,923
1971	40,889	1,818,944	+ 4.1	1,430,325	388,619	705,000,000	32,289
1972	50,143	2,244,377	+ 23.4	1,782,737	461,640	840,000,000	35,797
1973	59,578	2,630,952	+ 17.2	2,067,861	563,091	1,020,000,000	36,608
1974	63,535	2,786,489	+ 5.9	2,184,620	601,869	1,225,000,000	38,675
1975	66,308	2,829,105	+ 1.5	2,207,417	621,688	1,360,000,000	39,832
1976	75,532	3,220,151	+ 13.8	2,551,601	668,550	1,640,000,000	42,648
1977	83,030	3,433,667	+ 6.6	2,763,312	670,355	1,845,000,000	44,986
1978	92,034	3,670,309	+ 6.9	3,030,999	639,310	2,146,000,000	47,070
1979	98,676	3,960,531	+ 7.9	3,139,455	821,076	2,537,000,000	49,832

continued

Table 5-2. (continued)

Year	Average Daily Visitor Census	Visitors Staying Overnight or Longer				Visitor Expenditures In Hawaii ($)	Hotel Units
		Both Directions	% Change from Previous Year	Westbound[a]	Eastbound[b]		
1980	96,497	3,934,504	− 0.7	3,046,132	888,372	2,875,000,000	54,246
1981	95,968	3,934,623	—	2,974,791	959,832	3,200,000,000	56,769
1982	105,310	4,242,925	+ 7.8	3,278,525	964,400	3,700,000,000	57,968
1983	108,045	4,367,880	+ 2.9	3,395,880	972,000	3,974,000,000	58,765
1984	118,660	4,855,580	+ 11.2	3,721,380	1,134,200	4,582,000,000	62,448
1985	116,712	4,884,170	+ 0.6	3,708,610	1,175,560	4,900,000,000	65,919
1986	132,910	5,606,980	+ 14.8	4,256,390	1,350,590	5,500,000,000	66,308
1987	134,270	5,799,830	+ 3.4	4,204,010	1,595,820	6,600,000,000	69,012[d]

Sources: Hawaii (State) DPED 1987, Data Book, Table 211; Hawaii Visitors Bureau, Annual Report 1952–1987; Schmitt 1977, Tables 11.7 and 20.9.

Note: All expenditure figures are in current dollars. Additional details on visitor expenditures are available at the Research Department of the Hawaii Visitors Bureau.

NA Not available.

[a] Arriving from points east of Hawaii.

[b] Arriving from Asia or Oceania.

[c] Not reported as an annual count.

[d] Preliminary.

Table 5-3. Resident and De Facto Population by State and Counties, Hawaiʻi, 1970–1985

Population	1970 April 1	1980 April 1	1985 July 1	Percent Change			Annual Growth Rate		
				1970–1980	1980–1985	1970–1985	1970–1980	1980–1985	1970–1985
State Total									
Resident	769,913	964,691	1,053,900	25.3	9.2	36.9	2.3	1.7	2.1
De Facto	796,600	1,052,700	1,152,000	32.2	9.4	44.6	2.8	1.7	2.4
Counties:									
Hawaii									
Resident	63,468	92,053	109,200	45.0	18.6	72.1	3.7	3.3	3.6
De Facto	65,700	98,700	115,800	50.3	17.3	76.3	4.1	3.0	3.7
Honolulu									
Resident	630,528	762,565	814,600	20.9	6.8	29.2	1.9	1.3	1.7
De Facto	650,700	822,000	865,100	26.3	5.2	33.0	2.3	1.0	1.9
Kauai									
Resident	29,761	39,082	44,800	31.3	14.6	50.5	2.7	2.6	2.7
De Facto	31,800	46,100	55,600	45.3	20.6	74.8	3.7	3.6	3.7
Maui									
Resident	46,156	70,991	85,300	53.8	20.2	84.8	4.3	3.5	4.0
De Facto	48,400	85,900	115,500	77.3	34.5	138.6	5.7	5.6	5.7

Source: Hawaii (State) DPED 1987, Statistical Report 196, Table 1.

Table 5-4. Population Densities in Selected Areas of the World, 1983–1985

Area	Persons per Square Kilometer[a]	Area	Persons per Square Kilometer[a]
State of Hawaii (1985)	69	Asia	
County of Hawaii	11	Bangladesh	657[b]
County of Honolulu	560	China	108[b]
County of Kauai	35	Hong Kong	5,084
County of Maui	38	India	223[b]
		Indonesia	84[b]
		Japan	316
Countries (1983)		Korea, North	159[b]
		Korea, Republic of	406[b]
Africa		Pakistan	113[b]
Egypt	44[b]	Philippines	173[b]
Mauritius	486		
Nigeria	96[b]	Europe	
South Africa	25[b]	France	100
		Netherlands	352
America, North		Sweden	19
Canada	3	United Kingdom	228
Mexico	38[b]		
Puerto Rico	377	Oceania	
United States	25	American Samoa	174
		Australia	2
America, South		Fiji	37
Chile	15[b]	New Zealand	12
		Papua New Guinea	7[b]
		USSR	12

Sources: Hawaii (State) DPED, Statistical Report No. 190, Table 7; United Nations, Department of International Economic and Social Affairs, 1983, Table 3.

[a]Population per square kilometer of surface area. These figures do not reflect urban density or supporting power of a country's land and resources.

[b]Estimated.

Table 6–1. World Population, 1985[a]

Region or Country	Population Estimate (millions)	Crude Birth Rate	Crude Death Rate	Natural Increase (annual percent)	No. of Years to Double Population (in years)	Population Projection to A.D. 2000 (millions)	Population Projection to A.D. 2100 (millions)
World	4,942	27	11	1.7	41	6,157	10,445
Africa	583	45	16	2.8	24	872	2,477
Asia	2,876	28	10	1.8	39	3,579	5,749
North America	267	16	9	0.7	98	296	341
Latin America	419	31	8	2.3	30	563	915
Europe	493	13	10	0.3	248	508	547
USSR	280	20	11	0.9	79	311	376
Oceania	25	21	8	1.2	56	28	40
Hawai'i	1.1	17	5	1.2	30	1.3	3

Table 6-1. *(continued)*

Region or Country	Infant Mortality Rate[b]	Total Fertility Rate[c]	Percentage of Population Under Age 15/Over Age 65	Life Expectancy (years)	Per Capita Gross National Product (US$)[d]
World	82	3.7	35/6	62	2,760
Africa	118	6.3	45/3	50	740
Asia	86	3.7	37/4	59	940
North America	10	1.8	22/12	75	13,910
Latin America	62	4.1	38/4	65	1,900
Europe	14	1.8	22/13	73	8,230
USSR	31	2.4	25/10	69	6,760
Oceania	35	2.7	29/8	71	8,950
Hawai'i	9	2.1[e]	26/8	78[e]	15,826[f]

Sources: Hawaii (State) DPED 1986, Data Book, Tables 30, 56, 388; Statistical Report No. 190, Table 1; Population Reference Bureau 1986, World Population Data Sheet.

[a] April, 1986 for all areas except Hawai'i that reflects mid-1985 population figures.

[b] Infant deaths per 1,000 live births.

[c] Average number of children born to a woman during her lifetime.

[d] 1983 estimate.

[e] 1980.

[f] 1985 per capita gross state product.

NOTES

Preface

1. Frear 1947, p. 89.
2. Pukui and Elbert 1986, pp. ix–x.

Chapter I

1. Carlquist 1970, p. 3.
2. Bryan, E. H., Jr. 1954, p. 1.
3. Blumenstock and Price, in Kay 1972, p. 155.
4. Stearns 1966, pp. 1–3; University of Hawaii, Department of Geography 1983, p. 9.
5. Bryan, W. A. 1915, pp. 189–193.
6. Carlquist 1970, pp. 81–111.
7. Berger 1981, p. 15.
8. Fosberg, in Kay 1972, pp. 396–408.
9. Hubbell, in Kay 1972, pp. 390–391.
10. Kepelino and Kamakau, in Fornander 1974, p. 267.
11. Barrère 1961, pp. 422–425.
12. Malo 1951, pp. 3–5.
13. Johnson 1981, p. ii.
14. Fornander 1969, vol. 1, pp. 160–169.
15. Kamakau 1964, p. 3.
16. Johnson 1975, pp. iii, vi, 31–38.
17. Buck, in Handy et al. 1965, p. 23.
18. Emory 1974, p. 739.
19. Finney 1976, pp. 5–10.
20. Lindo and Mower 1980, pp. 21–22.
21. Finney 1979, pp. 7–12.

22. Fornander 1969, vol. 2, p. 8.
23. Lewis 1972, pp. 10–12.
24. Bellwood 1979, p. 303.
25. Sneider and Kyselka 1986, pp. 1–2.
26. Emory 1974, p. 745.
27. Holmes 1981, pp. 8–13.
28. Malo 1951, p. 6.
29. Elbert 1953, p. 169.
30. Fornander 1969, vol. 1, p. 55.
31. Luomala 1951, p. 10.
32. Howard, in Highland et al. 1967, p. 92.
33. Krauss 1974, pp. 5–6.
34. Kirch 1986, pp. 9–40.
35. Bell 1987, pp. 6, 56.
36. Kirch 1985, p. 47.
37. Buck, in Handy et al. 1965, p. 28.
38. Emory, in Handy et al. 1965, p. 320.
39. Stannard 1985, p. 30.
40. Schmitt and Zane 1977, pp. 1–5.
41. Peterson 1969b, pp. 9–11.
42. Kelly 1986, p. 18.
43. Baker 1917, pp. 62–70.
44. Kameʻeleihiwa 1986, pp. 33–43.

Chapter 2

1. Colum 1937, p. ix.
2. Kalākaua 1888, pp. 19–20.
3. Kalākaua 1888, p. 21.
4. The term *puaʻa* (hog) was applied to persons in ancient *mele* (songs or chants) as a poetical expression or religious connotation relating to the power of priests as mediators between God and man.
5. Fornander 1969, vol. 2, p. 25.
6. Wakakawa 1938, pp. 3–4.
7. Okahata 1971, pp. 5–7.
8. Fornander 1969, vol. 2, pp. 106–107. Quoted from *Moolelo Hawaii* by D. Malo.
9. Peirce 1940, p. 11.
10. Restarick 1930, pp. 6–29.
11. Jarves 1844, pp. 98–99.
12. Dahlgren 1916, p. 213.
13. Cook 1784, vol. 2, p. 191.
14. Fitzpatrick 1986, p. 15.
15. Cook 1784, vol. 2, p. 194.

16. Cook 1784, vol. 2, p. 230.
17. Beaglehole 1967, pp. 637–672.
18. Cook 1784, vol. 2, p. 230.
19. Schmitt 1968, pp. 19–20.
20. Schmitt 1986a, p. 1.
21. Dixon 1789, p. 267.
22. Stannard 1985, p. 30.
23. Ellis 1969, pp. 7–24.
24. Schmitt 1973, p. 8.
25. Schmitt 1968, p. 223.
26. Ellis 1979, p. 16.
27. Schmitt 1971, p. 239.
28. Schmitt 1969, pp. 66–86.
29. Kamakau 1964, p. 99.
30. Lee 1938, pp. 2–4.
31. Cook 1784, vol. 2, p. 196.
32. Beaglehole 1974, pp. 639, 678.
33. Clerke, in Beaglehole 1974, p. 678.
34. Bishop 1838, pp. 58–59.
35. Schmitt 1971, p. 239; 1973, p. 13; 1986, p. 4.
36. Adams, in Schmitt 1973, p. 15.
37. Loomis, in Westervelt 1937, p. 46.
38. Bishop 1838, p. 63.
39. Bishop 1838, p. 54.
40. Kamakau 1961, p. 237.
41. Ellis 1969, pp. 326–332.
42. Kamakau 1961, p. 234.
43. Kamakau 1961, p. 404.
44. Kuykendall 1938, p. 312.
45. Adams, in Schmitt 1968, p. 39.
46. Schmitt 1968, p. 39.
47. Schmitt 1977, p. 87.
48. Schmitt 1968, pp. 33, 45; 1977, p. 43.
49. Schmitt 1970, pp. 359–364.
50. Anderson 1864, p. 275.
51. Papa Ii 1973, pp. 163–164.
52. Thrum 1897, pp. 95–101.
53. Schmitt 1968, p. 33.
54. Hiscock 1935, p. 9.
55. Daws 1968, pp. 139–143.
56. Kuykendall 1967, pp. 136–137.
57. Mouritz 1943, pp. 9–11.
58. Gugelyk and Bloombaum 1979, p. 1.
59. Hiscock 1935, p. 78–79.
60. Alexander 1891, pp. 66–67.

61. Hawaii (Territory), Board of Health 1914, pp. 98–99.
62. Pukui, Haertig, and Lee 1972, pp. 141–142, 158.
63. Hormann 1954, p. 47.
64. Kalākaua 1888, pp. 64–65.

Chapter 3

1. Kuykendall 1953, p. 69.
2. Vandercook 1939, pp. 36–37.
3. Hawaiian Sugar Planters' Association (HSPA) 1926, pp. 9, 94–95.
4. HSPA 1926, p. 11.
5. Bird Bishop 1894, p. 101.
6. Kuykendall 1953, p. 178.
7. Adams 1937, p. 69.
8. Kanahele 1986, p. 28.
9. Linnekin 1985, p. 246.
10. Waihee, in *Honolulu Star-Bulletin,* February 17, 1987, Sec. 1, p. 2.
11. Bishop 1838, p. 59.
12. Bishop 1838, p. 62.
13. Adams 1937, p. 75.
14. Schmitt 1973b, p. 4.
15. Adams 1937, pp. 75–76.
16. Lind 1980, pp. 24–31.
17. Hawaii (State) DPED 1985, Statistical Report No. 180, pp. 1–8.
18. Petersen 1969, p. 873.
19. This figure was changed to 118,251 and 122,660 in later census adjustments. See U.S. Bureau of the Census, *1980 Census of Population,* PC80-1-B13, Table 15, and PC80-1-C13, Tables 58 and 59; and Hawaii (State) DPED 1985, Statistical Report No. 180, Table 1.
20. Hawaii (State) DPED 1985, Data Book, Table 24.
21. Schmitt 1967a, p. 474.
22. Howard 1974, pp. 20–21.
23. Young, in McDermott, Tseng, and Maretzki 1980, pp. 12–13.
24. Pukui, Haertig, and Lee 1979, p. 36.
25. Glick 1970, p. 280.
26. Blaisdell, in *Honolulu Star-Bulletin,* February 17, 1987, Sec. III, p. 19.
27. Chun 1986, p. 23.
28. Malo 1951, p. 95.
29. Schmitt 1967b, in *Hawaii Medical Journal,* Vol. 26, No. 6, July-Aug.
30. Gardner 1980, pp. 221–226.
31. Look, in *R & S Report* 1982, No. 38, p. 3.
32. Burch, in *R & S Report* 1983, No. 44, p. 3.
33. Blaisdell 1983, *Native Hawaiians Study Commission Report,* pp. 556–569.

34. Miike, in "Summary of Mortality Data on Native Hawaiians" (Draft), for U.S. Senate Committee on Indian Affairs, 1986, p. 6.

35. Burch, in *R & S Report* 1978, No. 23, p. 2.

36. Gardner and Schmitt, in *Hawaii Medical Journal,* 1978, Vol. 37, No. 10, p. 299.

37. Gardner, in *R & S Report* 1984, No. 7, pp. 6–7.

38. Kanahele, in *Social Process in Hawaii,* 1982, p. 21; see also Kanahele 1982, pp. 1–35.

39. Lueras and Chung 1981, p. 101.

40. Trask, in *Honolulu Star-Bulletin,* July 15, 1982, p. A–19.

41. Handy et al. 1965, p. 20.

42. Lake, quoted by Chapman, in *The Honolulu Advertiser,* June 21, 1984, p. A–3.

43. Whittaker 1986, pp. 4–5.

44. Campbell 1967, pp. 118–119.

45. Bushnell 1972, lecture notes.

46. Chambliss, in *Social Process in Hawaii* 1982, p. 113.

47. Lind 1980, pp. 23–24.

48. Hormann, in *Social Process in Hawaii* 1982, p. 32.

49. Hawaiian Mission Children's Society Committee 1969, pp. 7–13.

50. Hawaii Foundation for History and the Humanities 1973a, p. 11.

51. Felix and Senegal 1978, p. 113.

52. Hawaii (State) DPED 1985, p. 48.

53. Hawaii (Kingdom), Bureau of Immigration, 1886, p. 133.

54. Bowman 1980, in *The Honolulu Advertiser,* pp. C–1, 3; see also the historical novel of Norwegian immigration by I. and L. Clairmont, 1980.

55. Hormann 1931, pp. 65–83.

56. Wagner-Seavey 1980, p. 134.

57. Schweizer 1982, pp. 182–190.

58. Barratt 1987, pp. 29–116.

59. Peirce 1976, pp. 1–33.

60. Kuykendall 1938, pp. 55–60.

61. Mehnert 1939, pp. 61–68.

62. Ewanchuk 1986, p. 8.

63. McLaren 1951, p. 91.

64. Souza, in *Hawaiian Journal of History* 1984, pp. 158–167.

65. Souza and Souza 1985, pp. 10–26.

66. Hawaii (State) DPED 1987, p. 47.

67. Ivers 1909, p. 2.

68. The Caledonian Society of Hawaii 1986, p. 34.

69. Chapin, in *The Hawaiian Journal of History* 1979, p. 137.

70. Thrum 1905, pp. 44–45.

71. Lowe 1972, p. 21.

72. Char, W. J. 1974, pp. 3–9.

73. Kai 1974, pp. 39–72.

74. Vancouver 1801, pp. 112–113.

75. Diell, May 19, 1838. Other "foreigners" included: "200 to 250 Americans, 75 to 100 Englishmen, and a number of French, Spanish, Portuguese, and from various other countries."

76. Thrum 1905, p. 63.

77. Char, T. 1975, p. 37.

78. Char, T. 1975, p. 54.

79. Hill 1856, p. 305.

80. Glick 1980, pp. 3–4.

81. Hawaii (Kingdom), Bureau of Immigration, 1886, p. 5.

82. Char, T. Y. 1975, pp. 16, 60–61.

83. Kuykendall 1938, p. 329.

84. Young 1974, pp. 17–19.

85. Kuykendall 1953, p. 76.

86. Hillebrand 1972, p. 150.

87. Hawaii (Kingdom), Bureau of Immigration, 1886, pp. 16–17.

88. Kuykendall 1953, pp. 181–182.

89. Glick 1980, p. 11.

90. Hawaii (Kingdom), Bureau of Immigration, 1886, p. 22.

91. Daws 1968, pp. 201–206.

92. Hawaii (Territory) 1902, p. 81.

93. Kastens 1978, p. 61.

94. Kuykendall 1967, pp. 135–141.

95. Hawaii (Kingdom), Bureau of Immigration, 1886, p. 199.

96. Thrum 1894, pp. 75–78.

97. Glick 1980, p. 20.

98. Glick 1980, p. 21.

99. Lowe 1972, p. 25.

100. Glick 1980, p. 21–22.

101. Char, Walter F., Wen-Shing Tseng, Kwong-Yen Lum, and Jing Hsu, "The Chinese," in McDermott et al. 1980, pp. 52–72.

102. United Japanese Society of Hawaii 1971, pp. 5–7.

103. Wakukawa 1938, pp. 3–14.

104. Braden 1976, p. 86.

105. Stokes 1931, pp. 6–14.

106. Delano 1818, p. 400.

107. Soga 1931, pp. 15–19.

108. Odo and Sinoto 1985, p. 16.

109. Kuykendall 1966, p. 183.

110. Conroy and Miyakawa 1972, pp. 25–29.

111. Hawaii (Kingdom), Bureau of Immigration, 1886, p. 58.

112. Kuykendall 1967, p. 166.

113. Hawaii (Kingdom), Bureau of Immigration, 1886, p. 227.

114. Hawaii (Kingdom), Bureau of Immigration, 1886, p. 247.

115. Takaki 1983, pp. 42–43.

116. For a detailed account of the 1868 movement of laborers to Hawai'i and the government-sponsored 1885–1894 period of emigration, see Moriyama 1985, pp. 1–42.

117. Odo and Sinoto 1985, pp. 24–26.

118. Moriyama 1985, p. 39; Kotani 1985, p. 17.

119. Conroy 1973, pp. 123–127.

120. Japanese Chamber of Commerce, Honolulu, 1970, pp. 100–108.

121. Ethnic Studies Oral History Project 1981, pp. 52–58.

122. Matsumoto 1982, pp. 125–126.

123. Nordyke and Matsumoto 1977, p. 164.

124. Chuman 1976, pp. 30–33.

125. Wakukawa 1938, pp. 344–354.

126. Adams 1924, p. 17.

127. Moriyama 1985, pp. 138–139.

128. Lind 1967, p. 30.

129. Rogers and Izutsu 1980, p. 77.

130. Lind 1967, p. 97.

131. Yamamoto 1982, p. 68.

132. Ogawa 1978, pp. 477–495.

133. Hitch 1965, p. 4.

134. Hormann 1954, pp. 47–56.

135. Matsumoto 1982, p. 132.

136. An increase of immigration from Japan, which might be expected to accompany the high level of Japanese investment in residential real estate in Hawai'i since 1985, was not reported at the time of the preparation of this book.

137. Hazama and Komeiji 1986, p. 254.

138. Kamakau 1961, p. 304.

139. Greer 1986, p. 120.

140. Stewart 1970, p. 37. Although C. S. Stewart lists her name as "Betsy," in missionary documents it is frequently spelled "Betsey."

141. Hormann 1954, p. 48.

142. Tate 1962, pp. 251–252.

143. Hawaii (Kingdom), Bureau of Immigration, 1886, p. 143.

144. Adams 1945, p. 27.

145. Hawaii (State) DPED 1985, *Data Book,* Table 24.

146. Abe 1945, p. 36.

147. Hawaii (State) DPED 1985, *Data Book,* Table 24.

148. Jackson 1985, in *Honolulu Star-Bulletin,* February 19, 2:3.

149. Takara 1986, p. 3.

150. Daws 1968, p. 293.

151. Encyclopedia Britannica 1984, Vol. 14, p. 242.

152. Dorita 1954, pp. 3–11.

153. Junasa 1982, in *Social Process in Hawaii* 29:95.

154. Anderson 1984, p. 2.

155. Teodoro 1981, pp. 10–12.

156. Fuchs 1961, p. 143.

157. Cariaga 1936, p. 9.

158. Hormann 1954, p. 48.

159. Teodoro 1981, pp. 12–13.

160. Carino 1981, p. 1.

161. Sharma 1981, p. 11.

162. Wakukawa 1938, p. 187.

163. Clifford 1975, pp. 24–26.

164. Dionisio 1981, p. 36.

165. Teodoro 1981, p. 14.

166. Fuchs 1961, pp. 146–149.

167. Anderson 1984, pp. 22–24.

168. Alcantara 1981, pp. vii–ix.

169. Chuman 1976, p. 66.

170. Teodoro 1981, p. 30.

171. Alcantara 1981, p. 157.

172. Anderson 1984, pp. 68–69.

173. Agbayani et al. 1985, p. 3.

174. Nordyke 1973, p. 212.

175. Caces 1985, p. 61.

176. Dionesio 1981, p. 50.

177. Agbayani et al. 1985, p. 4.

178. Soriano 1982, in *Social Process in Hawaii* 29:170.

179. Agbayani et al. 1985, pp. 6–10.

180. Junasa 1982, in *Social Process in Hawaii* 29:103.

181. Kim, H. 1977, p. 3.

182. Patterson 1977, pp. 49–50.

183. Yang, S. L., in Lee, S. O. 1978, p. 16.

184. Yun, Yo-jun, in Kim, H. 1977, p. 36.

185. Patterson 1977, p. 383. A description of the early emigration from Korea including emigrant's places of origin, occupations, social characteristics, education, literacy level, and reasons for leaving Korea is presented by Patterson 1977, pp. 414–446. He also reviews the relationship of United States diplomacy, Hawai'i business interests, and Korean and Japanese response to the emigration process.

186. Choe, in Shin and Lee 1977, pp. 3–14.

187. Yang, in Lee, S. O. 1978, p. 16.

188. Kim, B. 1937, p. 85–86.

189. Harvey and Chung, in McDermott et al. 1980, p. 136.

190. Kim, H. 1977, pp. 47–51.

191. Kim, B. 1937, p. 83.

192. Chai, in Thomas and Keller 1981, pp. 330–331.

193. Choe, in Shin and Lee 1977, p. 9.
194. Kim, in Lee, S. O. 1978, p. 47.
195. Yang 1980, in *Social Process in Hawaii,* p. 93.
196. Lind 1938, p. 254.
197. Joun, in Lee, S. O. 1978, pp. 58–60.
198. Adams, Livesay, and Van Winkle 1925, p. 31.
199. Patterson 1979, p. 10.
200. Adams 1937, p. 188.
201. Ryu, in Kim 1977, p. 207.
202. See Chai 1986, pp. 1–43, for a review of a 1979 study of pre- and post-immigration Korean women for age, urban-rural origin, religion, socio-economic status, reasons for immigration, and length of residence in Hawai'i.
203. See Koo and Yu 1981, p. 4, for a discussion of overrepresentation of women and children among Korean immigrants to the United States.
204. Harvey and Chung, in McDermott et al. 1980, pp. 145–146.
205. Gardner, Wright, and Montenegro 1979, Table 11.
206. Chai 1983, pp. 171–172.
207. Franco 1987, p. 1.
208. Oliver 1951, p. 156.
209. Born 1973, in *Multicultural Center Publication No. 1,* p. 2.
210. Ala'ilima 1982, in *Social Process in Hawaii,* pp. 105–112.
211. Park 1972, p. 15.
212. Keesing 1956, p. 195.
213. Gray 1960, p. 263.
214. Born 1968, pp. 455–459.
215. Harbison, in Baker, et al. 1986, p. 90.
216. Franco 1987, p. 8.
217. Ala'ilima 1974, pp. 86–87.
218. Takeuchi 1983, in *Sunday Star-Bulletin and Advertiser,* p. G-1.
219. Franco 1984, pp. 16–18.
220. Hawaii (State) DPED 1973, p. 2.
221. Kuykendall 1953, pp. 77–78.
222. Lind 1982, in *Social Process in Hawaii,* p. 46.
223. Hawaii (Kingdom), Bureau of Immigration, 1886, p. 177.
224. Hawaii (Kingdom), Bureau of Immigration, 1886, p. 113.
225. Morton, Chung, and Mi 1967, p. 18.
226. Hawaii (State) DPED 1982 *Statistical Report 152,* p. 4.
227. U.S. Bureau of the Census 1983b.
228. Hawaii (State) DPED 1985 *Statistical Report 180,* Table 3.
229. Tack 1980, in McDermott et al., p. 200.
230. Liem and Kehmeier 1980, in McDermott et al, pp. 202–216.
231. Bliatout 1980, in McDermott et al., pp. 217–224.
232. Hawaii (State) DPED 1985 *Statistical Report 180,* Table 3.

Chapter 4

1. For a more comprehensive discussion of demographic information and statistics about Hawai'i, see Schmitt 1968 and 1977; Adams 1933; Lind 1980; Gardner, Nordyke, Schmitt, and Levin 1989; and Hawaii (State) DPED *Data Book* (annual).

2. Hawaii (State) DPED 1984 *Hawaii Population and Economic Projection and Simulation Model,* pp. 14–15.

3. Hawaii (State) DPED 1986 *Data Book,* Tables 2 and 3.

4. Hawaii (State) DPED 1987 *Statistical Report* 195, Table 1.

5. Hawaii (State) DPED 1984a, Tables 1 and 5.

6. Hawaii (State) DPED 1986 *Data Book,* Tables 4, 5, 6.

7. Hawaii (State) DPED 1987 *Statistical Report* 196, Table 1.

8. Schmitt and Silva 1984, pp. 39–46.

9. Hawaii (State) DPED 1985 *Statistical Report* 180, pp. 1–8.

10. Viele, in Hawaii (State) DOH 1983 *R & S Report* No. 44, p. 6.

11. Hawaii (State) DPED 1985 *Statistical Report* 180, Table 1.

12. Schmitt 1971, pp. 237–243.

13. Schmitt 1973a, p. 4.

14. Schmitt 1973b, pp. 1–49.

15. Schmitt 1968, pp. 46–114.

16. United States, Bureau of the Census 1981e, p. 3.

17. Hawaii (State) DPED 1986 *Data Book,* Table 22.

18. Hawaii (State) DPED 1985 *Statistical Report* 180, p. 5.

19. Adams 1945, p. 25.

20. Adams 1937, p. 113.

21. Gardner, Nordyke, Schmitt, and Levin 1989 (forthcoming), Table 6.

22. Hawaii (State) Office of the Governor 1982, p. 8.

23. See Black, Table 3-3.a, Figure 3-6; Chinese, Table 3-3.b, Figure 3-4; Filipino, Table 3-3.c, Figure 3-7; Hawaiian, Table 3-3.d, Figure 3-2; Part Hawaiian, Table 3-3.e, Figure 3-2; Japanese, Table 3-3.f, Figure 3-5; Korean, Table 3-3.g, Figure 3-8; Samoan, Table 3-3.h, Figure 3-9; White, Table 3-3.j, Figure 3-3; and Other, Table 3-3.k, Figure 3-10.

24. Schmitt 1977, pp. 651–655.

25. Daws 1968, pp. 252–253.

26. Hawaii (State) DPED 1986 *Data Book,* p. 365.

27. Schmitt 1977, p. 660.

28. Hawaii (State) DPED 1986 *Statistical Report* 192, p. 1.

29. Hawaii (State) DPED 1986 *Data Book,* Table 51.

30. Gardner, Nordyke, Schmitt, and Levin 1989 (forthcoming).

31. Gardner, Nordyke, Schmitt, and Levin 1989 (forthcoming), Table 24.

32. Hawaii (State) DPED 1986 *Data Book,* Table 65.

33. Schmitt and Strombel 1969, pp. 241–245.

34. Schmitt 1977, pp. xvii and 41.

35. For a comprehensive discussion of early marriage and divorce statistics in Hawai'i, see Schmitt 1968, pp. 193–215.

36. United States, Bureau of the Census 1983a, Table 205.

37. Hawaii (State) DPED 1986 *Data Book,* Table 95.

38. Glick 1970, p. 280.

39. Hawaii (State) DPED 1986 *Data Book,* Table 58.

40. United States, Department of Health and Human Services 1987b, p. 1.

41. United States, Department of Health and Human Services 1987c, p. 2.

42. Life expectancy figures for Hawai'i used in this volume are taken from Gardner 1984 and differ slightly from U.S. life expectancy tabulations, reflecting the use of death registration data of a two-year period surrounding the census year in contrast to similar data from a three-year period.

43. Gardner, Nordyke, Schmitt, and Levin 1989 (forthcoming).

44. Gardner 1984 (revised), p. 7.

45. Gardner 1980, pp. 222–226.

46. Gardner, Nordyke, Schmitt, and Levin 1989 (forthcoming).

47. Nordyke, Lee, and Gardner 1984, p. 2.

48. Daws 1968, pp. 251–311.

49. Hawaii (State) DPED 1984b, Table 13 and Table B–1.

50. Gardner 1980, p. 221.

51. Nordyke, Lee, and Gardner 1984, p. 34.

52. United States, Bureau of the Census 1983a, Table 200.

53. Hawaii (State) DPED 1985 *Statistical Report* 178, p. 8.

54. Nordyke, Lee, and Gardner 1984, p. 26.

55. Hawaii (State) Office of the Governor, EOA and CPHF 1982, p. 93.

56. Schmitt, in Hawaii (State) DOH 1982 *Population Report* No. 14, pp. 1–5.

57. United States, DHHS, Office of Human Development Services, AOA 1980 factsheet.

58. Schmitt 1968, pp. 175–192.

59. Schmitt, in Hawaii (State) DOH 1978 *Population Report* No. 10, pp. 2–3.

60. Hawaii (State) DPED 1986 *Data Book,* p. 10.

61. For earlier figures on migration history in Hawai'i, see Schmitt 1977, pp. 87–110.

62. Schmitt 1977, pp. 88–89.

63. Hood and Bell 1973, p. 4.

64. Fawcett and Carino 1987, pp. 110–111.

65. Arnold et al. 1987, p. 28.

66. Hawaii (State) Office of the Governor, State Immigrant Services Center 1982, p. 7.

67. Hawaii (State) DPED 1985 *Statistical Report* 178, pp. 1–11.

68. Hawaii (State) DPED 1985 *Statistical Report* 178, p. 7.

69. Hawaii (State) DPED 1986b *The Economy of Hawaii,* p. 29.

70. Hawaii (State) DPED 1986 *Statistical Report* 189, p. 1.
71. Hawaii (State) DPED 1978a *Economic Research Reports,* p. 1.
72. Hawaii (State) DPED 1978b *State Tourism Study. Economic Projections,* pp. 163, 183.
73. Retherford 1982, p. 17.
74. Hawaii (State) DPED 1984 *Hawaii Population and Economic Projection and Simulation Model, Updated State and County Forecasts,* Table 13.
75. Hawaii (State) Office of the Governor. Commission on Population and the Hawaiian Future 1977, p. 3.

Chapter 5

1. Thompson and Lewis 1965, p. 11.
2. Hawaii (State) DPED 1976 *Statistical Report No. 114,* pp. 39–44.
3. Gardner and Nordyke 1974, pp. 89–101.
4. Hawaii (State) DPED 1984a, pp. 9–12.
5. Hawaii (State) DPED 1978b, pp. 123, 163, 183.
6. Hawaii (State) DPED 1978a, pp. 1, 26.
7. Hawaii (State) DPED 1984a, p. 15.
8. Hawaii (State) DPED 1984a, Tables 12–17.
9. Hawaii (State) DPED 1984b, p. 3.
10. Hawaii (State) DBED 1988, pp. 2–6, 15, 30. These are preliminary projections; the final report was not completed for use at the time of publication of this book.
11. Hitch 1985, p. 83.
12. Hawaii (State) Office of the Governor, Commission on Population and the Hawaiian Future, p. 3.
13. Hawaii (State) DPED 1978c, p. 42.
14. Gardner, Nordyke, Schmitt, and Levin 1989 (forthcoming).
15. Schmitt 1977, p. 273.
16. First Hawaiian Bank 1984, p. 1.
17. Hawaii (State) DPED 1977, p. 77.
18. Hawaii (State) DPED 1978b, pp. 182–184.
19. Hawaii (State) DPED 1983.
20. Hawaii (State) DPED 1986 *Data Book,* Table 223.
21. *Honolulu Advertiser* 1988, A–13.
22. First Hawaiian Bank 1987b, p. 1.
23. Hawaii (State) DPED 1986, Tables 201 and 202; Hawaii Visitors Bureau, *Annual Report* 1952–1986.
24. Hawaii Visitors Bureau 1988, p. 4.
25. Hawaii Visitors Bureau 1985, *Annual Report,* Tables 10–14.
26. Hawaii (State) DPED 1986 *Data Book,* Table 220.
27. Hawaii Visitors Bureau 1988, pp. 4, 8.

28. Schmitt 1986b, p. 3.
29. Bank of Hawaii 1988, p. 5.
30. Twain (1908) in Frear 1947, opposite p. 243.
31. University of Hawaii, Department of Geography 1983, p. 108.
32. Babbie 1972, pp. 40–41.
33. Hawaii (State) DPED 1987 *Data Book,* Table 527.
34. Hawaii (State) 1986b, p. 6.
35. *Honolulu Advertiser* 1987a, A–14.
36. Bank of Hawaii 1983, p. 15.
37. Hawaii (State) DPED 1986 *Data Book,* pp. 273, 546, 551, 557.
38. Cooper and Daws 1985, pp. 3–9.
39. Cooper and Daws 1985, p. 450.
40. First Hawaiian Bank 1987a, p. 1.
41. Schmitt 1977, pp. 10 and 661.
42. Hawaii (State) DPED 1986 *Data Book,* p. 12.
43. First Hawaiian Bank 1987a, p. 1.
44. Bank of Hawaii 1984, pp. 1–3.
45. Lind 1984, pp. 38–41.
46. Trask 1984, pp. 122–123.
47. University of Hawaii, Department of Geography 1983, pp. 48–52.
48. Hawaii (State) DPED 1978d, pp. III–35, III–37, and IV–6.
49. Albu 1984, p. 1.
50. Keith 1982, p. 1.
51. Hawaii (State) DPED 1986b, p. 7.
52. Meadows et al. 1972, pp. 66–67.
53. Hawaii (State) DPED, Energy Resources Coordinator 1985, pp. 12–31.
54. Hawaii (State) DPED 1986 *Data Book,* p. 652.
55. University of Hawaii, Department of Geography 1983, p. 59.
56. Moberly and Mackenzie 1985, p. 1.
57. Farrell 1982, p. 257.
58. Hawaii (State) Office of the Governor, Office of Environmental Quality Control 1977, p. iii–iv.
59. Hawaii (State) Office of the Governor, Environmental Council 1983, pp. 7–8.
60. Hawaii (State) DPED 1986a Supplement, HRS Chapter 226, p. 3.
61. Hawaii (State) DBED 1988, p. 3.

Chapter 6

1. First Hawaiian Bank 1984, p. 1.
2. Hawaii (State) DBED 1988, p. 18.
3. Wright and Gardner 1983, p. 35.

4. Gardner 1984 (revised), p. 7; U.S. Department of Health and Social Services 1987, pp. 5, 10.

5. Hawaii, Office of the Governor, Commission on Population and the Hawaiian Future 1977, p. 6.

6. Hawaii (State) DPED General Plan Revision Program 1974, p. iii.

7. Hawaii (State) DPED 1986b, pp. 24–25.

8. Daws, in Lee 1974a, p. 143, and 1974b, pp. 6–8.

9. Creighton 1978, p. 356.

10. Hawaii (State) DBED 1988, p. 21.

11. Schmitt 1977, p. 117.

12. Chaplin and Paige 1973, p. 2.

13. Schmitt 1974, pp. 104–106.

14. Bank of Hawaii 1986, p. 18.

15. Stauffer 1984, p. 8.

16. First Hawaiian Bank 1987a, p. 1.

17. Hawaii (State) DPED 1985, p. 17.

18. Stauffer 1984, pp. 1–19.

19. First Hawaiian Bank 1987, p. 1.

20. Bank of Hawaii 1987, pp. 1–3.

21. Hardin, quoted in *The Honolulu Advertiser* 1971, p. A–18.

22. Burgess 1974, pp. 3–9.

GLOSSARY OF COMMON
DEMOGRAPHIC TERMS

abortion rate   The number of abortions per 1,000 women aged 15–44 years in a given year.

age-sex pyramid (population pyramid)   A graph showing the distribution of a population by age and sex, with the youngest at the base and oldest at the top; usually arranged by five-year groupings, with the males on the left, females on the right.

age-specific birth rate   The number of live births occurring each year per 1,000 women of a specified age (usually in terms of a five-year age group).

age-specific death rate   The number of deaths occurring each year per 1,000 persons of a specified age and sex (usually in terms of a five-year age group and given separately for male and female).

birth control   Practices employed by couples that result in a reduced likelihood of conception. This term is often used synonymously for contraception, fertility control, and family planning.

birth rate   A ratio of births to population; often used for crude birth rate (see also *age-specific birth rate; crude birth rate*).

Black   A person belonging to a dark-skinned race, especially of negroid Afro-American ancestry.

carrying capacity   The maximum sustainable size of a resident population in a given ecosystem.

census   A canvass of a given area for enumeration of a population, and the compilation of demographic, social, and economic information about that population at a specific time.

childbearing ages   The years during which a female is normally capable of producing children, usually considered to be either ages 15–44 or 15–49.

child-woman ratio   The number of children under 5 years of age per 1,000 women aged 15–44 or 15–49 years in a population.

civilian population The resident population, excluding members of the armed forces stationed in Hawai'i and all of their dependents (this contrasts with the method used by the *State Data Book,* which follows the U.S. census practice of including military dependents in the category of "civilian population").

cohort A group of people who experienced a demographic event at the same time, such as persons who are born at the same period (birth cohort) or who are married in the same year (marriage cohort).

crude birth rate The number of births in a year, per (usually) 1,000 total population.

$$\text{crude birth rate} = \frac{\text{number of births in a year}}{\text{mid-year population}} \times 1{,}000$$

crude death rate The number of deaths in a year, per (usually) 1,000 total population.

$$\text{crude death rate} = \frac{\text{number of deaths in a year}}{\text{mid-year population}} \times 1{,}000$$

death rate A ratio of deaths to population; often used for crude death rate (see also *age-specific death rate; crude death rate*).

de facto population The resident population, including all members of the armed forces and their dependents, plus all visitors present, minus residents who are temporarily absent. (On July 1, 1980, the Hawai'i de facto population was 1,052,659 persons; on July 1, 1987, it was estimated to be 1,199,000 persons.)

demography (From Greek: *demos* [people] and *graphie* [study]) The scientific study of human populations, including their births, deaths, migration, size, composition, distribution, and other socioeconomic characteristics, and the causes and consequences of changes in these factors.

density The average number of persons per unit of area (per square mile or per square kilometer).

$$\text{density} = \frac{\text{number of persons}}{\text{area}}$$

divorce rate The number of divorces per 1,000 population in a given year.

doubling time The number of years required for a population of an area to double its present size, given the current rate of population growth (see also *rate of growth*).

emigration The process of leaving one country to take up residence in another.

family planning The deliberate effort by men and women to regulate the number and spacing of births.

fecundity The biological capacity to reproduce.

fertility The number of births occurring to a woman, couple, group, or population (see also *age-specific birth rate; crude birth rate; general fertility rate; gross reproduction rate; net reproduction rate;* and *total fertility rate*).

general fertility rate   The number of live births in one year per 1,000 females of childbearing age (usually ages 15–44 or 15–49).

gross reproduction rate   The average number of daughters that would be born alive to a woman (or group of women) during her lifetime according to a given set of fertility rates, usually of a given year (the sum of single year, female, age-specific birth rates) (see also *total fertility rate*).

growth rate   See *rate of growth.*

illegitimacy rate   The number of illegitimate live births per 1,000 unmarried women aged 15–44 years in a given year.

illegitimacy ratio   The number of illegitimate live births per 1,000 live births in a given year.

immigration   The process of entering one country from another to take up permanent residence.

immigration rate   The number of immigrants arriving at a destination per 1,000 population at that destination in a given year.

infant mortality rate   The number of deaths of infants less than one year old per 1,000 live births in the same year.

in-migrant   A person who enters one administrative subdivision of a country (e.g., county or state) from another subdivision to take up residence.

labor force   All persons working or seeking employment at a given time, usually measured by age groups in a specific region.

life expectancy   The average number of additional years a person would live if current mortality trends were to continue. Most commonly cited as life expectancy at birth (calculated by using age-specific death rates).

life table   A tabulation of probabilities of death, survival, and length of life for various ages, males and females, racial groups, or other given populations.

marriage rate   The number of marriages per 1,000 population in a given year.

maternal mortality rate   The number of deaths to women owing to pregnancy and childbirth complications usually per 10,000 live births in a given year.

median age   The age which divides a population into two numerically equal groups with half the people younger than this age and half older.

migration   The movement of people across a specified boundary for the purpose of establishing a new permanent residence. International migration (migration between countries) is differentiated from internal migration (migration within a country).

morbidity   Sickness in a population.

mortality   Deaths in a population.

natural increase   The difference between the number of births and number of deaths in a given period (see also *rate of natural increase*).

net migration   The difference between the number of people who move to an area and the number who move out of that area in a given period.

net migration rate   The net effect of immigration and emigration on an area's population in a given time period, expressed as increase or decrease per 1,000 population of the area in a given year.

net reproduction rate   The average number of daughters that would be born to a woman (or group of women) if she passed through her lifetime from birth experiencing the age-specific fertility and mortality rates of a given year. This rate is similar to the gross reproduction rate, but it takes into account that some women will die before completing their childbearing years. A net reproduction rate of 1.00 means that at today's age-specific birth rates and age-specific death rates a generation of women would exactly replace themselves.

out-marriage   Marriage to a person of a different ethnic, national, or religious background.

out-migrant   A person who leaves one subdivision of a country to take up residence in another.

population   See also *civilian population; de facto population; resident population; stationary population.*

population density   See *density.*

population increase   The total increase in numbers resulting from the interaction of births, deaths, and migration in a population in a given period of time.

population policy   Direct and indirect governmental measures established to influence population size, growth, distribution, or composition.

population pyramid   See *age-sex pyramid.*

rate   The numerical expression of the relation of one variable to another during a given period of time—ordinarily a year. (Crude birth and death rates are based usually on 1,000 total population; infant death rates are based on 1,000 live births; and maternal mortality is based on 10,000 live births in a given year.)

rate of growth   The increase or decrease of a population during a period—usually a year—often expressed as a percentage of the population (a population rate of growth includes natural increase and net migration).

rate of natural increase   The rate at which a population increases (or decreases) in a given year owing to excess (or shortage) of births, usually expressed as a percentage of the base population.

ratio   The numerical expression of the relation of one variable to another without regard to a time period.

replacement level fertility   The level of fertility at which a cohort of women experiencing a certain year's age-specific rate would have only enough daughters to replace themselves in the population. In the more developed countries, a total fertility rate (TFR) of 2.1 is considered to be replacement level.

resident population   The population living in a designated area at a specified time. In Hawai'i, this figure includes the civilian population and members of the armed forces with their dependents, but it excludes visitors.

sex ratio The number of males per 100 females in a population.

stable population A population usually considered closed to migration whose rate of growth or decline is constant and in which the birth rates, death rates, and age-sex structure are also constant, with an unchanging age composition.

stationary population A stable population that does not increase or decrease in size (in which the birth rate equals the death rate).

total fertility rate The average number of children that would be born alive to a woman (or group of women) according to a set of fertility rates providing there is survival through the childbearing years (the sum of single year age-specific birth rates) (see also *gross reproduction rate; net reproduction rate*).

vital events Births, deaths, fetal deaths, marriages, and divorces.

vital statistics The statistics obtained by the registration of births, deaths, fetal deaths, marriages, and divorces by an official agency (in Hawai'i, the State Department of Health).

Whites Persons of American and European ancestry, including Britons, Germans, Norwegians, Swedes, and other northern Europeans. Tabulated by the U.S. census as "Caucasians" until 1970, this group gradually absorbed Portuguese, Spaniards, and Puerto Ricans, and, in 1980, Whites included responses such as Canadian, German, Italian, Lebanese, Polish, Cuban, Mexican, and Dominican.

zero population growth Growth rate of zero, achieved when births plus immigration equal deaths plus emigration.

REFERENCES

Adams, Romanzo C.
1924 *The Japanese in Hawaii*. New York: The National Committee on American Japanese Relations.

1933 *The peoples of Hawaii*. Honolulu: American Council, Institute of Pacific Relations.

1937 *Interracial marriage in Hawaii*. New York: Macmillan. Reprinted, Montclair, N.J.: Patterson Smith, 1969.

1945 Census notes on the Negroes in Hawaii prior to the war. *Social Process in Hawaii* 9/10 (7): 25–27.

Adams, Romanzo C., T. M. Livesay, and E. H. Van Winkle
1925 *The peoples of Hawaii*. Honolulu: Institute of Pacific Relations.

Agbayani, Amefil, Fred Arnold, Fe Caces, Benjamin Carino, James Fawcett, Robert Gardner, Julia Hecht, Rene Rivas, and David Takeuchi
1985 *Filipino immigrants in Hawaii: A profile of recent arrivals*. Honolulu: The East-West Population Institute, East-West Center, and Operation Manong, University of Hawaii. July.

Alaʻilima, Fay
1982 The Samoans in Hawaii. *Social Process in Hawaii* 29:105–112.

Alaʻilima, Fay and Vaiao
1974 Proposal for a Samoan Community Program. In Young, Nancy F., *Searching for the promised land: Filipinos and Samoans in Hawaii. Selected readings*. Honolulu: University of Hawaii General Assistance Center for the Pacific, College of Education.

Albu, Kathryn
1984 Water: Growth issue of the 80's. *Hawaii's 1,000 Friends Newsletter.* April. Honolulu.

Alcantara, Rubin R.
1981 *Sakada: Filipino adaptation in Hawaii*. Washington, D.C.: University Press of America.

Alexander, W. D.
1891 *A brief history of the Hawaiian people.* New York: American Book Company.

Anderson, Robert N., Richard Coller, and Rebecca F. Pestano
1984 *Filipinos in rural Hawaii.* Honolulu: University of Hawaii Press.

Anderson, Rufus
1864 *The Hawaiian Islands: Their progress and conditions under missionary labors.* Boston: Gould and Lincoln.

Ariyoshi, Koji (published as Koji, Ariyoshi)
1973 Nisei in Hawaii. *Japan Quarterly* 20 (4): 437–446.

Arnold, Fred, Benjamin V. Carino, James T. Fawcett, and Insook Han Park
1987 *The potential for future immigration to the United States: A policy analysis for Korea and the Philippines.* East-West Population Institute Working Paper No. 48. Honolulu: East-West Center.

Babbie, Earl R.
1972 *The maximillion report.* Honolulu: Citizens for Hawaii.

Baker, Albert S.
1917 Ahua a Umi. *Hawaiian Almanac and Annual for 1917* (also known as Thrum's Annual), pp. 62–70. Honolulu: Thomas G. Thrum, publisher.

Baker, Paul T., Joel M. Hanna, and Thelma S. Baker (eds.)
1986 *The changing Samoans.* New York: Oxford University Press.

Bank of Hawaii
1983 *Construction in Hawaii.* Honolulu.

1984 The impact of the military on Hawaii's economy. *Business Trends,* July/August. Honolulu.

1986 *Annual Economic Report.* Honolulu.

1987 High technology: The state's role. *Business Trends,* January/February. Honolulu.

1988 Long-range projections for Hawaii. *Business Trends,* March/April, pp. 5–6. Honolulu.

Barratt, Glynn
1987 *The Russian discovery of Hawai'i.* Honolulu: Editions Limited.

Barrère, Dorothy B.
1961 Cosmogonic genealogies of Hawaii. *Journal of the Polynesian Society* 70 (4): 419–428.

Beaglehole, J. C. (ed.)
1967 *The voyage of the* Resolution *and* Discovery *1776–1780.* London: The Syndics of the Cambridge University Press.

1974 *The life of Captain James Cook.* Stanford: Stanford University Press.

Bellwood, Peter
  1979 *Man's conquest of the Pacific.* New York: Oxford University Press.
  1987 *The Polynesians. Prehistory of an island people.* Revised edition. New York: Thames and Hudson, Inc.

Berger, Andrew J.
  1981 *Hawaiian birdlife.* Honolulu: The University Press of Hawaii.

Bird, Isabella (also known as Isabella Bird Bishop)
  1894 *Six months among the palm groves, coral reefs, and volcanoes of the Sandwich Islands.* First American edition reprinted from the fifth English edition. New York: G. P. Putnam's Sons.

Bishop, Artemas
  1838 An inquiry into the causes of decrease in the population of the Sandwich Islands. *The Hawaiian Spectator* 1:52–66.

Bishop, S. E.
  1888 *Why are the Hawaiians dying out?* Honolulu: Honolulu Social Science Association paper. November.

Blaisdell, Richard Kekuni
  1983 *Native Hawaiian Study Commission Report, Health Section* I:556–569, June 23. Washington, D.C.: U.S. Department of the Interior.
  1987 Old Hawaiians enjoyed general good health. *Honolulu Star-Bulletin,* February 17, III–19.

Bliatout, Bruce Thowpaou
  1980 The Hmong from Laos. In McDermott, Tseng, and Maretzki, *People and cultures of Hawaii.* Honolulu: The University Press of Hawaii.

Born, Ted Jay
  1968 American Samoans in Hawaii: A short summary of migration and settlement patterns. *Hawaii Historical Review* 2 (12): 455–459.

Bowman, Pierre
  1980 The forgotten immigrants: The Scandinavians in Hawaii. *The Honolulu Advertiser,* October 7, C-1,3.

Braden, Wythe E.
  1976 On the probability of pre-1778 Japanese drifts to Hawaii. *Hawaiian Journal of History* 10:75–89.

Brooks, Lee M.
  1948 Hawaii's Puerto Ricans. *Social Process in Hawaii* 12:46–57.

Bryan, E. H., Jr.
  1954 *The Hawaiian chain.* Honolulu: Bernice P. Bishop Museum.

Bryan, William Alanson
  1915 *Natural history of Hawaii.* Honolulu: The Hawaiian Gazette Co., Ltd.

Burch, Thomas A.
1978 Ethnicity and health in Hawaii, 1975. *R & S Report,* No. 23, August. Honolulu: Hawaii State Department of Health.
1983 Racial differences between linked birth and infant death records in Hawaii. *R & S Report,* No. 44, September. Honolulu: Hawaii State Department of Health.

Burgess, Eric (ed.)
1974 *The next billion years.* Moffett Field, Calif.: Ames Research Center, National Aeronautics and Space Administration.

Caces, Fe
1985 Personal networks and the material adaptation of recent immigrants: A study of Filipinos in Hawaii. Ph.D. dissertation, University of Hawaii.

Caledonian Society of Hawaii, Inc.
1986 *Speaking of Scots in Hawaii.* Honolulu: The Caledonian Society of Hawaii, Inc.

Campbell, Archibald
1967 *A voyage around the world from 1806 to 1812.* Reproduction of third American edition of 1822. Honolulu: University of Hawaii Press.

Cariaga, Roman
1974 The Filipinos in Hawaii: A survey of their economic and social conditions. Reprint of 1936 edition of *Social Science* 10(1). San Francisco: R and E Research Associates.

Carino, Benjamin V.
1981 *Filipinos on Oahu, Hawaii.* Papers of the East-West Population Institute, No. 72. Honolulu: East-West Center.

Chai, Alice Yun
1983 Sexual division of labor in the contexts of nuclear family and cultural ideology among Korean student couples in Hawaii. *Humboldt Journal of Social Relations* 10 (2): 153–174.
1986 Adaptive strategies of recent Korean immigrant women in Hawaii. Manuscript for Sharistanian, Janet (ed.) *Public dichotomy: Contemporary perspectives on women's public lives.* Westport, Conn.: Greenwood Press.

Chambliss, Randolph L.
1982 The Blacks. *Social Process in Hawaii* 29:113–115.

Chapin, Helen Geracimos
1979 From Sparta to Spencer Street: Greek women in Hawaii. *Hawaiian Journal of History* 13:136–156.

Chaplin, George, and Glenn D. Paige (eds.)
1973 *Hawaii 2000: Continuing experiment in anticipatory democracy.* Honolulu: The University Press of Hawaii.

Char, Tin-Yuke
1975   *The sandalwood mountains.* Honolulu: The University Press of Hawaii.

Char, Wai Jane
1974   Chinese merchant adventurers and sugar masters in Hawaii, 1802–1852. *Hawaiian Journal of History* 8:3–9.

Chuman, Frank F.
1976   *The bamboo people: The law and Japanese Americans.* Del Mar, Calif.: Publishers, Inc.

Chun, Malcolm Naea (translator)
1986   *Hawaiian medicine book, he buke la'au lapa'au.* Honolulu: Bess Press.

Clairmont, Ingrid and Leonard
1980   *Blood in the furrows.* Hicksville, N.Y.: Exposition Press.

Clifford, Dorita
1975   Motivation for Ilocano migration. *Proceedings of the Conference on International Migration from the Philippines, June 10–14, 1974.* Honolulu: East-West Population Institute, East-West Center.

Colum, Padraic
1937   *Legends of Hawaii.* New Haven: Yale University Press.

Coman, Katharine
1903   *The history of contract labor in the Hawaiian Islands.* New York: Macmillan.

Conroy, Francis Hilary
1973   *The Japanese expansion into Hawaii.* Reprint of the 1949 University of California Ph.D. dissertation. San Francisco: R and E Research Associates.

Conroy, Hilary, and Scott Miyakawa (eds.)
1972   *East across the Pacific.* Santa Barbara, Calif.: American Bibliographical Center, Clio Press.

Cook, Captain James (Captain James King for Volume III)
1784   *A voyage to the Pacific Ocean undertaken, by the command of His Majesty, for making discoveries in the northern hemisphere.* Volumes II and III. London: printed by order of the Lords Commissioners of the Admiralty by W. and A. Strahan for G. Nicol and T. Cadell, in the Strand.

Cooper, George, and Gavan Daws
1985   *Land and power in Hawaii. The democratic years.* Honolulu: Benchmark Books.

Creighton, Thomas
1978   *The lands of Hawaii: Their use and misuse.* Honolulu: The University Press of Hawaii.

Dahlgren, E. W.
1916 *Were the Hawaiian Islands visited by the Spaniards before their discovery by Captain Cook in 1778?* Stockholm: Almquist and Wiksells Boktryckeri-A.-B.

Davis, Eleanor H., and Carl D. Davis
1962 *Norwegian labor in Hawaii: The Norse immigrants.* Honolulu: Industrial Relations Center.

Daws, Gavan
1968 *Shoal of time.* Honolulu: The University Press of Hawaii.

DeFrancis, John
1973 *Things Japanese in Hawaii.* Honolulu: The University Press of Hawaii.

Delano, Amasa
1818 *Narrative of voyages and travels in the northern and southern hemispheres: Comprising three voyages round the world.* Second edition. Boston: E. G. House, printer.

Diell, John
1838 *Sandwich Island gazette.* 19 May. Honolulu.

Dionisio, Juan C.
1981 *The Filipinos in Hawaii: The first 75 years, 1906–1981.* Honolulu: Hawaii Filipino News Specialty Publications.

Dixon, Captain George
1789 *A voyage round the world, in 1785, 1786, 1787, and 1788.* Second edition. London: George Goulding.

Dorita, Mary
1954 Filipino immigration to Hawaii. Master's thesis, University of Hawaii.

Elbert, Samuel H.
1953 Internal relationships of Polynesian languages and dialects. *Southwestern Journal of Anthropology* 9 (2): 147–173.

Ellis, William (missionary)
1969 *Polynesian researches, Hawaii.* Reprint of the 1842 London edition. Rutland, Vt.: Tuttle.

1979 *Journal of William Ellis.* Reprint of the 1827 London edition, the 1917 Honolulu edition, and the 1963 Honolulu edition. Rutland, Vt.: Tuttle.

Emory, Kenneth P.
1974 The coming of the Polynesians. *National Geographic* 146 (6): 732–745.

Ewanchuk, Michael
1986 *Hawaiian ordeal, Ukrainian contract workers 1897–1910.* Winnepeg, Manitoba: M. Ewanchuk.

Farrell, Bryan H.
1982 *Hawaii, the legend that sells.* Honolulu: The University Press of Hawaii.

Fawcett, James T., and Benjamin V. Carino (eds.)
1987 *Pacific bridges. The new immigration from Asia and the Pacific Islands.* Staten Island, N.Y.: Center for Migration Studies.

Feher, Joseph, Edward Joesting, and O. A. Bushnell
1969 *Hawaii: A pictorial history.* Bernice P. Bishop Special Publication 58. Honolulu: Bishop Museum Press.

Felix, John Henry, and Peter R. Senecal (eds.)
1978 *The Portuguese in Hawaii.* Honolulu: Felix and Senecal.

Finney, Ben R.
1976 *Pacific navigation and voyaging.* Wellington, New Zealand: The Polynesian Society, Inc.

1979 *Hokule'a: The way to Tahiti.* New York: Dodd, Mead and Company.

First Hawaiian Bank
1984 Hawaii: A quarter-century of change. *Economic Indicators,* January/February. Honolulu.

1987a Foreign investment in Hawaii. *Economic Indicators,* January/February. Honolulu.

1987b Is Hawaii facing a potential labor shortage? *Economic Indicators,* March/April. Honolulu.

1987c The impact of declining defense spending in Hawaii. *Economic Indicators,* July/August. Honolulu.

Fitzpatrick, Gary L.
1986 *The early mapping of Hawai'i.* Honolulu: Editions Limited.

Fornander, Abraham
1969 *An account of the Polynesian race, its origin and migrations.* Reprint of 1878, 1880, and 1885 London editions (3 vols.). Rutland, Vt.: Tuttle.

1974 *Fornander collection of Hawaiian antiquities and folklore.* Vol. 6, pt. 2. Reprint of 1919 Honolulu edition. Millwood, N.Y.: Kraus Reprint Co.

Franco, Robert W.
1984 *A demographic assessment of the Samoan employment situation in Hawaii.* Report for East-West Population Institute and Commission on Population and the Hawaiian Future, East-West Center, Honolulu.

1987 *Samoans in Hawaii, a demographic profile.* Honolulu: East-West Population Institute, East-West Center.

Frear, Walter Francis
   1947 *Mark Twain and Hawaii*. Chicago: The Lakeside Press.

Fuchs, Lawrence H.
   1983 *Hawaii pono: A social history*. Reprint of 1961 edition. New York: Harcourt Brace Jovanovich.

Gardner, Robert W.
   1980 Ethnic differentials in mortality in Hawaii, 1920–1970. *Hawaii Medical Journal* 39 (9): 221–238.

   1984 Life tables by ethnic group for Hawaii, 1980. *R & S Report* 47(3). Honolulu: Hawaii State Department of Health.

Gardner, Robert W., Eleanor C. Nordyke, Robert C. Schmitt, and Michael J. Levin
   1989 *The demographic situation in Hawaii, revised edition*. Honolulu: East-West Population Institute, East-West Center.

Gardner, Robert W., and Robert C. Schmitt
   1978 Ninety-seven years of mortality in Hawaii. *Hawaii Medical Journal* 37 (10): 297–302.

Gardner, Robert W., Paul Wright, and Fred Montenegro
   1979 Asian female immigrants on Oahu, Hawaii. Paper presented at Women in the Cities Working Group, East-West Population Institute, Honolulu, Hawaii. March 15.

Glick, Clarence E.
   1970 Interracial marriage and admixture in Hawaii. *Social Biology* 17 (4): 278–291.

   1980 *Sojourners and settlers: Chinese migrants in Hawaii*. Honolulu: Hawaii Chinese History Center and The University Press of Hawaii.

Goto, Y. Baron
   1982 Ethnic groups and coffee. *Hawaiian Journal of History* 16:112–124.

Gray, J. A. C.
   1960 *Amerika Samoa: A history of American Samoa and its United States Naval Administration*. Annapolis: U.S. Naval Institute.

Greer, Richard A.
   1986 Blacks in old Hawaii. *Honolulu* 21 (5): 120–121, 183–184.

Gugelyk, Ted, and Mi Hon Bloombaum
   1979 *Maʻi hoʻokaʻawale*. Honolulu: University of Hawaii Social Science Institute.

Handy, E. S. Craighill, Kenneth P. Emory, Edwin H. Bryan, Peter H. Buck, John H. Wise et al.
   1965 *Ancient Hawaiian civilization*. Reprint of 1958 Wellington, New Zealand, edition. Rutland, Vt.: Tuttle.

Handy, E. S. Craighill, and Mary Kawena Pukui
1972 *The Polynesian family system in Ka'u, Hawaii.* Reprint of 1958 Wellington, New Zealand, edition. Rutland, Vt.: Tuttle.

Harbison, Sarah F.
1986 The demography of Samoan populations. In Baker et al. *The changing Samoans.* New York: Oxford University Press.

Hardin, Garrett
1968 The tragedy of the commons. *Science* 162:1243–1248.

Hawaii Foundation for History and the Humanities
1973a *The Samoans in Hawaii: A resource guide.* Honolulu: Multi-Cultural Center, Publication 1.

1973b *Portuguese in Hawaii: A resource guide.* Honolulu: Ethnic Research and Resource Center, Publication 2.

Hawaii (Kingdom), Board of Health
1892 Report of Dr. R. B. Williams. *Annual Report,* Appendix B: 3–6. Honolulu.

Hawaii (Kingdom), Bureau of Immigration
1886 *Report of the president of the Bureau of Immigration to the legislative assembly of 1886.* Honolulu: Daily Bulletin Steam Printing Office.

Hawaii (Kingdom), General Superintendent of the Census
1878 Report. Honolulu.

1884 Report. Honolulu.

1891 Report, 1890. Honolulu: Bureau of Public Instruction.

Hawaii (Republic), General Superintendent of the Census
1897 Report, 1896. Honolulu: Department of Public Instruction.

Hawaii (State), Census Statistical Areas Committee
1985 *Report CTC-64.* Estimated population of Hawaii by districts, 1984. October 16.

Hawaii (State), Commission on
1973 Statewide Environmental Planning, Temporary Report. Honolulu.

Hawaii (State), Department of Business and Economic Development, Research and Economic Analysis Division
1988 *Revised long-range economic and population projections to 2010, State of Hawaii (Series M-K).* Preliminary report. January.

Hawaii (State), Department of Education, Office of Instructional Resources.
1973 *Our cultural heritage—Hawaii.* Honolulu: Governor's Committee on Hawaiian Text Materials.

Hawaii (State), Department of Health
1959– *Annual Report: Statistical Supplement.* Honolulu.

1973– *Population Report.* Honolulu. Published periodically.

1973– *R and S Report.* Honolulu. Published periodically.

1981   Health Surveillance Program. Special tables on population estimates, 1970 and 1980. October 31.

Hawaii (State), Department of Land and Natural Resources
1981   *State water resources development plan: A state functional plan.*
Honolulu.

Hawaii (State), Department of Planning and Economic Development
1963– *Statistical Report.* Honolulu. Published periodically.

1967– *State Data Book* (annual). Honolulu.

1970– *Statistical Memorandum.* Honolulu. Published periodically.

1973   Size and characteristics of the Samoan population of Hawaii. *Economic Research Report* 73–2. Honolulu.

1977   *A long-range population and economic simulation model for the
State of Hawaii (preliminary).* December 22.

1978a Long-range population and economic simulations and projections
for the state of Hawaii. *Economic Research Report* 78–1. March 1.
Honolulu.

1978b *State tourism study. Economic projections.* Honolulu.

1978c *The Hawaii state plan.* Honolulu.

1978d Limited physical resources. *State plan issue paper no. 4. State plan
project.* Honolulu.

1983   The economic impact of tourism in Hawaii: 1970–1980. *Economic
Research Report* 1983–2. April. Honolulu.

1984a *Hawaii population and economic projection and simulation model.
Updated state and county forecasts.* July. Honolulu.

1984b *Population and economic projections for the State of Hawaii, 1980–
2005.* July. Honolulu.

1985   *Quarterly statistical and economic report, third quarter.* Honolulu.

1986a *The Hawaii state plan* (revised). Honolulu.

1986b The economy of Hawaii. *Annual economic report and outlook.*
December. Honolulu.

Hawaii (State), Department of Planning and Economic Development,
Energy Resources Coordinator
1985–
1986   *Annual Report.* Honolulu.

Hawaii (State), Department of Planning and Economic Development,
Hawaii State Census Statistical Areas Committee
1984   *Report CTC-56.* Honolulu.

Hawaii (State), Office of the Governor, Commission on Population and the Hawaiian Future
1977   *Toward a preferred future. A population strategy.* Honolulu.

Hawaii (State), Office of the Governor, Environmental Council
1983   *Hawaii's environment: The ninth annual report of the Environmental Council, 1982.* Honolulu.

Hawaii (State), Office of the Governor, Executive Office on Aging and the Commission on Population and the Hawaiian Future
1982   *The elderly in Hawaii: A data digest of persons 60 and over.* Honolulu.

Hawaii (State), Office of the Governor, Office of Environmental Quality Control
1977   *Toward a better Hawaii.* Honolulu.

Hawaii (State), Office of the Governor, State Immigrant Services Center
1982   *Immigrants in Hawaii.* Honolulu.

Hawaii (Territory)
1902   Report of the Commissioner of Labor. Honolulu.

Hawaii (Territory), Board of Health
1900–ㅤ*Annual Report.* Honolulu.

1920   *Report of the president.* Births by nationalities. Honolulu.

Hawaii Visitors Bureau
1952–ㅤ*Research Report* (annual). Honolulu.

1988   Highlights of Japanese visitors to Hawaii, 1987. *Asia-Pacific Market Brief, No. 3.* April 22. Honolulu.

Hawaiian Mission Children's Society Committee
1969   *Missionary album, sesquicentennial edition, 1820–1870.* Honolulu: Hawaiian Mission Children's Society.

Hawaiian Sugar Planters' Association
1926   *Story of sugar in Hawaii.* Honolulu: Hawaiian Sugar Planters' Association.

Hazama, Dorothy Ochiai, and Jane Okamoto Komeiji
1986   *Okage same de: The Japanese in Hawaii 1885–1985* Honolulu: Bess Press.

Highland, Genevieve A., Roland W. Force, Alan Howard, Marion Kelly, and Yoshihiko H. Sinoto (eds.)
1967   *Polynesian culture history. Essays in honor of Kenneth P. Emory.* Bernice P. Bishop Special Publication 56. Honolulu: Bishop Museum Press.

Hill, Samuel S.
1856   *Travels in the Sandwich and Society Islands, 1849.* London: Chapman and Hall.

Hillebrand, William
1972   Chinese immigration: A letter to the Board of Immigration, 1865. *The Hawaiian Journal of History* 6:142–155.

Hiscock, Ira V.
1935   *A survey of public health activities in Honolulu, Hawaii.* Honolulu: Chamber of Commerce of Honolulu with the cooperation of the Committee on Administrative Practice of the American Public Health Association.

Hitch, Thomas K.
1965   Up the occupational ladder. Manuscript prepared for *Paradise of the Pacific,* July 26.

1985   Continuing funding for tourism. *Proceedings, governor's tourism congress, December 10 and 11, 1984.* Honolulu: Hawaii (State) Department of Planning and Economic Development.

Holmes, Tommy
1981   *The Hawaiian canoe.* Hanalei, Hawaii: Editions Limited.

Honolulu Advertiser
1971   A population debate. *The Honolulu Advertiser,* December 26, A-18.

1987   A change of HART? *The Honolulu Advertiser,* February 13, A-14.

1988   All but 2.9 percent of the State's employable population is working. *The Honolulu Advertiser,* October 27, A-13.

Honolulu (City and County),
1971   Board of Water Supply 2020 Plan. Honolulu.

Hood, David R., and Bella Z. Bell
1973   In-migration as a component of Hawaii population growth: Its legal implications. *Legislative Reference Bureau Report 2.* Honolulu.

Hormann, Bernard L.
1931   The Germans in Hawaii. Master's thesis, University of Hawaii.

1948a Racial statistics in Hawaii. *Social Process in Hawaii* 12:27–35.

1948b Racial complexion of Hawaii's future population. *Social Forces* 27 (10): 68–77.

1954   A note on Hawaii's minorities within minorities. *Social Process in Hawaii* 18:47–56.

1982   The Haoles. *Social Process in Hawaii* 29:32–44.

Howard, Alan
1967   Polynesian origins and migrations. In Highland et al. *Polynesian Culture History.* Honolulu: Bishop Museum Press.

1974   *Ain't no big thing.* Honolulu: University Press of Hawaii.

Inouye, Daniel
1967   *Journey to Washington.* Englewood Cliffs, N.J.: Prentice Hall, Inc.

Ivers, Richard
1909 Statement on immigration for the federal immigration commission. Honolulu: Board of Immigration.

Jackson, Miles M.
1985 Records trace Hawaii's Blacks back to 1810. *Honolulu Star-Bulletin,* February 19, 2–3,8.

Japanese Chamber of Commerce, Honolulu, Historical Publication Committee
1970 *The rainbow: A history of the Honolulu Japanese Chamber of Commerce.* Honolulu: Japanese Chamber of Commerce.

Jarves, James Jackson
1844 *History of the Sandwich Islands.* Second edition. Boston: James Munroe and Company.

Johnson, Rubellite Kawena
1981 *Kumulipo: The Hawaiian hymn of creation.* Vol. 1. Honolulu: Topgallant Publishing Co., Ltd.

Johnson, Rubellite Kawena, and John Kaipo Mahelona
1975 *Nā inoa hōkū: A catalogue of Hawaiian and Pacific star names.* Honolulu: Topgallant Publishing Co., Ltd.

Junasa, Bienvenido D.
1982 Filipino experience in Hawaii. *Social Process in Hawaii* 29:95–104.

Kai, Peggy
1974 Chinese settlers in the village of Hilo before 1852. *Hawaiian Journal of History* 8:39–72.

Kalākaua, David
1888 *The legends and myths of Hawaii.* New York: Charles L. Webster and Company.

Kamakau, Samuel M.
1961 *Ruling chiefs of Hawaii.* Honolulu: Kamehameha Schools Press.

1964 *Ka po'e kahiko: The people of old.* Special Publication 51. Honolulu: Bishop Museum.

Kame'eleihiwa (Dorton), Lilikalā K.
1986 Land and the promise of capitalism. Ph.D. dissertation, University of Hawaii.

Kanahele, George S.
1982a *Hawaiian renaissance.* Honolulu: Project Waiaha.

1982b The new Hawaiians. *Social Process in Hawaii* 29:21–31.

1986 *Kū kanaka (stand tall): A search for Hawaiian values.* Honolulu: University of Hawaii Press and Waiaha Foundation.

Kastens, Dennis A.
1978 Nineteenth century Chinese Christian missions in Hawaii. *Hawaiian Journal of History* 12:61–67.

Kay, E. Alison (ed.)
1972 *A natural history of the Hawaiian Islands. Selected readings.* Honolulu: The University Press of Hawaii.

Keesing, Felix
1956 *Elite communication in Samoa.* Palo Alto: Stanford University Press.

Keith, Kent M.
1982 Petroleum management, conservation, and alternate energy development in Hawaii. Lecture presented to the American Water Works Association, Hawaii Section, conference on May 6. Honolulu.

Kelly, Marion
1986 Dynamics of production intensification in pre-contact Hawaii. Paper presented to World Archeological Congress, London, England. September.

Kent, Noel
1983 *Hawaii: Islands under the influence.* New York: Monthly Review Press.

Kim, Bernice B. H.
1937 *The Koreans in Hawaii.* Master's thesis, University of Hawaii.

Kim, Hyung-chan (ed.)
1977 *The Korean diaspora: Historical and sociological studies of Korean immigration and assimilation in North America.* Santa Barbara, Calif.: American Bibliographical Center, Clio Press.

Kim, Hyung-chan, and Wayne Patterson
1974 *The Koreans in America, 1882–1974.* Dobbs Ferry, N.Y.: Oceana.

Kim, Lloyd Y. S. (ed.)
1978 *75th anniversary of Korean immigration to Hawaii.* Honolulu: The Diamond Jubilee Committee.

Kirch, Patrick Vinton
1985 *Feathered gods and fishhooks: An introduction to Hawaiian archeology and prehistory.* Honolulu: University of Hawaii Press.

1986 Rethinking East Polynesian prehistory. *Journal of the Polynesian Society* 95:9–40.

Kittleson, David
1985 *The Hawaiians. An annotated bibliography.* Honolulu: Social Science Research Institute, University of Hawaii.

Koji, Ariyoshi; see Ariyoshi, Koji

Kotani, Roland
1985 *The Japanese in Hawaii: A century of struggle.* Honolulu: The Hawaii Hochi, Ltd.

Krauss, Beatrice H.
1974 *Ethnobotany of the Hawaiians.* Honolulu: Harold L. Lyon Arboretum, University of Hawaii.

Kuykendall, Ralph S.
1938 *The Hawaiian kingdom. Vol.1, 1778–1854: Foundation and transformation.* Honolulu: University of Hawaii Press.

1953 *The Hawaiian kingdom. Vol. 2, 1854–1874: Twenty critical years.* Honolulu: University of Hawaii Press.

1967 *The Hawaiian kingdom. Vol. 3, 1874–1893: The Kalakaua dynasty.* Honolulu: University of Hawaii Press.

Kuykendall, Ralph S., and A. Grove Day
1961 *Hawaii: A history from Polynesian kingdom to American state.* Englewood Cliffs, N.J.: Prentice-Hall.

Kyselka, Will
1971 *The Hawaiian sky.* Honolulu: Pacific Books-Hawaii.

Lake, Maiki Aiu
1984 Advice. Quoted by Don Chapman, *The Honolulu Advertiser,* June 21, A–3.

Lasker, B.
1931 *Filipino immigration to the continental United States and to Hawaii.* Chicago: University of Chicago Press. Reprinted by Arno Press and the New York Times, 1969.

Lee, David B.
1974a Where are we going? An interview with Mr. Gavan Daws. *Honolulu* 9 (5): 100–101, 136–142.

1974b The gloom of a haole historian. *Hawaii Observer,* May 28, pp. 6–8.

Lee, Richard K. C.
1938 *A study of the venereal disease problem in the Territory of Hawaii.* Honolulu: Territorial Board of Health.

Lee, S. O.
1978 *75th anniversary of Korean immigration to Hawaii, 1903–1978.* Honolulu: 75th Anniversary of Korean Immigration to Hawaii Committee.

Lewis, David
1972 *We, the navigators.* Honolulu: The University Press of Hawaii.

Liem, Nguyen Dang, and Dean F. Kehmeier
1980 The Vietnamese. In McDermott, Tseng, and Maretzki, *People and Cultures of Hawaii.* Honolulu: University of Hawaii Press.

Lind, Andrew W.
1938 *An island community.* Chicago: University of Chicago Press.

1946 *Hawaii's Japanese: An experiment in democracy.* Princeton, N.J.: Princeton University Press.

1967 *Hawaii's people.* Third edition. Honolulu: University of Hawaii Press.

1968 *An island community: Ecological succession in Hawaii.* New York: Greenwood Press Publishers. Reprint of 1938 edition by University of Chicago Press.

1980 *Hawaii's people.* Fourth edition. Honolulu: The University Press of Hawaii.

1982 The immigration of South Sea Islanders. *Social Process in Hawaii* 29:45–49.

Lind, Ian Y.
1984 Ring of steel: Notes on the militarization of Hawaii. *Social Process in Hawaii* 31:25–48.

Lindo, Cecilia Kapua, and Nancy Alpert Mower
1980 *Polynesian seafaring heritage.* Honolulu: The Kamehameha Schools and the Polynesian Voyaging Society.

Linnekin, Jocelyn
1985 *Children of the land.* New Brunswick, N.J.: Rutgers University Press.

Look, Mele A.
1982 A mortality study of the Hawaiian people. *R & S Report* 38:1–7. Honolulu: Hawaii State Department of Health.

Lowe, C. H.
1972 *The Chinese in Hawaii: A bibliographic survey.* Taipei: China Printing, Ltd.

Lueras, Leonard, and Nedra Chung (eds.)
1981 *Hawaii.* Hong Kong: Apa Productions.

Luomala, Katharine
1951 *The menehune of Polynesia and other mythical little people of Oceania.* Honolulu: Bishop Museum Bulletin 203.

McArthur, Norma
1968 *Island populations of the Pacific.* Honolulu: University of Hawaii Press.

McDermott, John F., Jr., Wen-Shing Tseng, and Thomas W. Maretzki (eds.)
1980 *People and cultures of Hawaii: A psychocultural profile.* Honolulu: The University Press of Hawaii.

McLaren, Nancy A.
1951 Russian immigration: Hawaii. Master's thesis, University of Hawaii.

Malo, David
1951 *Hawaiian antiquities.* Honolulu: Bishop Museum Press.

Matsumoto, Y. Scott
  1982 Okinawa migrants to Hawaii. *Hawaiian Journal of History* 16:125–133.

Meadows, Donella H., Dennis L. Meadows, Jorgen Randers, and William W. Behrens, III
  1972 *The limits to growth*. New York: New American Library.

Mehnert, Klaus
  1939 *The Russians in Hawaii, 1804–1819*. University of Hawaii Bulletin 18 (6): 1–86.

Miike, Lawrence
  1986 Summary of mortality data on native Hawaiians. *Technical memorandum on native Hawaiian health status*. (Draft) July 31. Washington, D.C.: Office of Technology Assessment, United States Congress.

Moberly, R., and F. T. Mackenzie
  1985 Climate change and Hawaii: Significance and recommendations. Paper HIG-85-1. Hawaii Institute of Geophysics, University of Hawaii. Honolulu.

Moriyama, Alan Takeo
  1985 *Imingaisha: Japanese emigration companies and Hawaii, 1894–1908*. Honolulu: University of Hawaii Press.

Morton, Newton E., Chin S. Chung, and Ming-Pi Mi
  1967 *Genetics of interracial crosses in Hawaii*. New York: S. Karger.

Mouritz, A.
  1943 *A brief world history of leprosy*. Revised edition. Honolulu: A. Mouritz.

Nordyke, Eleanor C.
  1969 Hawaii's most underrated problem—overpopulation. *Beacon Magazine of Hawaii* 9 (2): 12–15.

  1973 In-migration versus fertility as factors in Hawaii's population growth. *Hawaii Medical Journal* 32 (4): 207–212.

Nordyke, Eleanor C., Richard K. C. Lee, and Robert W. Gardner
  1984 *A profile of Hawaii's elderly population*. Paper 91. Honolulu: East-West Population Institute, East-West Center.

Nordyke, Eleanor C., and Y. Scott Matsumoto
  1977 The Japanese in Hawaii: A historical and demographic perspective. *The Hawaiian Journal of History* 11:162–174.

Odo, Franklin, and Kazuko Sinoto
  1985 *A pictorial history of the Japanese in Hawai'i 1885–1924: Commemorating the centennial of the first arrival of government contracted Japanese laborers in Hawaii*. Honolulu: Hawai'i Immigrant Heritage Preservation Center, Department of Anthropology, Bernice Pauahi Bishop Museum.

Ogawa, Dennis M.
1973 *Jan ken po: The world of Hawaii's Japanese Americans.* Honolulu: Japanese American Research Center, Japanese Chamber of Commerce.

1978 *Kodomo no tame ni—for the sake of the children: The Japanese American experience in Hawaii.* Honolulu: The University Press of Hawaii.

Okahata, James H. (ed.)
1971 *A history of Japanese in Hawaii.* Honolulu: The United Japanese Society of Hawaii.

Oliver, Douglas L.
1958 *The Pacific islands.* Cambridge: Harvard University Press.

Papa Ii, John
1973 *Fragments of Hawaiian history.* Honolulu: Bishop Museum Press.

Park, Chai Bin.
1972 *Population statistics of American Samoa.* Honolulu: East-West Population Institute, East-West Center.

Park, Chai Bin, Robert W. Gardner, and Eleanor C. Nordyke
1979 Life tables by ethnic group for Hawaii, 1920–1970. *R and S Report.* No. 26. June. Revised, 1980.

Patterson, Wayne
1977 *The Korean frontier in America: Immigration to Hawaii, 1896–1910.* Ph.D. dissertation, University of Pennsylvania.

1979 Upward social mobility of the Koreans in Hawaii. Paper presented at the Center for Korean Studies Conference on Korean Migrants Abroad, January 8–11, University of Hawaii, Honolulu.

Peirce, Henry A.
1940 *The Spanish discovery of the Hawaiian Islands: Evidences of visits by Spanish navigators during the sixteenth century.* Paper presented to California Academy of Sciences on June 7, 1880. Honolulu: Hawaiian Printing Co., Ltd.

Petersen, William
1969a The classification of subnations in Hawaii: An essay on the sociology of knowledge. *American Sociological Review* 34:863–877.

1969b *Population.* Second edition. New York: Macmillan.

Pierce, Richard A.
1976 *Russia's Hawaiian adventure, 1815–1817.* Kingston, Ontario: The Limestone Press.

Population Reference Bureau
1985 *World population data sheet, 1985.* Washington, D.C.: Population Reference Bureau.

Pukui, Mary Kawena, and Samuel H. Elbert
    1986 *Hawaiian dictionary.* Revised and enlarged edition. Honolulu: University of Hawaii Press.

Pukui, Mary Kawena, Samuel H. Elbert, and Esther T. Mookini
    1976 *Place names of Hawaii.* Revised and enlarged edition. Honolulu: The University Press of Hawaii.

Pukui, Mary Kawena, E. W. Haertig, and Catherine A. Lee
    1972 *Nānā I Ke Kumu (look to the source).* Volume II. Honolulu: Hui Hanai, Queen Liliʻuokalani Children's Center.

Restarick, Henry B.
    1930 *The discovery of Hawaii.* Paper presented to the Hawaiian Historical Society, July 20, Honolulu.

Retherford, Robert D.
    1982 *Migration and unemployment in Hawaii.* Paper 79. East-West Population Institute, Honolulu: East-West Center.

Rogers, Terence A., and Satoru Izutsu
    1980 The Japanese. In McDermott, Tseng, and Maretzki, *People and cultures of Hawaii.* Honolulu: The University of Hawaii Press.

Sakihara, Mitsugu
    1975 The Okinawan immigrants. *Honolulu Star-Bulletin.* January 29, A15.

Schmitt, Robert C.
    1967a Differential mortality in Honolulu before 1900. *Hawaii Medical Journal* 26 (6): 537–541.

    1967b How many Hawaiians? *Journal of the Polynesian Society* 76 (4): 467–475.

    1968 *Demographic statistics of Hawaii: 1778–1965.* Honolulu: University of Hawaii Press.

    1969 Catastrophic mortality in Hawaii. *Hawaiian Journal of History* 3:66–86.

    1970 The Okuʻu: Hawaii's greatest epidemic. *Hawaii Medical Journal* 29 (5): 359–364.

    1971 New estimates of the pre-censal population of Hawaii. *Journal of the Polynesian Society* 80 (2): 237–243.

    1972 The Samoan population of Hawaii. Memorandum. State of Hawaii Department of Planning and Economic Development, February 9.

    1973a The changing definitions of race in Hawaii. State of Hawaii Department of Planning and Economic Development and Department of Health, *Population Report* No. 1.

    1973b The missionary censuses of Hawaii. *Pacific Anthropological Records,* No. 20. Honolulu: Bishop Museum.

1974 Population policy in Hawaii. *Hawaiian Journal of History* 8:90–110.

1977 *Historical statistics of Hawaii.* Honolulu: The University Press of Hawaii.

1978 Immigration trends in Hawaii. Hawaii (State) Department of Health, *Population Report* No. 10, September.

1981 Early Hawaiian statistics. *The American Statistician* 35 (1): 1–3.

1982 Extreme old age in Hawaii. Hawaii State Department of Health, *Population Report* No. 14, November.

1984 Origins of the Hawaii Visitors Bureau research program, 1911–1950. University of Hawaii, School of Travel Industry Management and Social Science Research Institute, Tourism Research Publications, Occasional Paper No. 7.

1986a Private correspondence to David Stannard on pre-contact population. March 3.

1986b Estimates and projections of the de facto population. Paper prepared for the annual meeting of the Federal-State Cooperative Program for Population Projections, San Francisco, California, April 2.

Schmitt, Robert C., and Carol L. Silva
1984 Population trends on Kahoolawe. *The Hawaiian Journal of History* 18:39–46.

Schmitt, Robert C., and Rose C. Strombel
1969 Marriage and divorce in Hawaii before 1870. *Hawaiian Historical Review, selected readings.* Honolulu: Hawaiian Historical Society.

Schmitt, Robert C., and Lynn Y. S. Zane
1977 How many people have ever lived in Hawaii? Unpublished manuscript. Hawaii State Department of Planning and Economic Development Library.

Schweizer, Niklaus R.
1982 *Hawaii and the German speaking peoples.* Honolulu: Topgallant Publishing Co., Ltd.

Sharma, Miriam
1981 Why labor leaves the Philippines: Migration to Hawaii 1906–1946. Paper presented at the Second Philippine Studies Conference of the Philippine Studies Program, University of Hawaii, Honolulu, Hawaii, June 27–30.

Shin, Myongsup, and Daniel B. Lee
1977 Korean immigrants in Hawaii: A symposium on their background history, acculturation and public policy issues. Honolulu: Korean Immigrant Welfare Association of Hawaii and Operation Manong, College of Education, University of Hawaii.

Sneider, Cary, and Will Kyselka
1986   *The wayfinding art, ocean voyaging in Polynesia.* Berkeley: University of California.

Soga, Y.
1931   Japanese account of the first recorded visit of a shipwrecked Japanese to Hawaii. *Papers of the Hawaiian Historical Society,* no. 18, pp. 15–19.

Soriano, Fred
1982   Filipino Hawaiian migration and adaptation: New paradigms for analysis. *Social Process in Hawaii* 29:163–179.

Souza, Blaze Camacho
1984   Trabajo y tristeza (work and sorrow): The Puerto Ricans of Hawaii, 1900 to 1902. *Hawaiian Journal of History* 18:156–173.

Souza, Blaze Camacho, and Alfred P. Souza
1985   *De Borinquen A Hawaii Nuestra Historia. From Puerto Rico to Hawaii.* Honolulu: Puerto Rican Heritage Society of Hawaii.

Stannard, David E.
1985   Fruitful and populous islands: A new look at the pre-haole population of Hawaii. Unpublished manuscript, Department of American Studies, University of Hawaii.

Stauffer, Robert H.
1984   The tragic maturing of Hawaii's economy. *Social Process in Hawaii* 31:1–24.

Stewart, C. S.
1970   *Journal of a residence in the Sandwich Islands during the years 1823, 1824, and 1825.* Facsimile reproduction of the 1830 London edition (third edition). Honolulu: University of Hawaii Press.

Stokes, John F. G.
1931   Iron with the early Hawaiians. *Papers of the Hawaiian Historical Society* No. 18, pp. 6–14.

Tack, Cheryl
1980   The people of Indochina. In McDermott, Tseng, and Maretzki, *People and Cultures of Hawaii.* Honolulu: The University Press of Hawaii.

Takaki, Ronald
1983   *Pau Hana: Plantation life and labor in Hawaii 1835–1920.* Honolulu: University of Hawaii Press.

Takara, Kathryn
1986   *Blacks.* Unpublished manuscript. Ethnic Studies Program, University of Hawaii.

Takeuchi, Floyd
1983   Isle Samoans find integration difficult. *Star-Bulletin and Advertiser,* May 8, G–1.

Teodoro, Luis V., Jr.
  1981 *Out of the struggle: The Filipino in Hawaii.* Honolulu: The University Press of Hawaii.

Thomas, Hilah F., and Rosemary Skinner Keller (eds.)
  1981 *Women in new worlds.* Nashville: Abingdon Press.

Thompson, Warren S., and David T. Lewis
  1965 *Population problems.* New York: McGraw-Hill.

Thrum, Thomas George
  1879 Census of the Hawaiian Islands, 1872. *Hawaiian almanac and annual for 1879.* Honolulu.

  1894 Chinese immigration to the Hawaiian Islands. *Hawaiian almanac and annual for 1894.* Honolulu.

  1897 *Hawaiian almanac and annual for 1897.* Honolulu.

  1905 The sandalwood trade of early Hawaii. *Hawaiian almanac and annual for 1905.* Honolulu.

Trask, Haunani-Kay
  1982 A Hawaiian view of Hawaiian problems. *Honolulu Star-Bulletin,* July 15, A–19.

  1984 Hawaiians, American colonization, and the quest for independence. *Social Process in Hawaii* 31:101–136.

United Nations, Department of International Economic and Social Affairs
  1985 *Demographic yearbook 1983.* New York: United Nations.

United Okinawan Association of Hawaii, Ethnic Studies Oral History Project
  1981 *Uchinanchu: A history of Okinawans in Hawaii.* Honolulu: Ethnic Studies Program, University of Hawaii.

United States, Bureau of the Census
  1913 *Thirteenth census of the United States, 1910: Abstract of the census with supplement for Hawaii.* Washington, D.C.: Government Printing Office.

  1922 *Fourteenth census of the United States, 1920.* Vol. 3, *Composition and characteristics of the population by states.* Washington, D.C.: Government Printing Office.

  1931 *Birth, stillbirth, and infant mortality statistics for the birth registration area of the U.S., 1930.* Washington, D.C.: Government Printing Office.

  1932 *Fifteenth census of the United States, 1930: Outlying territories and possessions.* Washington, D.C.: Government Printing Office.

  1943 *Sixteenth census of the United States, 1940: Population. Second series, characteristics of the population, Hawaii.* Washington, D.C.: Government Printing Office.

1953 *Census of population: 1950.* Vol.2, *Characteristics of the population.* Part 52, Hawaii. Washington, D.C.: Government Printing Office.

1961 *Census of population, 1960: General characteristics, Hawaii.* Final report PC(1)-13B. Washington, D.C.: Government Printing Office.

1962 *Census of population, 1960: Detailed characteristics, Hawaii.* Final report PC(1)-13D. Washington, D.C.: Government Printing Office.

1963 *Census of population, 1960: Subject reports, nonwhite population by race.* Washington, D.C.: Government Printing Office.

1971a *Census of population, 1970: Number of inhabitants, Hawaii.* Final report PC(1)-A13. Washington, D.C.: Government Printing Office.

1971b *Census of population, 1970: General population characteristics, Hawaii.* Final report PC(1)-B13. Washington, D.C.: Government Printing Office.

1971c *Census of population, 1970: General social and economic characteristics, Hawaii.* Final report PC(1)-C13. Washington, D.C.: Government Printing Office.

1972 *Census of population, 1970: Detailed characteristics, Hawaii.* Final report PC(1)-D13. Washington, D.C.: Government Printing Office.

1973a *Census of population, 1970: Subject reports, Japanese, Chinese, and Filipinos in the United States.* Final report PC(2)-1G. Washington, D.C.: Government Printing Office.

1973b *Census of population, 1970: Population and distribution of races by county, age, and sex, Hawaii.* Special tabulation.

1975 *Historical statistics of the United States, colonial times to 1970. Part 1.* Washington, D.C.: Government Printing Office.

1981a *Census of population, 1980: Census tracts by age and sex, Hawaii. Summary tape file 1A.* Special tabulation.

1981b *Census of population, 1980: Number of inhabitants, Hawaii.* PC80-1-A13. *Hawaii.* Washington, D.C.: Government Printing Office.

1981c *Statistical abstract.* 102nd edition. Washington, D.C.: Government Printing Office.

1981d *Census of population, 1980: General population characteristics, United States.* PC 80-1-B1. Washington, D.C.: Government Printing Office.

1981e *Census of population, 1980. Supplementary reports. Race of the population by states: 1980.* PC 80-S1-3. Washington, D.C.: Government Printing Office.

1982a *Census of population, 1980. General population characteristics, Hawaii.* PC 80-1-B13. Washington, D.C.: Government Printing Office.

1982b *Census of population, 1980. General social and economic character-istics, Hawaii.* PC80–1–C13. Washington, D.C.: Government Printing Office.

1983a *Census of population, 1980. Detailed population characteristics, Hawaii.* PC80–1–D13. Washington, D.C.: Government Printing Office.

1983b *Census of population, 1980: Asian and Pacific Islander population by state, 1980.* PC80–S1–12. Washington, D.C.: Government Printing Office.

1983c *Census of population and housing, 1980: Census tracts, Hawaii.* PHC80–2. Washington, D.C.: Government Printing Office.

1983d *Census of population and housing, 1980: Public-use microdata sample A, Hawaii.* Special tabulation by Hawaii State Department of Planning and Economic Development, Honolulu.

1984   *Census of population, 1980: Residence in 1975 for states by age, sex, race, and Spanish origin.* PC80–S1–16. Washington, D.C.: Government Printing Office.

1986   *Statistical abstract of the United States, 1986.* 106th Edition. Washington, D.C.: Government Printing Office.

1987   *Census of population, 1980: Summary characteristics of the Black population for states and selected counties and places.* Supplementary report. PC80–S1–21. Washington, D.C.: Government Printing Office.

United States, Census Office
1901   *Twelfth census of the United States, 1900: Population, part 1.* Washington, D.C.: Government Printing Office.

1902   *Twelfth census of the United States, 1900: Population, part 2.* Washington, D.C.: Government Printing Office.

United States, Department of Health, Education and Welfare
1931– *Vital Statistics of the United States.* Annual. Washington, D.C.: Government Printing Office.

United States. Department of Health and Human Services, Office of Human Development Services, Administration on Aging (AOA)
1980   *Facts about older Americans.* DHHS Publication No. 80–20006. Washington, D. C.: Government Printing Office.

United States. Department of Health and Human Services (DSSH), Public Health Service, National Center for Health Statistics
1984   *Vital statistics of the United States, 1980: Life tables.* Vol. II, Sec. 6. Washington, D.C.: Government Printing Office.

1987a *Vital statistics of the United States, 1984: Life tables.* Vol. II, Sec. 6. DHHS Publication No. 87–1104. Washington, D.C.: Government Printing Office.

1987b *Vital statistics report.* Vol. 35, No. 12. Washington, D.C.: Government Printing Office.

1987c Some trends and comparisons of United States life-table data: 1900–1981. *U.S. decennial life tables for 1979–81.* Vol. 1, No. 4. DHHS Publication (PHS) No. 87–1150–4. Washington, D.C.: Government Printing Office.

University of Chicago (ed.)
1967 *Encyclopedia Britannica.* Vol. 17. Chicago: Encyclopedia Britannica, Inc.

University of Hawaii, Department of Geography
1983 *Atlas of Hawaii.* Second edition. Honolulu: University of Hawaii Press.

Vandercook, John W.
1939 *King cane: The story of sugar in Hawaii.* New York: Harper and Brothers Publishers.

Viele, Marie
1983 Coding of race on vital records in Hawaii. Hawaii State Department of Health, *R & S Report* No. 44, Honolulu.

Wagner-Seavey, Sandra E.
1980 Effect of World War I on the German community in Hawaii. *Hawaiian Journal of History* 14:109–140.

Waihee, John
1987 Hawaiian harmony urged for all. *Honolulu Star-Bulletin,* February 17, 1–2.

Wakukawa, Ernest K.
1938 *A history of the Japanese people in Hawaii.* Honolulu: The Toyo Shoin.

Westervelt, William D.
1937 *Copy of the journal of E. Loomis.* Honolulu: University of Hawaii, Loomis Journal Committee.

Whittaker, Elvi
1986 *The mainland Haole: The White experience in Hawaii.* New York: Columbia University Press.

Wright, Paul
1979 Residents leave paradise: A study of outmigration from Hawaii to the mainland. Ph.D. dissertation, University of Hawaii.

Wright, Paul, and Robert W. Gardner
1983 *Ethnicity, birthplace, and achievement: The changing Hawaii mosaic.* East-West Population Institute, Paper 82, East-West Center, Honolulu.

Yamamoto, George K.
1982 The Japanese. *Social Process in Hawaii* 29:60–69.

Yang, Sarah Lee
  1982   Koreans in Hawaii. *Social Process in Hawaii* 29:89–94.
Young, Benjamin B. C.
  1980   The Hawaiians. In McDermott, Tseng, and Maretzki, *People and cultures of Hawaii.* Honolulu: The University Press of Hawaii.
Young, Margaret
  1974   *Hawaii's people from China.* Honolulu: Hogarth Press.
Young, Nancy Foon (ed.)
  1974   *Searching for the promised land: Filipinos and Samoans in Hawaii. Selected readings.* Honolulu: University of Hawaii General Assistance Center for the Pacific, College of Education.

INDEX

Page numbers for illustrations and demographic tables are in italics

313